TEACHING THE PRIMARY CURRICULUM

Sara Miller McCune founded SAGE Publishing in 1965 to support the dissemination of usable knowledge and educate a global community. SAGE publishes more than 1000 journals and over 800 new books each year, spanning a wide range of subject areas. Our growing selection of library products includes archives, data, case studies and video. SAGE remains majority owned by our founder and after her lifetime will become owned by a charitable trust that secures the company's continued independence.

Los Angeles | London | New Delhi | Singapore | Washington DC | Melbourne

TEACHING THE PRIMARY CURRICULUM

EDITED BY
COLIN FORSTER AND RACHEL EPERJESI

Los Angeles | London | New Delhi
Singapore | Washington DC | Melbourne

Los Angeles | London | New Delhi
Singapore | Washington DC | Melbourne

SAGE Publications Ltd
1 Oliver's Yard
55 City Road
London EC1Y 1SP

SAGE Publications Inc.
2455 Teller Road
Thousand Oaks, California 91320

SAGE Publications India Pvt Ltd
B 1/I 1 Mohan Cooperative Industrial Area
Mathura Road
New Delhi 110 044

SAGE Publications Asia-Pacific Pte Ltd
3 Church Street
#10-04 Samsung Hub
Singapore 049483

Editor: James Clark
Assistant editor: Diana Alves
Production editor: Nicola Carrier
Copyeditor: Samantha Lacey
Proofreader: Leigh Smithson
Indexer: Author supplied
Marketing manager: Dilhara Attygalle
Cover design: Naomi Robinson
Typeset by: C&M Digitals (P) Ltd, Chennai, India
Printed in the UK

First published 2020

Library of Congress Control Number: 2019943758

British Library Cataloguing in Publication data

A catalogue record for this book is available from the British Library

ISBN 978-1-5264-5901-5
ISBN 978-1-5264-5902-2 (pbk)

TABLE OF CONTENTS

ABOUT THE EDITORS

Much to the surprise of anyone who meets him now, when he was a young man, **Colin Forster** spent two years working as an outdoor activities instructor, and it was during this time that he developed an interest in education. He began his primary teaching career in south-west London before moving to Gloucestershire, where he continued to gain school leadership experience. He is currently a senior lecturer in primary education at the University of Gloucestershire, where he has gained considerable experience of primary teacher education course leadership and in supporting students, at both undergraduate and postgraduate level, with research projects focused on improving practice. His areas of interest include primary science, behaviour management and action research, and he has undertaken research into children's experience of homework in the primary years.

Rachel Eperjesi knew she wanted to be a teacher from the age of five. However, some rather poor careers advice led her to embark on a medical degree, which quickly resulted in her declaring it 'too messy' and she decided to follow her heart into teaching instead. After completing a BEd Hons, Rachel taught in Foundation Stage and Key Stage 1 (also quite messy) in Gloucestershire, as well as undertaking English consultancy for the local authority. She now works at the University of Gloucestershire, lecturing in primary English and professional studies, as well as currently leading the School Direct PGCE Primary course. Rachel has supported many students, both undergraduate and postgraduate, with research projects focusing on improving their educational practice.

ABOUT THE CONTRIBUTORS

Richard Brice has enjoyed a successful teaching career spanning nearly thirty years and has always had a strong interest in the use of technology across the primary age phase. In primary schools he was subject leader for IT and design and technology; in his role as senior lecturer in primary education at the University of Gloucestershire, he has specialised in teaching computing and design and technology on the undergraduate and postgraduate primary Initial Teacher Education courses. Working with his colleague, Lindsay Evans, Richard is closely involved in the Cheltenham Primary Computing at School (CAS) community and is a Science, Technology, Engineering and Mathematics (STEM) Continuing Professional Development (CPD) associate facilitator.

Barbara Brown has developed her knowledge as a teacher and tutor through study and practice with a central focus on the access of all children to physical education. Children have been at the heart of her learning journey, enabling her to share knowledge and practice of working with children in mainstream and special schools with teachers, including student teachers on undergraduate and postgraduate Initial Teacher Education courses at the University of Gloucestershire. She has adopted a developmental approach to teaching physical education, which recognises the individuality and diversity that underpin all children's movement skill development, health, fitness and well-being. This inclusive approach embraces the teaching of all children and enables teachers to engage in personalised provision with a focus on pupil progress.

Cathy Burch is a senior lecturer in primary education at the University of Gloucestershire, specialising in teaching primary languages to undergraduate and postgraduate Initial Teacher Education students.

Lindsay Evans developed a strong interest in the use of technology across the primary age phase during a teaching career spanning over twenty years. In her role as senior lecturer in primary education at the University of Gloucestershire, she specialises in teaching computing on the undergraduate and postgraduate primary Initial

Teacher Education courses. She is leader of the Cheltenham Primary CAS community and a STEM CPD associate facilitator.

Ruth Hollier is a senior lecturer in primary education at the University of Gloucestershire. Having previously enjoyed a rewarding career as a primary school teacher and Deputy Head, Ruth now teaches primary mathematics across undergraduate and postgraduate Initial Teacher Education courses and has been involved in an Education Endowment Foundation (EEF)-funded national research project into developing children's mathematical reasoning. Ruth also supports professional development in mathematics for primary teachers through extensive work with the GLOW Maths Hub, for which she is a Strategic Board member.

Emma Howell began her career working as a class teacher in a range of infant and primary schools, specialising as a school mentor, before moving into Initial Teacher Education. After ten years as a senior lecturer in the primary mathematics team, Emma now leads the primary partnership and school experience aspects of Initial Teacher Education at the University of Gloucestershire. Emma continues her interest in primary mathematics through ongoing work with the GLOW Maths Hub.

Simon Hyde-White taught in a variety of primary schools over twenty years before fulfilling his longstanding desire to work with the future generation of teachers by becoming a senior lecturer in primary education at the University of Gloucestershire. Simon delivers the provision for religious education on the undergraduate and postgraduate Initial Teacher Education courses and has led student research in local primary schools, exploring how best to develop religiously literate pupils who are able to fully embrace and contribute positively to future society.

Jackie McNeil taught in a range of primary schools for over twenty years before becoming a senior lecturer in primary mathematics at the University of Gloucestershire. She teaches mathematics to students on undergraduate and postgraduate Initial Teacher Education courses, as well as leading CPD for primary teachers and teaching assistants through the GLOW Maths Hub.

Alice Parkin is a senior lecturer in primary education at the University of Gloucestershire. After teaching in a number of primary schools, Alice moved into Initial Teacher Education. She teaches music and art and design on primary undergraduate and postgraduate courses and also teaches on the secondary postgraduate art and design Initial Teacher Education course.

Jude Penny worked for 16 years as a primary school teacher and science lead in London, before joining the University of Gloucestershire as a senior lecturer in primary education. Her specialist areas are science and PSHE on the postgraduate and undergraduate Initial Teacher Education programmes. Jude's research interests include dialogic teaching and teachers' questioning; she also has a passion for Philosophy for Children (P4C) and supports accredited training for student teachers.

Joanna Rigg started her career in primary education as a class teacher in a mining village in Barnsley. Over the next thirty years, she built on this experience, teaching across the full primary age range in a variety of settings, from inner city to small village. Her final post in school was as a headteacher in Oxfordshire. She now teaches on the undergraduate and postgraduate Initial Teacher Education courses at the University of Gloucestershire. Her particular subject focus is geography and she also contributes to professional studies modules. Joanna is committed to the provision of a broad and balanced curriculum in primary schools that inspires and motivates children to love learning.

Kate Thomson is a senior lecturer in primary education at the University of Gloucestershire, specialising in teaching history and English on undergraduate and postgraduate Initial Teacher Education courses. She began her career teaching in a range of primary schools, before working as Advisory Teacher for history and geography in Gloucestershire. Kate now leads the foundation subjects team at the University of Gloucestershire and is a University Teaching Fellow.

Tracey Wire is a senior lecturer in primary education at the University of Gloucestershire, specialising in teaching history, English and PSHE (with a particular interest in relationships and sex education) with undergraduate and postgraduate Initial Teacher Education students. She has over twenty years of experience working in primary and secondary schools and universities.

ACKNOWLEDGEMENTS

We would like to thank everyone who has encouraged or supported us and contributed to our work in the creation of this book.

We would like to thank all of our students, from whom we learn so much every year, and in particular those students who kindly gave their permission for us to use examples of their teaching in the case studies in this book. We would also like to thank our partnership schools, staff, children and parents for hosting our student teachers and for giving permission for evidence from teaching and learning episodes to be included in this book.

It has been a privilege and a pleasure to collaborate with our wonderful colleagues from the primary education team at the University of Gloucestershire on this book. We would like to thank them for their hard work and dedication.

Finally, we would like to thank our respective families for their patience and support.

PUBLISHER'S ACKNOWLEDGEMENTS

Table 3.1: Computing in The National Curriculum – a guide for primary teachers (Computing At School, Naace), *https://community.computingatschool.org.uk/resources/2618/single*, ISBN number: ISBN978-1-78339-143-1

Figure 3.3: *www.barefootcas.org.uk* and Crown Copyright 2014 (OGL). Barefoot gratefully acknowledges the work of Julia Briggs and eLim team at Somerset County Council for their contribution to the poster. The positioning Statement for Barefoot computing project is:

Barefoot – the free, curriculum based, computational thinking programme for primary school children from BT and Computing At School.

1

INTRODUCTION

COLIN FORSTER AND RACHEL EPERJESI

In this book, we present an explicit and uncompromising message: that children are intelligent beings, that they should be treated as such and that primary school teachers have a responsibility to develop children's intelligence through engaging them in meaningful and purposeful educative experiences. Throughout, we aim to explore how each subject in the curriculum can be engaged with to provide good opportunities for intelligent learning. Student teachers often begin their training with an unspoken model of the teacher as the dominant intellectual force within the classroom, the one with all the questions and all the right answers. The cohering theme that will come through every chapter of this book will be that teachers should aim not to dominate the intellectual activity within the classroom and should aim to offer children meaningful opportunities to raise questions, challenge ideas, create solutions, apply learning, articulate and justify ideas and give thoughtful answers to meaningful questions: in short, to develop a range of higher order intellectual skills.

In this chapter, we will explore the purpose of primary schools, how the curriculum impacts on what happens in schools, and the significant role that teachers play in interpreting the curriculum to engage children in meaningful, valuable and valued learning experiences that demonstrate that children are respected as intelligent and active agents in their own education.

PRIMARY EDUCATION: WHAT ARE WE TRYING TO ACHIEVE?

Most countries in the developed world spend billions of pounds, dollars, euros or other currencies, per year, on primary education and it is seen as an important part of a government's policy agenda. What is it that they hope is being achieved as a result of this huge political and financial investment and, more importantly, what is actually being achieved and is it of long-term value?

In the United Kingdom, compulsory education for the masses is still a relatively new idea, invented by the Victorians, and the world has been changing at an incredible rate since those early days. Education that was supposed to be emancipatory and seen as an enormous privilege has, by its very nature, created the risk that, for many

CRITICAL TASK 1.1

The point of education

What do you see as the main purpose of education? To what extent was this achieved in your own experience in school? Reflect on these questions and make notes; you may wish to refer back to these notes when completing other critical tasks.

children and young people, it could be seen as an imposition on their personal liberty and they might feel restricted by the institutionalisation of schools. For many children, education is something that is 'done' to them: they are not invited to participate but forced to do so and this fundamentally changes the nature of the 'contract' made between schools and their main 'clients'.

Do children know what we are trying to achieve through their education? Do they see school as an exciting journey of self-realisation and personal development or, as suggested by Holt (1982), a series of tasks to be completed so that they are allowed to go out for lunch ...

For thousands of years, long before the notion of schools, 'learning' was absolutely central to our survival as humans. What should I do if I find myself facing a lion? Which berries are good to eat and which are poisonous? How do I make my arrows as straight and sharp as possible? How much food will I need to survive the winter? The passing on of 'survival expertise' was absolutely central to life and completely relevant: learning about the real world was undertaken in the real world.

In the twenty-first century, schools are so much a part of our shared cultural experience and have developed such an embedded role in our societies that we do not often stop to ask whether our current systems are 'fit for purpose'. Put simply, the current educational model is this: in order to prepare children for life in the real world, we put them in a box for twelve years. We call this box 'school'. In this box, we teach them about things that some nameless 'experts' think they should know.

The good news is that primary schools are vibrant, creative places and individual primary teachers have a good degree of professional autonomy about how they approach teaching and learning. As a result, teachers can make decisions about the kind of impact that they want to have on children's development. Children's time in primary school can have a life-enhancing effect if teachers hold a clear vision about the really important things that they want children to learn.

THE CURRICULUM

In the previous section, we considered the nature and purpose of education. In this section, we consider 'the curriculum' and how this guides our work as primary teachers.

In England, most primary schools are required to follow the National Curriculum (Department for Education (DfE), 2013), which sets out 'subject content for those subjects that should be taught to all pupils' (DfE, 2013: 5). It also states that schools must 'teach religious education to pupils at every Key Stage' and 'must make provision for a daily act of collective worship . . . [and] for personal, social, health and economic education' (DfE, 2013: 5). The document states that the National Curriculum is part of the wider 'school curriculum', which comprises 'all learning and other experiences each school plans for its pupils' (DfE, 2013: 5). Free schools and academies have more flexibility and can adopt their own curriculum, but the reality is that many of these schools also follow the National Curriculum, perhaps because Ofsted (2018: 42) considers 'the design, implementation and evaluation of the curriculum, ensuring breadth and balance and its impact on pupils' outcomes and their personal, development, behaviour and welfare' when making inspection judgements.

The Department for Education (DfE, 2013: 5) states that all state-funded schools must 'offer a curriculum which is balanced and broadly based and which:

- promotes the spiritual, moral, cultural, mental and physical development of pupils at the school and of society, and
- prepares pupils at the school for the opportunities, responsibilities and experiences of later life'.

Here, the DfE is referring to the wider 'school curriculum', of which the National Curriculum is one part. The aspects of the wider school curriculum that sit alongside the National Curriculum are sometimes referred to as 'the hidden curriculum' or the 'co-curriculum'. While the National Curriculum tends to dominate the focus of many schools, some might suggest that the hidden curriculum is even more important, in terms of equipping pupils with 'life skills' and preparing them for employment. James (2018) suggests that there is 'a growing awareness of the importance of social and emotional skills', claiming that not only are these important in their own right as skills for life, but that they can also support children in becoming more effective learners within education. For example, children who have developed the skill of resilience in other situations will be able to apply their resilience to their learning, willing to take risks and to persevere when they find something challenging. Analysing the results of the Global University Employability Survey, Baker (2017) identifies that employers list communication as the most important quality they are looking for in new employees, closely followed by problem-solving/critical thinking, adaptability, initiative, collaboration and creativity. Resilience and social awareness also feature in the top ten. Knowing the properties of a cylinder or having the ability to distinguish between a simile and a metaphor did not feature on the list at all ... In this book, we explore ways in which the National Curriculum can be taught in order to develop these desirable qualities.

In recent years, significant debate has taken place in relation to whether a knowledge-based curriculum is more effective than a skills-based curriculum. In a speech in 2017, Nick Gibb (School Standards Minister) suggested opponents to a knowledge-based approach propose that it can lead to 'entrenching [of] social divisions', whereas supporters propose that a knowledge-rich curriculum can help to close the gap for pupils from disadvantaged backgrounds (Gibb, 2017). The reality is that, while the current National Curriculum is undoubtedly more knowledge-based than its predecessor, it is intended to 'promote the development of pupils' knowledge, understanding and skills' (DfE, 2013: 6). Our own view is that any curriculum should always include a balance of knowledge, understanding and skills: what value is knowledge without any skills with which to make use of the knowledge? How can pupils develop skills in a meaningful way, if not drawing upon knowledge? It is the development of these alongside each other that can truly promote and develop children's own intelligence.

The content of the National Curriculum, in previous versions, the current version and subsequent versions (because curricula will come and go, to be replaced with versions that are deemed by policy makers to be 'better' than the previous), is also worthy of consideration. The vast majority of primary-aged pupils in England will be following a curriculum that has been designed by a relatively small group of adults, drawn from a narrow range of fields, focusing on content that they consider to be most important for primary-aged pupils to learn. Postman and Weingartner (1969: 34) suggest that any statutory curriculum is inherently focused upon children learning 'somebody else's answers to somebody else's question'. So whose curriculum is it? Who is it for? The important thing to remember is that the National Curriculum is just a document. During your teaching career, it will undoubtedly be reviewed and adapted and you will have little control over that, beyond engaging with consultation opportunities during periods of review. What you *can* control is the way in which you interpret and transact the curriculum; that is in your hands and we will now go on to consider the role of the teacher.

CRITICAL TASK 1.2

Memorable moments: the role of emotion in learning

Think back to your time in primary school and make a note of your most vivid memories. Try to unpick why these memories have stayed with you for so long when so many have been forgotten.

HOW TO BE A REALLY EFFECTIVE PRIMARY SCHOOL TEACHER

To be a really effective primary school teacher, you need to be clear about what you are trying to achieve. Are you trying to develop children to be polite and compliant or respectful and intellectually challenging? Are you trying to teach children stuff or inspire them to learn stuff? Are you trying to help them remember some facts from the curriculum or lead them on a journey of discovery that is relevant to their lives?

Being clear about the 'higher goals' of teaching is important and something to hold on to in the day-to-day business of the job. It is also important to reflect, regularly, on how your work as a teacher is going and whether there is a good match between your goals and your actual impact. Here are some general principles that great primary school teachers draw on in developing and reflecting on their practice:

Empathy: First and foremost, it is important to put yourself 'in the shoes' of the children: try to imagine what the 'lived experience' is like for the learners in your classroom. Remember that children are real live human beings, with all the emotional responses that we experience: boredom, frustration, joy, inspiration, anger, anxiety, glee, calmness, confidence, irritation, disengagement, excitement … the list goes on. When planning any learning opportunity, ask yourself how it will feel for the learners.

Partnership: Aim to see the children as co-owners of the curriculum, the learning environment, the learning process and the intellectual activity engaged with in your classroom. Of course, by the end of the school day, you may feel mentally exhausted as a result of all the thinking that you have done to support the children's learning; but you should also aim to send the children home with their brains fizzing nicely from the intellectual stimulation during the day.

Problem-solving: It is often said that teachers have to be creative and able to find solutions to problems. We believe this to be true but, drawing on the previous point, we propose that children should be given a role in the problem-solving process. Do not come up with ten brilliant ideas to support the children's learning: come up with one idea that will allow the *children* to come up with ten brilliant ideas to progress their own learning.

Humility: As a reflective teacher, you will recognise that you will not get everything right and be willing to admit when things have not worked out as you had hoped. Be willing to apologise to parents, to your colleagues and, most importantly, to the children. Just as you will be empathetic and aware of children's emotional responses, you should aim to share your 'humanness' with them, including your flaws and your determination to learn from your mistakes as you strive to be an effective teacher.

Determination: Teaching is an incredibly busy job, with multiple and competing demands made on your time and attention. Once you have decided what kind of teacher you want to be, you need to hold on to this very tenaciously and then stay focused on the children's development as intellectual beings. Reflect on your practice, learn from the children, and stay determined to provide rich, positive and child-centred learning opportunities.

CRITICAL TASK 1.3

How do you see yourself teaching?

When you imagine yourself 'teaching', what do you imagine the children doing? Are they hanging on your every word or identifying their own topics for discussion?

CRITICAL TASK 1.4

New school: blank slate

If you had the opportunity to open a brand new school and design your own curriculum from scratch, how would you approach this? Which subjects would you have in your curriculum? Would you have a curriculum? How would you organise the timetable? What role would the children have in negotiating the approach to learning?

HOW TO READ THIS BOOK

This book has been written by subject experts and has a very clear focus on effective primary practice. Each of the following chapters (with the exception of the final chapter) focuses on a different subject of the National Curriculum, exploring the distinctive elements of the subject and effective pedagogical approaches appropriate to it.

Each chapter also explores a key pedagogical issue, applicable across the curriculum, which is discussed in relation to the chapter's subject drawn from the National Curriculum. At the end of each chapter, the applicability of the pedagogical issue to other curriculum areas is considered.

Throughout the book, there will be the opportunity to reflect on some case studies and critical tasks, often based on real examples of student teachers grappling with the development of new and challenging aspects of their own professional practice.

In the final chapter, we will review some of the key issues identified throughout the book and look ahead to the development of education in the twenty-first century.

RESPONSE TO CRITICAL TASK 1.1

The point of education

In this task, we invited you to reflect on what you see as the main purpose of primary education. We asked some Postgraduate Certificate in Education (PGCE) student teachers this question at the beginning of their course. Here are some of their responses:

The main purpose of primary education is:

- to explore ideas and make sense of the unknown

(Continued)

- to open as many doors as possible to children
- to teach pupils how to learn and how thinking is important in all aspects of life
- to inspire a love of learning and a passion for finding out new information
- to learn to embrace and celebrate difference, culture and success
- to ensure that the future of humanity is properly equipped to open doors to all possibilities...

RESPONSE TO CRITICAL TASK 1.2

Memorable moments: the role of emotion in learning

We asked you to explore why it is that some memories of our time in primary school are so vivid, when there must be thousands of hours of experience that we cannot recall specifically. We suggest that experiences that provoke a heightened emotional response are more likely to stay with us when other memories fade. So, we predict that most of your long-term memories are from times when you were anxious, excited, sad, scared, happy, humiliated, inspired, intrigued ... the list goes on.

This is not just a trivial oddity. This is a really important point to remember if you aspire to be a great teacher. Always remember that the children in your class are small human beings, with all of the emotional responses that we experience as adults. If you ignore children's emotions in your teaching, you are missing out on a really powerful aspect of their learning. To be clear, we are not arguing, here, that you should aim to make your teaching 'interesting': that should be a minimum requirement. We are arguing that your teaching should engage children as social and emotional beings.

SUMMARY FOR THIS CHAPTER

In this chapter, we have considered how our current education system has evolved and some of the purposes of education. We have reflected on the nature of the curriculum and the role of the teacher in interpreting and translating it into meaningful and significant learning opportunities that put children at the centre of the process. We have considered some of the attributes of great teachers and outlined ways in which this book may support your development towards becoming an outstanding teacher.

FURTHER READING

Forster, C. and Eperjesi, R. (2017) *Action research for new teachers: evidence-based evaluation of practice*. London: SAGE Publications.

This book provides a clear guide to action research, a methodology that supports teachers in evaluating and improving key aspects of their own practice.

The Children's Society: 'Good Childhood Report'. Available at: www.childrenssociety.org.uk/what-we-do/resources-publications (Accessed: 23 April 2019).

This annual report sheds light on what life is like for children and young people in the UK. It often makes for uncomfortable reading and is an important indicator of trends over time.

Wenger, E. (1998) *Communities of practice*. New York: Cambridge University Press.

This book explores a theory that emphasises the social nature of learning in professional contexts. It is a valuable tool for new teachers, to support them in reflecting on who influences them and whether this influence is always a good thing.

REFERENCES

Baker, S. (2017) 'The global university employability ranking 2017', *Times Higher Education*, 16 November. Available at: www.timeshighereducation.com/features/which-countries-and-universities-produce-most-employable-graduates (Accessed: 23 April 2019).

Department for Education (DfE) (2013) *National curriculum in England: key stages 1 and 2 framework document*. London: DfE.

Gibb, N. (2017) 'The importance of knowledge-based education'. Available at: www.gov.uk/government/speeches/nick-gibb-the-importance-of-knowledge-based-education (Accessed: 23 April 2019).

Holt, J. (1982) *How children fail*. 2nd edn. London: Penguin Books.

James, D. (2018) 'Why you need to know about the "hidden curriculum", and how to teach it', *TES*, 22 January. Available at: www.tes.com/sponsored/smart-technologies/why-you-need-know-about-hidden-curriculum-and-how-teach-it-sponsored (Accessed: 23 April 2019).

Ofsted (2018) *School inspection handbook: handbook for inspecting schools in England under section 5 of the Education Act 2005*. Manchester: Ofsted.

Postman, N. and Weingartner, C. (1969) *Teaching as a subversive activity*. London: Penguin Books.

2

ART AND DESIGN

MODELLING TO PROMOTE CREATIVITY

RACHEL EPERJESI WITH ALICE PARKIN

OBJECTIVES

- To explore the distinctive nature of primary art and design.
- To consider how teachers can make effective use of modelling to promote children's creativity.
- To reflect on the application of modelling to promote creativity in some other subjects within the primary curriculum.

In this chapter, we explore the distinctive nature of primary art and design and consider what it has to offer children, both as part of their primary education and their wider life. We will consider some key principles for teaching art and design effectively. We will also consider how skilful modelling can be used by teachers within primary art and design to promote children's creativity. We will conclude the chapter with some consideration of ways in which modelling can be used to promote creativity in other curriculum subjects.

WHAT IS DISTINCTIVE ABOUT TEACHING AND LEARNING IN ART AND DESIGN?

The purpose of the art and design curriculum is to 'engage, inspire and challenge pupils, equipping them with the knowledge and skills to experiment, invent and create their own works of art, craft and design' (DfE, 2013: 176). Cox et al. (2007: 29) suggest that the potential value can be even greater: 'through a rich curriculum and responsive teaching, children should learn more about themselves and their world through art and design as well as learning about art and design'. However, Ofsted (2012) identified that teaching of art and design was good or better in only one third of the primary schools inspected between 2008 and 2011, suggesting that the rich potential of the subject is not being fully optimised. We will, therefore, explore some key principles for effective learning and teaching in art and design.

PROCESS, RATHER THAN PRODUCT

We would agree with Barnes' (2015: 161) suggestion that there is a significant difference between 'doing art activities' with children and 'teaching art'. It is important that our teaching of art and design is focused on children's learning, by which we mean that our teaching must enable children to make progress in their art and design knowledge, skills and understanding. While we can certainly celebrate and value children's finished pieces of artwork (the 'product'), it is the 'process' leading up to finished pieces in which the most significant learning takes place. Through our approaches, we must communicate the importance of process to the children, showing that we value it more highly than the product, in our planning, teaching and assessment. Our learning objectives and success criteria should focus on what children are learning to do, rather than on what they are producing. The teaching strategies we employ should place emphasis on the development of knowledge, skills and understanding. Our assessment should focus on each child's progress in these elements, rather than on their finished work.

What we choose to display can also send powerful messages about what we value. There is no doubt that skilfully displaying artwork (both the children's and that produced by others) can contribute to an inviting and visually stimulating learning environment. However, producing artwork purely for the purposes of display overlooks the importance of learning, which should be at the heart of all that we do. Consider using your displays to showcase the process of learning, not just the product. Initial idea sketches, pieces that demonstrate skills development, captions of children's oral and written responses, and photographs of the children engaged in learning in art and design lessons can all be valuable additions to our displays. Ensure that you also think carefully about whose work you are displaying; if the focus is on process, rather than product, all children's progression in art and design should be valued and displayed. That does not mean that every display has to include something from every child; instead you should ensure that, over time, you are not sending any inadvertent messages to children about the value you place on their individual learning journey.

Many schools teach art through cross-curricular learning and teaching. This can have many benefits for children, when the links between subjects are strong and purposeful. However, we should ensure that art and design does not get 'consumed' by the other subjects it is being linked to; it is all too easy for art and design to simply become a means of communicating what has been learnt in the other subjects. That may sometimes be appropriate, but should not be the sum total of a child's art and design education. Ask yourself what specific art and design knowledge, skills or understanding children are developing through your art lesson, in order to ensure it is really art; the word 'developing' is important here, as applying previously learnt knowledge, skills or understanding is not the same as extending these or developing new ones.

ADDRESS ALL ASPECTS OF THE NATIONAL CURRICULUM AIMS FOR ART AND DESIGN

Before we continue, we would like you to consider Critical task 2.1:

CRITICAL TASK 2.1

Verbs connected to the art and design curriculum

Make a list of all the verbs that you would expect to see in the National Curriculum for art and design. Then compare your list with the curriculum, making sure that you look at the purpose and aims, as well as the subject content for Key Stage 1 and Key Stage 2.

When you completed Critical task 2.1, we are fairly confident that you included verbs such as *draw*, *paint*, *design* and *make*. However, did you also include verbs such as *explore*, *analyse* and *evaluate*, which are explicitly included in the aims of the National Curriculum for art and design (DfE, 2013)? Whichever subject you are teaching, it is important that the ways in which you teach the identified subject content enable you to also meet the aims for the subject. Of the four art and design aims, only two relate to the potentially 'messier' aspects of art and design; it is important that the other two do not get forgotten.

One way to ensure that your teaching of art covers all aspects of the National Curriculum is to follow the approach outlined by the National Society for Education in Art and Design (NSEAD), in its framework for planning and assessment in primary art and design, in which it identifies four key progress objectives (NSEAD, 2014: 3):

- Generating ideas: the skills of designing and developing ideas.
- Making: the skills of making art, craft and design.
- Evaluating: the skills of judgement and evaluation.
- Knowledge: knowledge of technical process and cultural context.

It would not be practical to cover all of these elements in a single session and therefore we should seek to plan and teach art and design through units of work, in which carefully considered lesson sequencing contributes to progression. While the first three of these elements may often be addressed in that order in a unit of work (but not always: sometimes we might begin with evaluation of the work of others), the fourth element, knowledge, will be developed throughout the entire unit, underpinning the development of children's skills.

CREATE A CLASSROOM CLIMATE THAT FOSTERS CREATIVITY

In addition to developing knowledge, skills and understanding, art and design can also offer valuable opportunities for children to develop creativity, defined by the National Advisory Committee on Creative and Cultural Education (NACCCE) as 'imaginative activity fashioned so as to produce outcomes that are both original and of value' (NACCCE, 1999: 30). Craft (2002: 51) proposes that there are two types of creativity, 'Little c creativity' and 'Big C Creativity', going on to suggest that while 'Big C Creativity' might relate to high-level creativity, perhaps engaged in by established artists, 'Little c creativity' is within the grasp of every child within our classes; of course, this depends on the effectiveness of the teaching. If we can foster creativity within art and design, not only will this have a positive impact on learning in this subject, children may also be able to transfer their creativity to other subjects and their life outside school.

In the second half of this chapter, we will explore modelling as a particular strategy for promoting creativity. The classroom climate that we establish is also a significant factor. One of the key aspects to address is ensuring that your classroom is one in which experimenting and making mistakes is not just acceptable, but valued as an important part of the learning process. Indeed, as Adams (1996: 324) proposed: 'Creativity is allowing yourself to make mistakes. Art is knowing which ones to keep.' So, for example, children might experiment with different ways of shaping clay or creating patterns in clay, before creating their own piece of clay sculpture. The way that we respond to children's experimentation and to what they themselves might regard as failures/mistakes is crucial. Praising children's efforts, finding something positive to say about something they are disappointed with (e.g. 'I can see you're unhappy with the shape, but I really like the way that you have used different amounts of paint and used your brush in different ways to create texture; you could use that approach again') and explicitly demonstrating that, even as the teacher, you also need to experiment, reject ideas and make decisions, will all have a positive impact.

Of course, we need to ensure that we allocate plenty of time for experimenting and for evaluating or reflecting upon our efforts; we may need to include time to teach children how to evaluate their own efforts. The way in which we organise the physical environment will also be significant. Ogier (2017: 39) suggests that the environment should enable children to 'make independent choices … with materials and resources that can be easily accessed'.

WORK ALONGSIDE CHILDREN

The potential benefits of working alongside children go far beyond the importance of seeing the teacher as part of their 'community of artists'. We can, both explicitly and through our own artwork, remind children of the success criteria, of skills and techniques, of the visual and tactile elements to consider as they work. We can encourage them to reflect and to make decisions, providing support with this where it is needed. We can provide feedback, ask questions to encourage children to think imaginatively, make accurate use of artistic vocabulary (e.g. vocabulary related to visual and tactile elements, such as shading, pattern and texture) and encourage children to do the same. Ofsted (2010: 5–6) identified that:

> Teachers were seen to promote creative learning most purposefully and effectively when encouraging pupils to question and challenge, make connections and see relationships, speculate, keep options open while pursuing a line of enquiry, and reflect critically on ideas, actions and results.

These approaches could certainly be applied in art and design, to promote creative learning, as we work with and alongside children.

PEDAGOGIC FOCUS FOR THIS CHAPTER: MODELLING TO PROMOTE CREATIVITY

In this section, we will focus on how teachers can use modelling to promote creativity within art and design. For some, this might sound like an impossible notion, asking how children can possibly produce something imaginative and original, if the teacher has provided a model, identifying a tension between a directed approach and a child-centred approach. However, Key and Stillman (2009: 95) suggest that 'it is possible to support creative outcomes with direct intervention … employed in a supportive and encouraging environment', and we will now explore how that can be achieved.

DEMONSTRATE SKILLS AND TECHNIQUES

Firstly, it is important to recognise that there is a difference between 'modelling' and 'providing a model'; the latter suggests a 'product', whereas the former can be used very effectively to emphasise 'process'. When seeking to develop children's creativity through art and design, we would certainly wish to avoid a 'make yours look exactly the same as mine' approach, but an approach with no direction at all is unlikely to lead to progression in learning for many pupils. Balance is, therefore, the key idea here (Barnes, 2015).

Modelling is likely to be a very familiar teaching strategy to most primary teachers and student teachers, but perhaps more so in other subjects, such as English. In art and design, we can use modelling to demonstrate skills and techniques that we would like children to learn how to use, without tightly controlling what they then go on to do with them. Remember that modelling is most effective when it is accompanied by talk, as well as the physical modelling; provide a 'running commentary' of what you are doing and why, to help children to make sense of what they are witnessing and to understand how they could use the same techniques. Just as in other curriculum subjects, it is important to gradually shift the control during modelling, so while you may be doing all of the work initially, children can become more involved, offering suggestions or providing the explanation to accompany your physical modelling.

Given that children need to observe *how* you are working, rather than *what* you have done, it is important that all children can see you during the modelling. Additionally, some of what you will be modelling may be small in scale and so you should use your professional judgement about when to model with the whole class and when to model with groups of children. Of course, in order to model effectively, it is important that you are confident, so do ensure that your subject knowledge is secure and that you have practised, ahead of time, the skills and techniques that you intend to model. This will help you to identify what children might find more challenging and how to overcome such challenges, so that you can explicitly address these within your modelling.

CASE STUDY 2.1

In this example, Gosia, an undergraduate student teacher, is working through a unit of work on drawing with her Year 2 class. In science, the class has been focusing on animals and their habitats and Gosia has noticed that the children have been particularly interested in the birds visiting the school's nature area. She has therefore decided to use the theme of 'birds' as a vehicle to develop children's skills in using shading to convey texture. Gosia has gathered the class on the carpet, facing the flipchart.

Gosia: So, I'm going to show you how we can use different types of pencil and use them in different ways to shade our birds to show the different textures. Make sure you are watching so you can have a go afterwards.

[*Gosia selects a pencil and draws an arc on the flipchart.*]

Gosia: Let's imagine that is the bird's chest. We noticed that often looks quite fluffy, so I am going to use this pencil to shade it.

[*Gosia begins to shade, using the side of the pencil and using her finger to smudge some sections. She then instructs the children to go to their tables and have a go, using the materials she has provided.*]

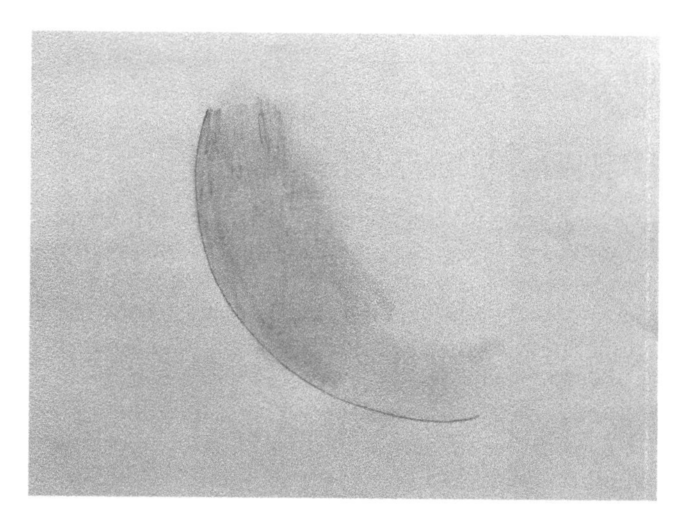

Figure 2.1 Gosia's demonstration of shading

(Continued)

Student teacher evaluation: Gosia was disappointed in her modelling, noting that she did not explain how she selected which pencil to use and did not provide a running commentary while modelling. She noted that children found it difficult to practise the shading techniques modelled, with many of them expressing frustration.

Expert critique: Despite her disappointment, there are some positives to note. Gosia did ensure that her modelling focused on skills and techniques, rather than trying to produce a completed drawing of a bird. She also emphasised the focus to the children at the start. However, she did not check that all children could see; while drawing and shading, Gosia's body blocked the view of a number of children and, although she stood back from time to time, those children missed the physical demonstration of how to shade. As she identified, Gosia was mostly silent while modelling, missing the opportunity to explain exactly what she was doing, how she was doing it and why.

Later in the session, when Gosia realised that some children were really struggling, she led another modelling session with a small group, which was much more effective, as she ensured that the children were all able to see and she provided more of a commentary to accompany her physical actions, as well as asking children to comment on the effects of her different actions. Gosia now needs to apply the same principles to her whole-class modelling.

DEMONSTRATE EXPERIMENTATION AND DECISION-MAKING

In addition to modelling skills and techniques, there is enormous value in also modelling experimentation and decision-making. 'Thinking aloud' as you work can enable you to demonstrate how artists try different things, how they reflect upon and evaluate their experiments and how they make decisions about how to proceed: 'Hmm, I wonder how it would look if I tried that technique with a larger brush ... ? I'm going to try it. I like it, as it seems to make the colours stand out more, but the texture is not so obvious. I think for this particular project, capturing the texture is more important, so I think I'll go with the smaller brush, but I'll remember how it worked with a larger brush for another time.'

Being willing to try different things, reflecting on and evaluating these, and making decisions on the basis of those reflections, are all important aspects of the creative process and for wider life. One of the central themes of this book is a desire to support children in becoming independent thinkers, able to reflect on their efforts and actions and to make considered choices, rather than become carbon-copies of each other. How wonderful that art and design can provide such a purposeful and enjoyable vehicle for doing so, provided we model these aspects for children effectively.

PROVIDE TIME AND OPPORTUNITIES FOR CHILDREN TO PRACTISE WHAT HAS BEEN MODELLED

Many children will need time to practise and experiment with the skills and techniques that you are modelling for them, before applying them to a particular outcome. We would not expect children to watch someone demonstrate some dance choreography then immediately perform the same choreography to an audience, no matter how effective the demonstration: we would allocate time for them to practise, and the same should be true in art and design.

The use of sketchbooks can be a valuable tool for encouraging children to experiment and to practise, and their use is explicitly stated within the National Curriculum subject content for art and design in Key Stage 2 (DfE, 2013). The 'status' that we give to these books is important; they should be valued as much as, if not more than, final pieces of artwork, so it can be helpful if they are different from the sorts of exercise books children might be using in other subjects. It is also helpful if you have your own sketchbook and make regular use of this. Where the use of sketchbooks is valued and the teacher acts as a positive role model for their use, many children progress beyond using them when asked to in art and design lessons, choosing to use them at other times, such as during reward time or when looking at leaves as part of a forest school session.

The format of sketchbooks will vary from school to school, with differences in factors such as size, type of cover, type of paper and so on; remember that, despite the name, sketchbooks are not just for practising drawing, so the thickness and quality of the paper is particularly significant. Whatever you decide upon, you will probably end up wishing at some point that you had selected something different; for example, you might want children to experiment on a larger scale than will fit in their sketchbooks, but if your sketchbooks are very large, they can be difficult for children to manipulate and challenging to store. Accompanying a physical sketchbook with an electronic sketchbook, where each child has a folder on the computer to store photographs of their experimentation that will not fit in their physical sketchbook, can be one way of overcoming this issue (Edwards, 2013); the electronic sketchbook can also be a valuable place to keep a record of transient artwork (e.g. patterns made with natural materials, such as shells, stones, leaves and so on) and artwork created using digital technologies.

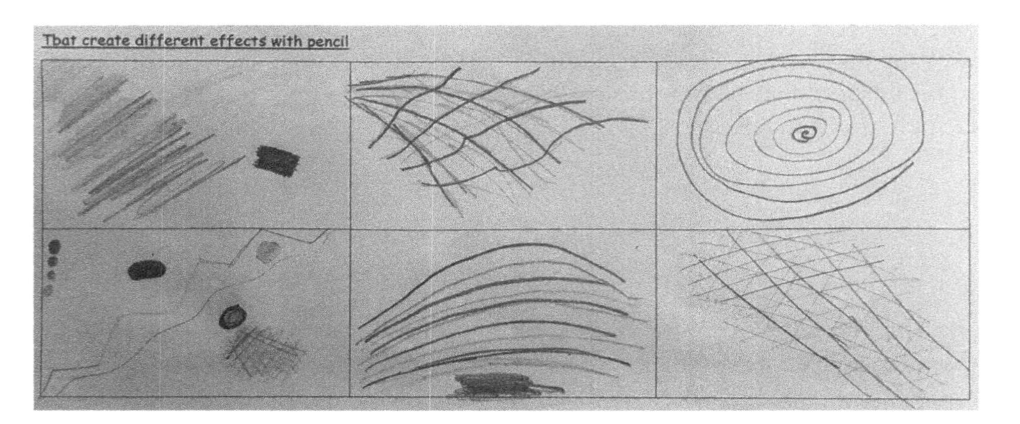

Figure 2.2 Ned's sketchbook: exploring pencil effects

As can be seen from Ned's sketchbook (Figure 2.2), he has been asked to use his sketchbook to explore ways of using pencils to create different effects. He has been creative in his approach, considering line, shape and shading, and the framework provided indicates that he is actively expected to experiment with different techniques, rather than being provided with a blank page which he could have filled with a single technique. Similarly, Kelly has been provided with a paper strip with four boxes to experiment with different techniques for shading. This has then been stapled into her sketchbook so that she can refer to it when drawing and shading a rabbit, to remind her of the techniques she has practised (Figure 2.3).

Figure 2.3 Kelly's sketchbook: investigating and applying shading techniques

The impact of time and opportunities to practise what has been modelled can be seen very clearly in Figure 2.4, which shows two pieces from Taylor's sketchbook. In the first piece, the teacher has modelled different techniques for shading (as Gosia did in Case study 2.1), before asking the children to select a leaf from the playground then draw and shade it in their sketchbooks. Taylor has carefully drawn the leaf's shape, including a hole, then made use of different approaches to shade the leaf. Other pieces in the sketchbook exemplify further experimentation with shading. In the second piece, Taylor has been asked to use shading to recreate a colour image in monochrome. The progress Taylor has made in shading is very clear. Different techniques, including different amounts of pressure, and different pencils have been used to indicate very clearly where changes in the colour/texture of the character's clothing exist. The use of shading to represent the folds in the ear is particularly impressive.

Figure 2.4 Taylor's sketchbook: progression in shading skills

COMPLEMENT YOUR OWN MODELLING WITH A VARIED RANGE OF OTHER PIECES

One of the previously suggested potential challenges (and, sometimes, a criticism) of using a modelling approach is that it can have a negative impact on children's creativity, possibly leading to children trying to copy or replicate the teacher's model. As has been outlined, modelling skills, techniques, experimentation and decision-making, rather than a product, can help to overcome this potential challenge. Another strategy is to ensure that your modelling is not the only example presented to children. Sharing other examples (whether these are finished or unfinished, by established artists or amateurs), which exemplify the same skills and techniques as those being modelled, will help children to see that there are many possible outcomes.

It can, therefore, be helpful to build up a bank of your own artwork, and that of other children you have taught (obviously ensuring that you have children's permission to use their work in this way and that you anonymise it, if asked). It is important that this bank includes some pieces that were for the purposes of practising and experimentation, as well as 'finished' pieces. Remember that the focus, here, is on the skills and techniques you want children to use, so discussion and evaluation need to be directed as such. If your aim is for children to develop their own skills in shading, sharing your own quick sketch of a magpie in the school garden and exploring how your shading technique might have been improved is going to impact on children's learning much more positively than identifying that it looks more like a seagull.

It is also valuable to share examples created by established artists, not only to provide further opportunities to see how skills and techniques can be used creatively in a wide range of ways, but also to help children develop their own artistic identity as they begin to recognise that even the most renowned artists make use of exactly the same sorts of skills and techniques. Indeed, one of the aims of the National Curriculum (DfE, 2013: 176) is that pupils should 'know about great artists, craft makers and designers'. Watts (2007: 136) draws parallels between art and design, and English, suggesting that 'artists' work could potentially be essential to the art and design curriculum in much the same way that writers' work is essential to the literacy curriculum'.

Engaging with the work of others could mean looking at a reproduction or image of the work in the classroom. Alternatively, it could involve visiting an art gallery to see an original piece, hosting a visit from an artist or engaging with an 'artist-in-residence', whether that be in the school or in another setting.

CRITICAL TASK 2.2

Engaging with the work of others

Consider the benefits and limitations of looking at an original piece of artwork in a gallery, compared with looking at a reproduction or image of the piece in the classroom.

Selecting which artists and which pieces to share with children is an important consideration. Edwards (2013: 43) suggests that it is the responsibility of teachers 'to give children a rich and varied experience of the work of artists, craftspeople and designers'. Therefore, we need to consider factors such as gender, current artists and artists from history, location, type of art, theme of artwork, and so on. However, it is equally important to consider your learning intentions; remember to focus on the knowledge, skills and understanding that you want children to develop when making your selections.

CASE STUDY 2.2

In this example, Farouq, a postgraduate student teacher, is working with his class of Year 4 children on a unit of art and design work focusing on painting, using colour and shapes to convey emotions. The aim is for the children to build up to producing their own modern artwork, selecting an emotion of their choice to convey. In previous lessons, Farouq has effectively modelled how to mix colours, how to pair colours together to create particular effects and how to use brushes of different sizes to create recognisable geometric shapes. Farouq has noticed that some of the children are reluctant to work at larger scales, often painting small pieces in one corner of a larger piece of paper. In this lesson, Farouq has decided to share Kandinsky's (1913) 'Colour Study: Squares with Concentric Circles' with the children and has asked them to experiment with creating their own versions in their sketchbooks, providing the opportunity to practise mixing and combining colours, practise painting a particular shape, and to encourage them to fill the page by firstly creating a grid of squares with a pencil and ruler, before then filling each square.

Student teacher evaluation: Farouq was pleased with the children's engagement in the session, noting that 'they were happy to keep trying different things and to persevere when the colour they mixed wasn't quite right'. When asked what he thought had contributed to that, he was able to identify that working alongside them in his own sketchbook had been significant. He was also pleased that he had shared with the children that Kandinsky had never intended this to be a final piece of artwork; instead, Kandinsky had been experimenting with colour, to use as a reference point, when creating a larger painting. In previous lessons, Farouq had identified which children had particularly struggled to mix colours and paint two

(Continued)

colours alongside each other without them bleeding into each other; he had worked closely with these children in this lesson, modelling the careful application of each colour, with a dry, fine brush, and he felt that this had been particularly successful.

Expert critique: Farouq was right to be pleased with his teaching in this lesson. He had a clearly defined focus on skills and techniques, following on from modelling these in previous lessons. His selection of Kandinsky's piece was inspired, as it provided a model of the visual elements and painting skills that the children were learning about, and also emphasised to the children that all artists, even very famous ones, experiment and practise, valuing this part of the creative process. Farouq further emphasised this by working in his own sketchbook, while skilfully modelling again for a particular group of children. His use of 'running commentary' and 'thinking aloud' was particularly helpful in this lesson, to support his modelling.

RESPONSE TO CRITICAL TASK 2.2

Engaging with the work of others

In this task, we asked you to consider the benefits and limitations of looking at an original piece of artwork in a gallery, compared with looking at a reproduction or image of the piece in the classroom. It is likely that you focused on being able to truly appreciate factors such as size and texture when viewing an original piece, in ways that reproductions and images can rarely replicate. You may also have identified the sometimes 'awe-inspiring' nature of visiting an art gallery and how this might positively impact on children's own artistic identity. On the other hand, you may have recognised that engagement with original pieces will be fleeting, whereas reproductions and images can be visible in the classroom throughout the duration of the particular lesson or unit of work. You may also have noted the potential barriers or additional challenges involved in taking children to visit art galleries, such as financial restrictions and risk assessment. Just as in many aspects of teaching, there is no 'right answer'. As a teacher, you must make a considered judgement about which approach to use in any given situation. Over the course of their primary education, children should have opportunities to engage with the work of artists in a range of ways and settings.

APPLICATION OF THE PEDAGOGIC FOCUS TO OTHER SUBJECTS

We have considered how to make use of modelling to promote children's creativity within art and design, and the same approaches could be employed in modelling to promote creativity in other subjects. For example, modelling is a technique that is frequently used in teaching writing in English. Again, if we are to encourage children's creativity and avoid them copying the teacher's model, it is important that the modelling is carried out with the children, focusing on specific aspects of the writing process, rather than the finished piece. The use of WAGOLLs (What A Good One Looks Like) seems to be increasing in primary schools; perhaps sharing What A Good One *Might* Look Like could promote children's creativity even more effectively (although we appreciate WAGOMLL does not trip off the tongue so easily).

Modelling can also be used very effectively to promote creativity in physical education. For example, the teacher might model how to undertake particular gymnastic movements (e.g. rolls, balances) and give children plenty of time to practise those movements, before then asking children to create their own gymnastic sequences, in which they combine the movements modelled and practised in different ways. Children may also vary aspects such as level and speed, in order to ensure that their sequence is imaginative and original.

SUMMARY FOR THIS CHAPTER

In this chapter, we have explored some key principles involved in teaching art and design effectively, focusing on the value of process, rather than product. We have also considered how modelling can be used effectively in art and design, both to extend children's knowledge, skills and understanding, and to promote children's creativity.

When teaching art and design, do:

- emphasise the value of process, rather than product, focusing on the development of children's knowledge, skills and understanding
- ensure that each unit of work addresses all aspects of the National Curriculum aims for art and design
- create a classroom climate that fosters creativity
- work alongside children.

When engaging in modelling to promote creativity, do:

- demonstrate the skills and techniques that you would like children to develop and use
- explicitly demonstrate the experimentation and decision-making process that artists engage in

- provide time and opportunities for children to practise what has been modelled, before they apply it to their own creative works
- complement your own modelling with a varied range of other pieces that exemplify the skills and techniques being modelled.

FURTHER READING

The following sources may be helpful in further developing your subject knowledge and understanding of effective pedagogy:

Barnes, R. (2015) *Teaching art to young children*. 3rd edn. Abingdon: Routledge.

The third edition of this popular text provides practical advice, supported by images throughout. The chapter on talk provides some valuable strategies for making use of talk when modelling and when working alongside children, to promote their creativity.

Edwards, J. (2013) *Teaching primary art*. Abingdon: Routledge.

Filled with practical and reflective activities to undertake, this text covers everything you could need to know about teaching art and design in primary schools. There is a particularly useful section that defines the visual and tactile elements of art, such as colour, line, tone and so on, as well as a chapter that focuses explicitly on teaching strategies, such as modelling.

Ogier, S. (2017) *Teaching primary art and design*. London: Learning Matters.

This excellent text provides a comprehensive, yet accessible, overview for teachers of art and design in the primary school. Emphasising the importance of creativity, it also provides valuable information about the main art processes, such as drawing, painting, printmaking and sculpture.

REFERENCES

Adams, S. (1996) *The Dilbert principle: a cubicle's-eye view of bosses, meetings, management fads and other workplace afflictions*. London: Boxtree.

Barnes, R. (2015) *Teaching art to young children*. 3rd edn. Abingdon: Routledge.

Cox, S., Herne, S. and McAuliffe, D. (2007) 'Art and design in foundation and primary settings' in Cox, S. and Watts, R. (eds.) *Teaching art and design 3–11*. London: Continuum, pp. 11–30.

Craft, A. (2002) *Creativity and early years education: a lifewide foundation*. London: Continuum.

Department for Education (DfE) (2013) *The national curriculum in England: key stages 1 and 2 framework document*. London: DfE.

Edwards, J. (2013) *Teaching primary art*. Abingdon: Routledge.

Kandinsky, W. (1913) *Colour study: squares with concentric circles* [Watercolour, gouache and crayon on paper]. Available at: www.wassilykandinsky.net/ (Accessed: 23 April 2019).

Key, P. and Stillman, J. (2009) *Teaching primary art and design*. Exeter: Learning Matters.

National Advisory Committee on Creative and Cultural Education (1999) 'All our futures: creativity, culture and education'. Available at: http://sirkenrobinson.com/pdf/allourfutures.pdf (Accessed: 23 April 2019).

National Society for Education in Art and Design (NSEAD) (2014) 'The national curriculum for art and design; guidance: EYFS, Primary KS1–2: a framework for progression, planning for learning, assessment, recording and reporting'. Available at: www.nsead.org/downloads/NSEAD_Assessment_Framework_KS1_2.pdf (Accessed: 23 April 2019).

Ofsted (2010) 'Learning: creative approaches that raise standards'. Available at: https://webarchive.nationalarchives.gov.uk/20141116012722/http://www.ofsted.gov.uk/node/2405 (Accessed: 23 April 2019).

Ofsted (2012) 'Making a mark: art, craft and design education, 2008 to 2011'. Available at: www.gov.uk/government/publications/art-craft-and-design-education-making-a-mark (Accessed: 23 April 2019).

Ogier, S. (2017) *Teaching primary art and design*. London: Learning Matters.

Watts, R. (2007) 'Using artists' work' in Cox, S. and Watts, R. (eds.) *Teaching art and design 3–11*. London: Continuum, pp. 136–55.

3

COMPUTING

DEVELOPING COMPUTATIONAL THINKING

RICHARD BRICE AND LINDSAY EVANS

OBJECTIVES

- To explore the distinctive nature of primary computing in the National Curriculum.
- To consider pedagogical approaches for developing computational thinking.
- To reflect on opportunities to apply computational thinking across the primary curriculum.

In this chapter, we will examine how primary computing is distinctive from, yet beneficial to, other subjects, as 'computational thinking' is a widely applicable skill across the curriculum. Discussion will focus on the ways in which coding and related activities can lead to the development of higher order thinking as pupils produce a workable solution to a specific problem. Papert (2002) described computing as 'hard fun'; activities that are appropriately challenging can provide opportunities for children to learn through collaboration and to become more resilient learners.

Computing is a subject that is highly relevant to the world in which today's children are growing up. Coding a simple game that can be played on their mobile device encourages children to become producers, rather than simply consumers of other people's content. As it is a relatively new subject in the primary curriculum, teaching primary computing often involves venturing into slightly uncharted waters where ideas are still being tried and tested. In the next section, we will endeavour to outline some pedagogical approaches that we have found to be particularly successful in teaching computing in the primary school, drawing on our own experiences of working with student teachers and pupils, demonstrating that teaching the computing curriculum successfully is perfectly achievable for the non-specialist teacher. We will then consider the value of developing children's computational thinking skills and explore some approaches for doing so. The chapter will conclude with some consideration of ways in which these skills can be developed and applied in other curriculum subjects.

WHAT IS DISTINCTIVE ABOUT TEACHING AND LEARNING IN COMPUTING?

To answer that question, it is important to firstly understand the content of the 2014 National Curriculum for computing and the rationale behind significant changes from the previous ICT curriculum, which had become outdated, lacking both challenge and relevance. The change was driven largely by The Royal Society (2012), which lamented the decline in knowledge and understanding of computer science, with children instead learning Information Communication Technology (ICT), synonymous with Office applications and a lack of intellectual rigour. The IT industry was also concerned that it would face an increasingly difficult challenge to recruit graduates with the skills required to compete in the twenty-first century (Livingstone and Hope, 2011). The proposed solution was the explicit teaching of computer science concepts, starting at primary school level. It is not the intention for all children to have a career in computer science, but, in studying this subject, children are required to work and think in particular ways; this is reflected in the underlying principle of the National Curriculum for computing, in that 'a high-quality computing education equips pupils to use computational thinking and creativity to understand and change the world' (DfE, 2013: 178).

The primary computing curriculum could be described as containing three main aspects: computer science, information technology and digital literacy. Table 3.1 shows how the curriculum content can be sorted into these strands for ease of interpretation (Humphreys, 2015: 6).

Table 3.1 National Curriculum by strand

	KS1	KS2
CS	Understand what algorithms are; how they are implemented as programs on digital devices; and that programs execute by following precise and unambiguous instructions. Create and debug simple programs. Use logical reasoning to predict the behaviour of simple programs.	Design, write and debug programs that accomplish specific goals, including controlling or simulating physical systems; solve problems by decomposing them into smaller parts. Use sequence, selection and repetition in programs; work with variables and various forms of input and output. Use logical reasoning to explain how some simple algorithms work and to detect and correct errors in algorithms and programs. Understand computer networks, including the internet; how they can provide multiple services, such as the World Wide Web. Appreciate how [search] results are selected and ranked.
IT	Use technology purposefully to create, organise, store, manipulate and retrieve digital content.	Use search technologies effectively. Select, use and combine a variety of software (including internet services) on a range of digital devices to design and create a range of programs, systems and content that accomplish given goals, including collecting, analysing, evaluating and presenting data and information.
DL	Recognise common uses of information technology beyond school. Use technology safely and respectfully, keeping personal information private; identify where to go for help and support when they have concerns about content or contact on the internet or other online technologies.	Understand the opportunities [networks] offer for communication and collaboration. Be discerning in evaluating digital content. Use technology safely, respectfully and responsibly; recognise acceptable/unacceptable behaviour; identify a range of ways to report concerns about content and contact.

Source: Computing in The National Curriculum – a guide for primary teachers (Computing At School, Naace), https://community.computingatschool.org.uk/resources/2618/single, ISBN number: ISBN978-1-78339-143-1

The latter two strands bear some similarities to the previous curriculum, with information technology (IT) involving the application of technology to learning across the curriculum in order to create content and digital literacy (DL) concerning using technology in a safe and responsible manner. These ideas will probably resonate with the ICT lessons you may have experienced in your own education. Although there were elements of computer science (CS) in the previous curriculum (some teachers were valiantly teaching children to control devices such as programmable toys, or the Logo turtle on screen, or to use flow charts and control boxes to work motors and LEDs on peripherals such as traffic lights and lighthouses), Ofsted (2011: 9) found insufficient provision of opportunities for children to develop understanding and use of programming, particularly at Key Stage 2.

Potential explanations for these findings might have been lack of teacher subject knowledge and lack of appropriate resources. If these problems are to be avoided with the new computer science aspects of the curriculum, then significant development may potentially be required for existing teachers and trainee teachers in terms of both subject knowledge and pedagogy. An updated report from The Royal Society (2017) still identifies challenges in relation to teacher confidence and lack of opportunities for professional development.

DEMYSTIFYING COMPUTER SCIENCE FOR THE PRIMARY TEACHER

The computer science strand of the National Curriculum requires explicit teaching of the fundamentals of computing. This may initially seem daunting to non-specialist teachers, who are unlikely to have been taught this at school and may, therefore, have little idea of what this entails. However, once a basic understanding of the principles that underpin the new curriculum is gained, it is possible to see that these ideas are not as complicated as might be imagined. The aim is to prepare children for life in the real world by providing them with an approach to solving problems that offers opportunities to work collaboratively, with increasing independence from the class teacher, to develop what many teachers might call 'thinking skills', labelled as 'computational thinking' in the National Curriculum. In our experience, pupils tend to thrive on these sorts of problem-solving activities, finding them very rewarding.

CRITICAL TASK 3.1

Understanding key vocabulary

Look at the computer science strand of the National Curriculum. Highlight any words that you are not familiar with and look up their definitions.

UNDERTAKING SHARED CODING

It might be helpful to compare the teaching of computing with the teaching of English, a subject more familiar to many teachers, with an established pedagogy. Research by Waite (2018a) has identified traits common to both subjects. In English, the teacher selects texts that are appropriate for their class, in terms of complexity and pupil interest, and reads to and with the children to support their reading and comprehension development. Similarly, teachers need to work alongside pupils to teach them how to read and understand code, before they can be expected to write it. When it comes to English, pupils often generate a story plan for their writing and planning should also be the starting point for computing work. Just as teachers would guide pupils in English by exploring word meanings and providing support with vocabulary or sentence structure, in the teaching of computing, we need to jointly explore how specific code blocks might behave. During shared writing in English, we write together, honing our ideas and exploring new words and structures. Likewise, when writing code together as a class, we need to try out new code or develop and improve existing code; we would call this 'shared coding'. Equally, when children are writing independently in English, we might provide children with word banks specific to that genre or context for support. When coding, we might provide useful code blocks to explore for a particular purpose; this is called 'guided exploration' (Waite, 2018b).

One of the aims of the National Curriculum for computing (DfE, 2013: 178) is that pupils must 'have repeated practical experience of writing computer programs in order to solve ... problems'. This suggests the need to learn to code: that is, to write instructions using computer languages to make something happen on a screen. However, the intention is not simply to teach children to code, but to enable them to develop transferable thinking skills ('computational thinking') that can be applied across the curriculum. In short, this means approaching problems in a logical and systematic manner, rather like a computer and, in order to achieve this, teaching approaches specific to computing are required. Children need opportunities to work together, with increasing tenacity, accepting that there is not necessarily only one way to solve a problem. They should be encouraged to talk, to explain their thinking and to justify decisions. With guidance, they can improve their initial solutions to make them more precise and concise. The focus should be more on the learning process than on the final outcome, and this can prove challenging for some teachers. It may seem easier to provide code for children to copy and have a working outcome, than to provide opportunities for them to achieve their own solution through trial and error, with the teacher giving guidance through questioning and activities that promote computational thinking. In our experience, while some children initially find the idea challenging that there is not necessarily a right answer, with appropriate encouragement and support to seek their own working solutions they often embrace the opportunity.

TEACHING WITH UNPLUGGED ACTIVITIES

An emerging pedagogical approach is the use of 'unplugged' activities, which can be usefully undertaken to explore computational ideas away from the computer. This is not a new idea: Bell et al. (1998) have been advocating this approach for many years, but the idea has gained additional momentum since the changes to the curriculum took place. Jarman (2015: i) identifies that 'many important concepts can be taught without using a computer' and that 'sometimes the computer is just a distraction from learning'. He goes on to suggest that teaching computer science 'using programming first … can be a significant barrier to getting into the really interesting ideas in computer science'. Through undertaking some of the excellent activities available on the CS Unplugged website (https://csunplugged.org), many teachers have realised that some of the fundamental ideas of computer science can be made accessible to much younger pupils than might have been previously assumed.

In our own experience, understanding and the subsequent application of a concept can often be more successful if unplugged activities have been undertaken first, to develop understanding of a fundamental concept without the potential barrier of the computer software itself. These activities can take a variety of forms, such as drama, games and puzzles, but essentially involve working through a potential solution to a problem. Children can consider whether or not that solution is likely to be successful and the activities then provide opportunities for unplugged debugging, through fixing errors that are easier to spot in a more familiar situation. For example, you may have seen programmable toys such as a Bee-Bot. It can be very useful when young children are learning to use such devices for them to 'act out' the commands available first, through taking turns to pretend to be the Bee-Bot, precisely following the instructions given by another child. This develops understanding that the instructions (algorithm) need to be accurate, precise and in a particular order. Children can learn to 'debug': that is, spot and correct the error when their instruction did not achieve the intended outcome. Algorithms can be recorded using words, pictures or symbols to represent the particular actions. Children can then apply this understanding when working with the programmable toys or with computer software that controls an on-screen bot.

CASE STUDY 3.1

In this case study, Bryony, an undergraduate student teacher in the second year of training, is exploring the use of unplugged activities to develop children's ability to work logically and systematically when programming in Scratch. The children have previous experience in using Scratch and moving the sprite (character) around the screen using 'move x steps' instructions, and Bryony has identified that many children hold some misunderstandings in the use of the 'point in direction' block. Consequently, Bryony predicts that the children may have difficulty in coding the arrow keys to control the sprite. She therefore provides a simple unplugged activity in the hall, using a masking tape maze and direction cards, for the children to practise 'controlling' each other using the correct terminology that they will use, later, in Scratch: for example, 'when the right key is pressed, point in direction ninety and move three steps'. Bryony hopes that this will support the children's understanding of the decomposed algorithm and the individual code blocks. She also aims to reinforce the idea that algorithms must contain clear instructions. Back in the classroom, she provides the children with laminated copies of the relevant code blocks for them to sequence the algorithm for one of the arrow keys.

Figure 3.1 Unplugged masking tape activity

Student teacher evaluation: Bryony commented that, from carrying out this activity, she had learnt that using this unplugged method 'allowed the children to step away from the computer' and put themselves in the role of the sprite (on-screen character) and the programmer. As they physically moved and commanded each other, errors and misconceptions were easier for them to spot and debug. She identified that the unplugged activity offered her 'a window into their thinking'. Bryony noted that, back in the classroom after completing the masking tape maze activity, the children were quickly able to sequence and edit the laminated code and then successfully apply and test this in their game. She commented that she was not sure they would have been able to achieve this so readily without the unplugged activities. Bryony was therefore pleased with the approach that she took, but reflected that she could have used a more complicated maze for a greater level of challenge.

(Continued)

Figure 3.2 Scratch code pieces

Expert critique: We have observed student teachers using Scratch with Key Stage 2 pupils for several years, and have noticed that controlling the sprite using arrow keys frequently presents a stumbling block for pupils and a temptation for the teacher to resort to providing code to copy to get the games to work. Bryony's own understanding of the software enabled her to anticipate this potential problem. By taking a step back, unplugging and moving away from the computer, the children were able to understand more clearly how to control the sprite. When observing Bryony's lesson, it was clear to see that through undertaking the unplugged activity, pupils' engagement and confidence grew and pupils were empowered to take control of the program. Their later work on screen proved far easier to achieve as the paired pupils worked independently of the teacher. We agree with Bryony that the unplugged activity could have been extended to provide more challenge.

CRITICAL TASK 3.2

Unplugged activities

Consider other unplugged activities that could be undertaken away from the computer that would allow children to develop a sequence of instructions to achieve something.

PEDAGOGIC FOCUS FOR THIS CHAPTER: DEVELOPING COMPUTATIONAL THINKING

Earlier in this chapter, we highlighted the underlying principle of the National Curriculum for computing, that 'a high-quality computing education equips pupils to use computational thinking and creativity to understand and change the world' (DfE, 2013: 178).

SO WHAT EXACTLY IS 'COMPUTATIONAL THINKING'?

Computational thinking is not explicitly identified in the National Curriculum content, but implied within the wording. Looking carefully, phrases such as 'understand what algorithms are', 'use logical reasoning', 'solve problems by decomposing them into smaller parts' and 'debug' (DfE, 2013: 179) are prevalent, suggesting the need for a unique way of thinking to understand the digital world in a deeper way.

A widely accepted interpretation of computational thinking was first articulated by Papert (1994) and again more recently by Wing (2006: 33), who stated that 'computational thinking is a way of solving problems, designing systems, and understanding human behaviour that draws on concepts fundamental to computer science'. This suggests that we need to think like a computer to solve real world problems, breaking down a problem into small stages or looking for patterns.

Computing at Schools (CAS) is a grass roots organisation which was set up to support and develop excellence in the teaching of computing in schools, with the Barefoot project developing resources specifically to support primary schools to teach computer science concepts. The Barefoot CAS Computing model of Computational Thinking (2014) (Figure 3.3) advocates six different concepts developed through five approaches to learning, to develop children's thinking skills. It proposes that concepts of logic, evaluation, algorithms, patterns, decomposition and abstraction can be developed through tinkering, creating, debugging, persevering and collaborating.

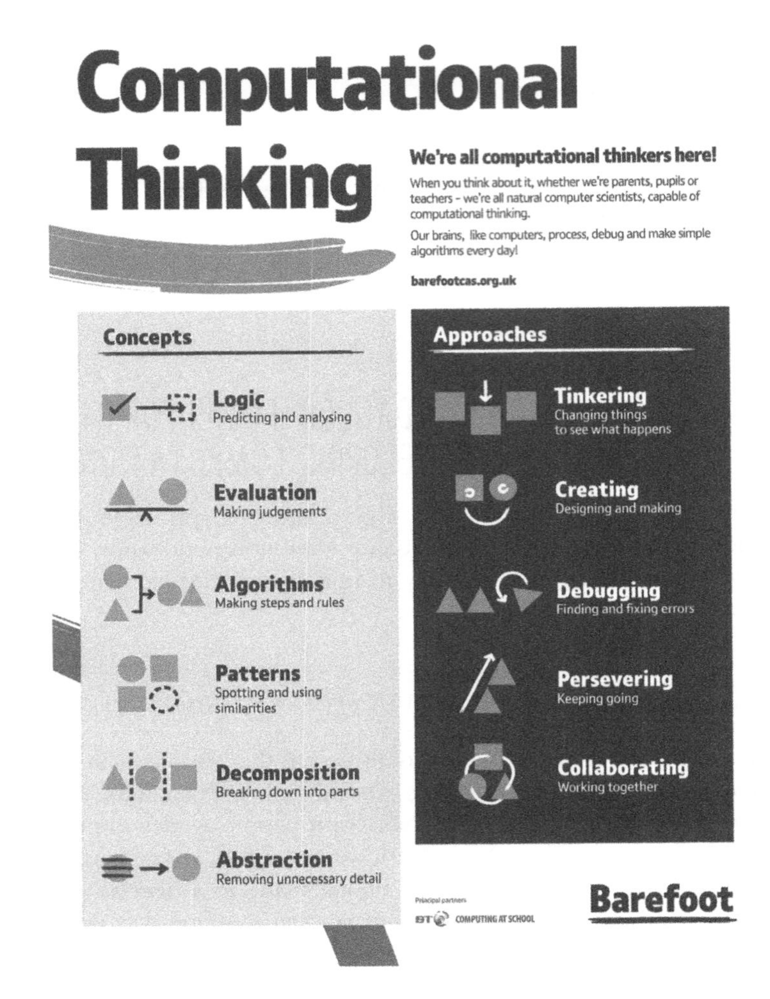

Figure 3.3 Computational thinking poster

INTERPRETING THE TERMINOLOGY OF COMPUTATIONAL THINKING

In Table 3.2, we have provided some clear definitions of terms, with some examples to further clarify meaning.

In our opinion, the concepts outlined by Barefoot provide a good starting point for teachers new to the subject. You can see from Table 3.2 that many of the concepts, such as using logical reasoning, spotting patterns and evaluating outcomes, are already familiar from subjects such as mathematics and design and technology. These are also ideas that can be developed without the use of technology. For example, the

Table 3.2 Defining and exemplifying concepts of computational thinking

Word	Definition	Example
Logic	Being able to explain why something happens.	Children's games such as four-in-a-row or noughts and crosses, that require logical thinking. Predicting whether the Bee-Bot will reach the intended goal.
Evaluation	Making systematic, objective judgements.	Decide which is the most effective route for a Bee-Bot to reach the park on a play mat.
Algorithm	A sequence of instructions or set of rules to get something done.	Any classroom routines, such as getting changed for PE. A set of instructions to get the Bee-Bot to the park.
Patterns	Looking for similarities or trends, leading to formulation of rules.	Times tables and spellings. Spot the difference.
Decomposition	Breaking tasks into smaller, more readily solvable chunks.	Getting ready for school involves: getting dressed, eating breakfast, brushing teeth and packing bag, all of which can be further broken down to generate clear instructions.
Abstraction	Deciding which details to focus on and which to ignore.	Drawing a road sign requires absolute simplicity so the message is communicated in an instant. The London tube map is another example.

writing of an algorithm might involve the everyday example of sequencing the instructions for making a recipe, for which precise amounts of ingredients are required to be used in a specific order if the outcome is to be successful. Developing this idea and involving technology might lead us to write a set of instructions for a Bee-Bot to enable it to drive along a play mat road and park in a garage.

What is perhaps less clear from this model is how we, as teachers, enable children to apply approaches such as tinkering, creating, debugging, persevering and collaborating to develop computational thinking concepts, and we will now explore this further.

COLLABORATING THROUGH PAIRED PROGRAMMING

We believe that collaborative learning is invaluable in computing so that pupils can build on each other's ideas and discuss solutions or code, spot errors, debug to correct errors and evaluate progress. However, pairing children appropriately can be a challenge. We have probably all seen children who dominate the computer while the other child becomes bored and disengaged with the learning.

One solution that we advocate is the paired programming pedagogy that has been developed in the IT industry over the last twenty to thirty years. The key idea is that both programmers are actively engaged in the task, with one physically writing code while the other checks the code for errors as it is typed in, taking a more holistic view. Roles are switched frequently and programmers are expected to maintain a dialogue.

In a classroom learning situation, there are clear advantages in terms of the reduction of low-level errors, particularly when coding, and a move towards independence and resilience among pupils as they take more responsibility for debugging and improving their code and thinking computationally; after all, two heads are better than one. Paired programming is no silver bullet, though, and requires a consistent and systematic approach to get the children working effectively. After many years of using this pedagogy, O'Donohoe (2018) has outlined some useful guidelines, suggesting that roles are clearly defined as the 'driver' and the 'navigator', with the driver using the keyboard and mouse and the navigator guiding the driver. Rules for each role need to be clearly negotiated with pupils, particularly that of the navigator, with which pupils are less likely to be familiar. Navigator skills such as spotting errors, making suggestions for improvements and looking for alternative solutions should be regularly reinforced and celebrated. For pupils, a five-minute time limit for each role works well, regularly swapping throughout the lesson.

Once this approach has been established as a clear expectation in the classroom, it frees the teacher from low-level 'firefighting' and enables a productive, developmental dialogue with each pair of pupils, periodically stopping for a mini-plenary to discuss common issues or celebrate notable successes.

CASE STUDY 3.2

Jamie is an undergraduate student teacher, in the first year of his training. While the paired programming pedagogy is often associated with work on computers, Jamie decides to explore this approach with a class of children in Year 3 using Probots, a programmable toy, with the children sharing one Probot between two of them. In a previous session, Jamie had encountered problems with pupils not supporting each other effectively; for example, he noticed that when it was the second partner's turn to code the Probot, they would often delete the first partner's code and start again, rather than debugging and improving the existing code. In this lesson, the children are learning how to input instructions into the Probot to navigate a course on a mat that Jamie has designed. They have a variety of challenges to complete that require them to use commands such as 'Forward X' or 'Back X' (number of centimetres) and 'Right X' or 'Left X' (degrees of turn). To overcome the previous issues he had identified, Jamie decides to implement a 'driver, navigator' rule, whereby the pupil holding the Probot is the 'driver' but can only input the commands in negotiation with the 'navigator'. Jamie also provides each navigator with a mini-whiteboard and pen to record instructions to dictate to the driver. After five minutes, roles are swapped, with the aim that both children assume responsibility for the code.

Student teacher evaluation: Jamie identified that the benefits of this approach were clear as he noticed the children talking to each other a lot more. He observed 'navigators' writing suggestions for code on the white-board and also using this to debug, crossing things out and changing them as the Probot ran the instructions.

Figure 3.4 Navigator whiteboard

Jamie identified that there was definitely an increase in collaboration and more effective code development to achieve the desired outcome in this lesson. However, he realised he should have clarified the role of the navigator more clearly, regularly reinforcing this, as there were still some pairs of children who found co-operation difficult. He also noted that, in the future, he would look more closely at how the children were paired. On this occasion, the teacher had paired the pupils beforehand and their mathematical knowledge and understanding was quite diverse; Jamie felt that, for some pairs, this had a negative impact.

Expert critique: It is hard to develop skills such as logical reasoning unless you are engaged in collaborative, ideally paired, practical activities through which you can share ideas, test ideas and modify to make improvements. This was the first time that the pupils had encountered the 'driver, navigator' pedagogy and, for most pairs, it seemed to work effectively. Jamie was right to identify that it is necessary to establish a clear set of rules for each role, particularly that of the navigator. If these rules are developed with the children, so that they have ownership of them, then they are more likely to be adhered to.

(Continued)

This might result in the creation of a poster to display on the classroom wall. The rules can then be applied for all paired programming work that the children undertake. This approach might also be applicable in other areas of the curriculum where children are expected to collaborate in pairs. It emulates the real world situations that they will find themselves in as adults, where being able to collaborate effectively in the workplace is an important skill.

The consideration of how to pair the children is an interesting one. The class teacher had paired the children, prior to Jamie's lesson, according to attainment in English; this proved to be problematic for some pairs, as this activity was highly mathematical in nature. It would have been more beneficial for them to have been paired according to attainment in maths. This may not always be the case in computing activities, but serious consideration should be given to how to pair children according to each task.

APPLICATION OF THE PEDAGOGIC FOCUS TO OTHER SUBJECTS

We have considered how to develop children's computational thinking skills; many of the concepts involved in computational thinking are transferable thinking skills, which can be readily applied and developed further in other curriculum subjects using some of the approaches identified as valuable for developing computational thinking. Two of the concepts associated with computational thinking are decomposition (breaking problems down into smaller, easier to access, chunks) and evaluation (making systematic, objective judgements). Before designing and making products of their own in design and technology, pupils should evaluate products by investigating, disassembling and tinkering with them, to identify the key components and how they function. For example, pupils evaluating a battery-powered model car in this way can see that there are three main parts: the chassis; the circuit (containing motor and battery); and the mechanism to transfer the energy to the driven wheels. As well as assisting children with the task of designing and making their own battery-powered model car, as each main part (or 'chunk') can be considered separately before combining them, pupils will also have developed their computational thinking skills.

Many of the concepts associated with computational thinking are also relevant to teaching and learning in mathematics. Identifying patterns (e.g. in times tables), applying logic (e.g. considering whether their solution to a calculation 'sounds about right'), decomposition (e.g. using place value to make calculations easier to undertake) and abstraction (e.g. using brackets in calculations) are all familiar concepts in mathematics, and, therefore, this subject offers excellent opportunities to further develop children's computational thinking skills and for them to apply these in meaningful situations.

SUMMARY FOR THIS CHAPTER

In this chapter, we have explored some key principles involved in teaching computing effectively, with particular emphasis on teaching computer science. We have considered the value of using unplugged activities and drawing on pedagogy from subjects such as English, where teachers undertake 'shared' activities with pupils. We have learnt that, through computing, children are required to develop their computational thinking skills and that the concepts and approaches underpinning computational thinking are transferable to many other subjects, as well as to real world scenarios. We have explored the importance of taking a collaborative approach, perhaps through paired programming, to enable pupils to focus on processes rather than outcomes, in order to further develop their computational thinking skills.

When teaching computing, do:

- use unplugged activities to develop children's understanding before using technology
- contextualise learning in the real world
- approach shared coding in the same manner as shared writing in English.

When developing children's computational thinking skills, do:

- focus on the process rather than the outcome
- look for opportunities to embed and develop computational thinking skills across the curriculum
- consider how to pair children and devise rules for an effective paired programming approach.

FURTHER READING 

The pace of change that reflects the nature of computing means that our best advice is to make use of reputable websites and Twitter to keep abreast of developments and to join some subject communities. The following sources may be particularly useful:

BT and Computing at School's 'Barefoot' website (https://barefootcas.org.uk/) provides free resources and workshops to primary school teachers throughout the UK. The website contains exemplar teaching activities, and a 'teach yourself concepts' section.

Caldwell, H. and Smith, N. (2017) *Teaching computing unplugged*. London: SAGE Publications.

This valuable text illustrates a range of ways in which unplugged activities might be used to support teaching of the computing curriculum.

(HelloWorld) magazine (https://helloworld.raspberrypi.org/)

This computing and digital making magazine for educators is published three times a year. It is free for educators and contains news, articles, lesson plans and information written by teachers, for teachers.

The National Centre for Computing Education's 'Computing at School' website (www.computingatschool.org.uk/)

This website provides useful classroom resources and has a community discussion section, where all questions are welcome. Computing at School also supports hubs all around the UK for teachers to join and attend meetings, which are a great way to share ideas and learn with colleagues who are teaching locally.

REFERENCES

Barefoot CAS (2014) 'Computational thinking'. Available at: www.barefootcomputing.org/resources/computational-thinking-poster (Accessed: 23 April 2019).

Bell, T., Witten, I.H. and Fellows, M. (1998) *Computer science unplugged: offline activities and games for all ages*. Christchurch: University of Canterbury.

Department for Education (DfE) (2013) *The national curriculum in England: key stages 1 and 2 framework document*. London: DfE.

Humphreys, S. (2015) *Computing in the national curriculum: a guide for primary teachers*. Available at: https://community.computingatschool.org.uk/resources/2618/single (Accessed: 23 April 2019).

Jarman, S. (2015) *Computer science unplugged: an enrichment and extension programme for primary-aged students*, created by Tim Bell, Ian H. Witten and Mike Fellows. Adapted for classroom use by Robyn Adams and Jane McKenzie. Available at: https://classic.csunplugged.org/wp-content/uploads/2015/03/CSUnplugged_OS_2015_v3.1.pdf (Accessed: 23 April 2019).

Livingstone, I. and Hope, A. (2011) 'Next Gen'. Available at: https://www.nesta.org.uk/report/next-gen/ (Accessed: 04 November 2019).

O'Donohoe, A. (2018) 'Bluffer's guide to pair programming pedagogy'. *(HelloWorld)*, 4 (Spring Term), pp. 82–5. Available at: https://helloworld.raspberrypi.org/issues/4 (Accessed: 23 April 2019).

Ofsted (2011) 'ICT in schools 2008–11: an evaluation of information and communication technology education in schools in England 2008–11'. Available at: https://assets.publishing.service.gov.uk/government/uploads/system/uploads/attachment_data/file/181223/110134.pdf (Accessed: 23 April 2019).

Papert, S. (1994) *The children's machine: rethinking school in the age of the computer*. New York: Harvester Wheatsheaf.

Papert, S. (2002) 'Hard fun'. Available at: www.papert.org/works.html (Accessed: 23 April 2019).

The Royal Society (2012) 'Shut down or restart? The way forward for computing in UK schools'. Available at: http://royalsociety.org/uploadedFiles/Royal_Society_Content/education/policy/computing-in-schools/2012-01-12-Computing-in-Schools.pdf (Accessed: 23 April 2019).

The Royal Society (2017) 'After the reboot: computing education in UK schools'. Available at: https://royalsociety.org/~/media/policy/projects/computing-education/computing-education-report.pdf (Accessed: 23 April 2019).

Waite, J. (2018a) 'Re-using familiar techniques'. *(HelloWorld)*, 6 (Autumn Term), pp. 74–5. Available at: https://helloworld.raspberrypi.org/issues/6 (Accessed: 23 April 2019).

Waite, J. (2018b) 'Shared coding, tinkering and other techniques for teaching programming'. *(HelloWorld)*, 4 (Spring Term), pp. 70–1. Available at: https://helloworld.raspberrypi.org/issues/4 (Accessed: 23 April 2019).

Wing, J. (2006) 'Viewpoint: Computational Thinking', *Communications of the ACM*, 49(3), pp. 33–5. doi: 10.1145/1118178.1118215

4

DESIGN AND TECHNOLOGY

USING REAL WORLD APPLICATIONS

RICHARD BRICE

OBJECTIVES

- To explore the distinctive nature of design and technology.
- To consider how teachers can make use of real world applications to enhance children's learning in design and technology.
- To reflect on opportunities to use real world applications in other subjects within the primary curriculum.

In this chapter, we will explore the distinctive and valuable nature of design and technology and some key aspects of effective teaching in this subject. We will consider how real world applications in design and technology can enhance learning through providing context and meaning. Design and technology inhabits a frequently misunderstood and rather lonely corner of the National Curriculum. This is a great pity as, in my experience, children often remark that design and technology is one of their favourite subjects. Design and technology provides opportunities to express scientific understanding and creativity through the creation of something that 'works'.

The key issue or barrier associated with design and technology is that many primary teachers are unlikely to have experienced sufficient design and technology, as pupils, to get a basic feeling for what it should entail. This is further compounded by a lack of research into effective pedagogy for teaching design and technology, unlike most other curriculum subjects, for which a plethora of research has been published. Thus, the first aim of this chapter is to offer a workable definition of the subject so that teachers and pupils can recognise design and technology lessons as distinct from art lessons or craft activities.

WHAT IS DISTINCTIVE ABOUT TEACHING AND LEARNING IN DESIGN AND TECHNOLOGY?

Pupils are living in an increasingly technologically sophisticated world and it is only right that their education reflects this (DfE, 2013). In the 1980s, Zanussi ran an amusing TV advert and coined the term 'The Appliance of Science' to describe its products. While some writers, including Hope (2006), see this analogy as over simplistic, we could define design and technology as applied science: this means using scientific knowledge and understanding to build objects that do something for someone. This might be, for example, light up, stand up, move, make a noise or carry something. Pupils can draw on knowledge of colour, texture and finish learnt in art lessons to add aesthetic appeal to the object being made. To ensure that the activity is design and technology and not art, we would ask whether the task involves designing and making a product for somebody and for a particular purpose. This is a key distinction: whereas the function of a piece of art is concerned solely with aesthetics, the design and technology product has to do something for someone and also be well finished so that it will appeal to that person. It is likely, therefore, that pupils will have to apply their art knowledge and skills to ensure the product is finished to a standard that is appropriate for the age and stage of the pupils involved.

CRITICAL TASK 4.1

Reflecting on your own experiences of design and technology

Can you remember undertaking any design and technology when you were at primary school? Reflect on what these lessons consisted of and what you learnt.

INTERPRETING THE NATIONAL CURRICULUM FOR DESIGN AND TECHNOLOGY

The National Curriculum for design and technology is organised into four themes or areas (DfE, 2013). While the design and technology programmes of study do not explicitly suggest starting with design, by placing it at the start of the list it might be tempting to start by designing in any unit of work. However, based on experience of teaching design and technology, working in a different order, as in the right-hand column in Table 4.1, can be much more effective.

Table 4.1 Areas of design and technology in the National Curriculum and a suggested order for teaching them

Original National Curriculum order		Suggested order	
1	Design	3	Evaluate by observation and disassembly tasks.
2	Make	4	Technical Knowledge: develop through direct teaching of skills and techniques.
3	Evaluate	1	Design: once pupils have the required knowledge to actually construct the object.
4	Technical Knowledge	2	Make the object to agreed criteria; e.g. the car should move and have an on/off switch.

Taking the approach on the right implies a longer unit of work, most likely around four to six sessions, starting with investigative work, feeding in skills and knowledge, which pupils are likely to be receptive to, as they are motivated to build the product. Design will involve a drawing with some labelling to reflect the age of the pupils. The main criteria from the teacher's perspective is that the design conveys the pupil's intentions and increasingly lists the resources required. Tackled in this manner, the design serves to maximise the chance of a successful outcome as impractical elements can be addressed at this stage. The final 'making' stage might represent less than half of the unit plan's time allocation, and this process will be exemplified in the case studies later in this chapter.

EVALUATION THROUGH DISASSEMBLY AND TINKERING

Investigative and disassembly activities are very useful and yet this aspect of design and technology is often overlooked in the rush to design and make something. In order to understand how something works, we invariably take it apart. In much the same way that adults may start to unscrew the bodywork panels of a broken vacuum cleaner to try to identify what is wrong with it, children need to explore materials and mechanisms to aid understanding and promote curiosity. Taking things apart often sparks questions from pupils, which can lead to higher order thinking as they try to work out how or why something does or does not work.

That children need to tinker and take things apart to find out how they work has been part of the design and technology curriculum from the outset, but, to make these activities successful, the teacher needs a confident grasp of the technological principles at hand, so that accessible examples can be used with pupils. For example, when exploring the topic of pulleys with Key Stage 1 pupils, a range of toys such as cranes and fishing rods are ideal to explore and identify the key components in a pulley system, such as an axle, a pulley, a string and a hook. As children initially play with and explore these objects, technical vocabulary and conceptual understanding may be introduced in a concrete and meaningful way. A useful way to manage these activities in a class setting is to set a drawing task, as this often prolongs pupils' attention; significant learning can occur through careful observation. In addition to introducing the concept or science behind the object (how it works), disassembly also reveals common assembly methods and items such as screws, pins and rivets, thus drawing attention to how it is made.

Older pupils could annotate their drawing with labels, or motion arrows to show which components move, plus a brief explanation of how it works, as in Figure 4.1. Counting and listing the components is another useful technique to focus observation. I would suggest that you specifically ask the pupils to refrain from shading and other artistic techniques to stress that the learning aim here is simply to understand how the object works.

At this point, having a teacher-created example of whatever the pupils are going to make is essential, as is a manufactured version of the same object. For example, when making torches with lower Key Stage 2 pupils, disassembling a simple shop-bought torch shows pupils that a typical torch has fewer than ten components. These are usually batteries, bulb, case, switch, strip connectors inside the case, the case itself, a reflective cone and a plastic screen. They also need to see a torch made from the

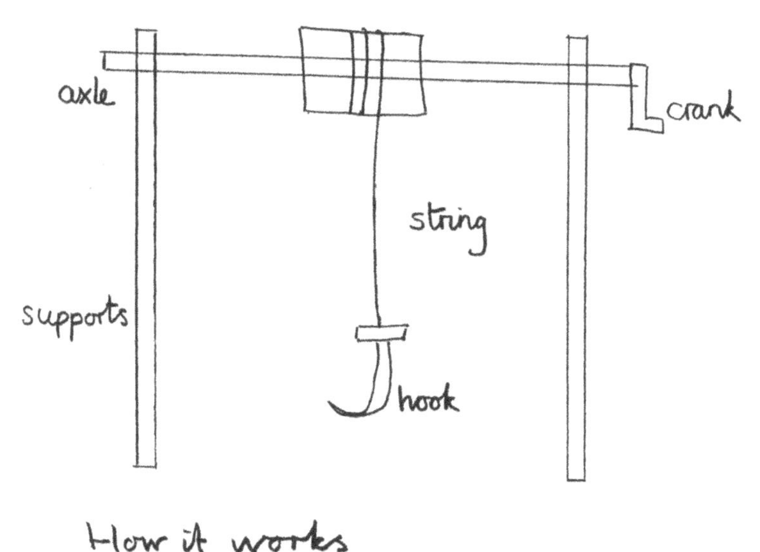

Figure 4.1 Pupil drawing of a pulley mechanism

materials they are likely to have at hand, which may be card, paper clips, paper fasteners and tin foil, as in Figure 4.2.

As before, pupils could disassemble the torches and produce a quick, labelled drawing of both the manufactured version and the example. However, we need to go beyond drawing to fully understand how something works; this could be achieved by asking the pupils to repair some 'broken' torches. The word 'broken' is a little misleading here, as the torches would have simple, repairable faults that pupils would encounter in the real world, such as having no batteries, flat batteries, batteries placed the wrong way round and, finally, a loose bulb.

Figure 4.2 Example of a teacher-created torch

As there is no obvious way to distinguish a flat battery from a fresh one, a simple battery tester is an essential and inexpensive tool for circuit work. Taking the torch apart explores the idea that the voltage of a typical battery is inadequate to power many common objects that require a higher voltage. Therefore, torches often use several batteries stacked nose to tail and this often influences the shape of a torch. At this point, pupils have sufficient knowledge and confidence to identify faults in a torch found at home. The learning has moved from the classroom to the real world, which is one of the reasons why design and technology can be such a useful way to explore science topics.

TECHNICAL KNOWLEDGE

Now that the pupils have some idea of what the product is made of and how it is put together, they may be eager to make something of their own. However, without some structured teaching it is likely that they will lack the skills and knowledge to make their own version. There is a balance here between letting pupils have free rein over the tools and resources as opposed to a more structured approach, where the class proceeds more or less at the same time; a more structured approach tends to work more effectively. Experience of teaching design and technology with children and adults has demonstrated that the range of expertise, usually based on prior experience, is wide and very difficult to predict. Whatever product we are making, we need to ensure that all pupils have the necessary skills and knowledge to make a basic version of that product. This will inevitably involve some construction and this is likely to be more successful if those construction skills are developed as a class, in what previous versions of the National Curriculum referred to as 'focused skills' and the current National Curriculum describes as 'technical knowledge'. Considering the previous example of a torch, this would require some teaching input on constructing circuits, simple switches and the actual container or body of the torch. Each of these aspects would be thoroughly covered by some demonstration and a worked example.

DESIGN

Some might question whether children can really 'be designers'. Provided that they are encouraged to use other people's work as a stimulus and have undertaken sufficient investigative activities to understand how the product is made, they can. Just as there is a fine line between being inspired by something and copying, designers in the real world are likely to have their own favourite designers, whose work may have provided inspiration. Teachers should understand that pupils need to see other people's ideas, in the same way that we learn music by playing other people's music initially. Once the skills and knowledge are in place, pupils will usually look carefully at other people's ideas but then go their own way.

Just as with other aspects of design and technology, the design process needs to be modelled and guided for pupils, in order to scaffold the development of their designing skills. For example, the teacher should model the need at the design stage to consider both function (to ensure that the design meets the agreed criteria for the product) and form (to ensure that it is aesthetically pleasing and likely to appeal to the intended user). Pupils should also be taught that design is usually an iterative process, with alterations made on the basis of self-assessment and feedback from others, so that the final design may look quite different from the initial one (Klapwijk, 2017).

MAKING

As well as being a distinct subject within the National Curriculum, design and technology augments the science and art curricula by providing opportunities for pupils to explore key ideas from these subjects in depth, through 'design and make' projects in contexts that are appropriate and appealing to pupils (Newton, 2005). In a typical design and technology project, the 'making' is not the major component and typically takes about a third of the allocated time, once the investigative, technical knowledge and design-based activities have been completed.

In terms of teacher preparation, Ofsted (2012: slide 16) identifies that, in the most successful design and technology projects, teachers use 'their own work to model ideas and to explain the methods they used to identify the problem or to tackle a task'. This approach will be discussed further in Case study 4.1. A teacher-created example sets a basic standard, offers an idea of what is achievable using the resources available and, finally, offers a valuable means of explaining the technical knowledge to be taught. For pupils in Key Stage 1, this could involve the design and construction of a moving toy, whereby pupils will learn that a simple paper fastener can be used to make the toy's head move up and down.

Pupils in Key Stage 2 could explore the way in which modern buildings are constructed from simple frames. They can choose themes such as bridges or buildings to explore these principles through activities that build technical knowledge and give them sufficient knowledge and understanding to build their own structure using the same principles, but using card instead of steel.

Table 4.2 Using structures to build bridges

Flat card	Card rolled into a tube	Card folded into square girders
Flat card can hold 80 g of weight across a 15 cm gap.	The same card, rolled into a tube, can hold 200 g across the same gap.	The same card folded into square girders can hold weight and a simple road of card can be laid across, as in most modern bridge designs, and the model can now support around 1 kg.

PEDAGOGIC FOCUS FOR THIS CHAPTER: USING REAL WORLD APPLICATIONS

If learning is to be authentic, it ought to develop knowledge, understanding and skills that can be identified in pupils' real lives outside of school. Thus, wherever possible, activities should explore and identify ideas and designed objects that are from that 'real' world, as opposed to the school science cupboard, in order to generate meaningful learning that can be applied in a variety of situations. Indeed, the National Curriculum (DfE, 2013: 181–2) is clear that pupils should 'work in a range of relevant contexts' in design and technology.

SELECTING APPROPRIATE REAL WORLD APPLICATIONS

In opting to use real world applications to support the teaching of design and technology, the teacher needs to carefully consider the contexts they select to use. The contexts should be familiar in some way to the pupils, so that it is applicable to their own lives, not just those of others (Milne, 2017). The contexts should also be interesting to pupils, sparking their curiosity and promoting genuine desire to find out more.

Of course, the contexts selected also need to offer the scope to address the curriculum requirements for design and technology.

CASE STUDY 4.1

In this example, Zara, an undergraduate student teacher, is undertaking her final placement in a small primary school with a class of Year 5 and 6 pupils. The class teacher has asked Zara to undertake some design and technology linked to their topic of 'transport', in which the children have explored local steam engines as examples of past technology and electrically powered vehicles as examples of future technology, drawing on advances developed by companies such as Tesla.

This is the first lesson of five in the design and technology unit of work and is an example of an 'evaluation' lesson, which aims to introduce the project and to build confidence and knowledge of concepts relevant to the creation of a model electrical car. The first part of the lesson involves pupils in investigating and identifying key components of toy cars and handmade electrical cars, such as wheels, axles, motors, batteries and switches. The second part of the lesson involves pupils being able to understand how these components work together, as the children aim to fix a 'broken' electrical car.

Student teacher evaluation: Zara was pleased that she had prepared a presentation to introduce some of the key ideas, including demonstrating the sort of car her parents drove when she was a child and what a car would have looked like 100 years ago. She felt that this also enabled her to focus the pupils' attention on the image of the Model T Ford to identify that most of the features we identify with modern cars were present a century ago. Zara noted that the pupils' comments were revealing. For example, they identified that four wheels was still the favoured option, the wheels on the old car looked like waggon wheels and, while the seats looked very comfortable ('like a sofa'), there were no windows.

In order that pupils could understand the difference between a push-along toy car and one with a motor that drove itself, they were asked to look closely and feel the 'free' axles of a push-along car compared to 'fixed' axles of the motorised car. The first task was to draw a quick sketch and label the toy cars to show they understood some new vocabulary such as 'axle' and 'chassis'. There were two examples on each table. Zara identified that pupils had no difficulty in identifying the features such as the wheels, axles and chassis.

(Continued)

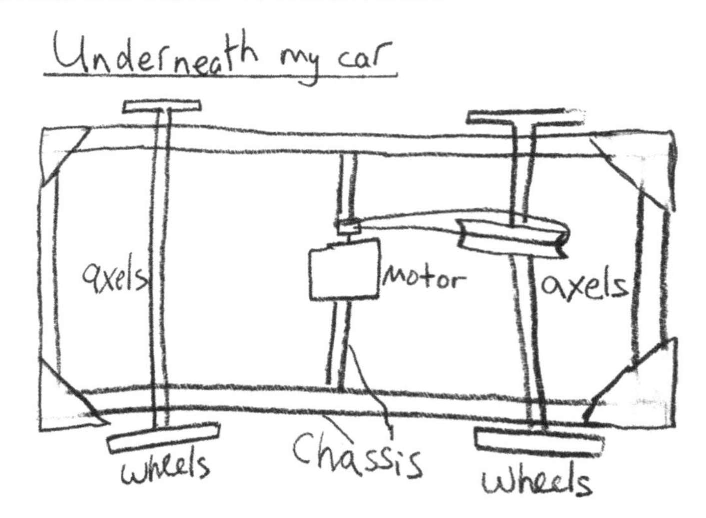

Figure 4.3 Pupil drawing of underside of car

The final task for the lesson was to fix the broken cars and Zara had been curious to see how pupils would cope with this. She had provided a small collection of motorised toy cars that she had made herself. Each of the cars had been deliberately sabotaged for the lesson, with a list of simple faults such as a flat battery, a missing elastic band or a wire disconnected. The task was simply to get the car going, and the only teaching input was a quick demonstration of how to use a battery tester. Zara commented that she was 'amazed how keen the pupils were to fiddle and try to understand how the cars worked and what might be wrong'. In fifteen minutes, the pupils were able to 'fix' all of the cars and list the faults they had discovered, with typical responses including 'pulley not connected to motor', 'flat battery', 'wire not attached'.

Expert critique: It was clear from observing the lesson that the pupils were highly motivated and did not want to stop at the end of the lesson. The real world application was relevant to the pupils' own lives and they were definitely interested in it. The guided approach to the evaluation worked well. Zara offered an appropriate balance of input, in terms of new vocabulary and how to use the battery tester, without 'giving the game away'. Letting pupils 'fix' the cars was empowering. They saw that the problem was not that complicated but did require their full attention and some thought. Once one group got a car working, the other pupils became even more determined. New vocabulary and concepts were being used in context, probably because

Zara had been consistent in her own use and modelling of this earlier in the lesson. Zara might have improved the lesson further by outlining the aim of the unit of work more clearly to the pupils (that they would be building their own battery-powered car) and by providing a purpose, to make the real world application more explicit from the outset.

EXPLOIT MEANINGFUL LINKS TO OTHER CURRICULUM SUBJECTS

Where appropriate, real world applications may be drawn from, or make links to, other subjects from the National Curriculum. Doing so is likely to make the real world application seem more authentic to pupils, as well as being an efficient use of time, as some of the knowledge, understanding and skills can be 'shared' across multiple subjects (Hope, 2018). However, links should only be made when these are purposeful; tenuous links, just for the sake of making a link, should be avoided. As outlined in the first part of this chapter, design and technology requires pupils to draw upon the knowledge, skills and understanding developed through science and art lessons, but other curriculum subjects may also provide the context for a real world application.

It should go without saying that your own subject knowledge needs to be secure, whatever you are teaching. When making links to other curriculum areas in design and technology, it is therefore crucial that your knowledge of both/all subjects is secure, if the potential benefits of making such links are to be achieved. In Case study 4.2, we return to Zara's class to explore the links between design and technology and science more fully.

CASE STUDY 4.2

Lesson two is focused on building pupils' technical knowledge of using circuits in design and technology and begins with a recap of the key ideas and vocabulary from the previous lesson. A discussion follows about how fuels such as petrol and diesel are used to power the engines in most cars, whereas electric cars use motors and batteries. Pupils are invited to look closely at motors which have been placed on each table. They are asked to identify the key elements, which are the case, the positive and negative tabs and the spindle going all the way through the motor.

(Continued)

The pupils are then handed a set of homemade circuits, which replicate the ones that will be used in the model cars, but with a bulb in place of a motor. Zara invites the pupils to loosen the bulb in the holder by a quarter of a turn, to demonstrate that components must be firmly attached to allow the electricity to flow. The fact that pupils can remove wires and see that the switch is simply two drawing pins and a paper clip is an effective way to demystify the circuit and build confidence.

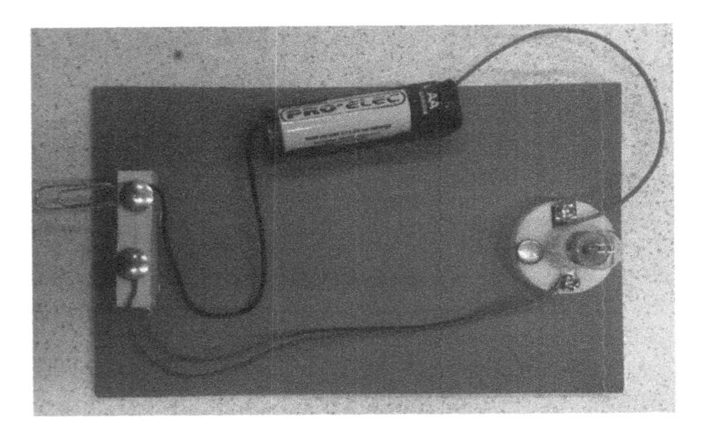

Figure 4.4 Example of homemade circuit

In the second part of the lesson, Zara demonstrates how to construct a simple circuit using a motor instead of a bulb, showing an example on the interactive whiteboard and building one 'live' in front of the class. Pupils use wire strippers successfully, most for the first time, and by the end of the lesson they have constructed circuits ready to be added to the frame of the car.

Student teacher evaluation: Zara commented that she was pleased with how this lesson had gone and was confident that the lesson had developed the pupils' technical knowledge. She confided that she had been apprehensive before teaching the lesson as she was not really sure about the pupils' prior knowledge in relation to circuits and that it was not an aspect of subject knowledge that she felt confident in.

Expert critique: Zara was right to be positive about this lesson. In terms of the sequence of lessons, she had continued to follow the 'evaluation, develop technical knowledge, design and make' approach outlined earlier in this chapter. In addition to identifying a real world application that linked to the history topic, Zara's lesson also provided a meaningful opportunity to extend pupils' scientific learning in relation to circuits.

Ofsted (2012: slide 25) noted that 'pupils had insufficient opportunities to learn about circuits ... in D&T'. It may be that, like Zara, many primary teachers lack confidence in their own subject knowledge in this area, which may lead them to avoid teaching it in design and technology. However, if we look at the National Curriculum for science (DfE, 2013), the requirements are modest and realistic. In Table 4.3, the programme of study requirements relating to circuits for Year 4, which the pupils would have previously addressed, are presented in the left-hand column (DfE, 2013: 164) and exemplified in relation to Zara's lessons in the right-hand column.

Table 4.3 Links between pupils' existing knowledge and understanding of circuits, and the opportunities to apply this in Zara's lessons

Science programme of study requirements, relating to circuits, for Year 4	Exemplification in relation to Zara's lessons
• identify common appliances that run on electricity	For example, many household items and the model cars being made.
• construct a simple series electrical circuit, identifying and naming its basic parts, including cells, wires, bulbs, switches and buzzers	All pupils made a circuit to power their car in lesson two.
• identify whether or not a lamp will light in a simple series circuit, based on whether or not the lamp is part of a complete loop with a battery	All pupils carried out fault-finding in lessons one and two as they fixed circuits and then made one of their own.
• recognise that a switch opens and closes a circuit and associate this with whether or not a lamp lights in a simple series circuit	Pupils made their own on/off switch to control their car. During the lesson, push spring switches were shown to model the type of switch that might be used in a car horn. A rotary switch was also shown to model a typical radio volume control.
• recognise some common conductors and insulators, and associate metals with being good conductors	Making the switches using drawing pins and paper clips covered this concept thoroughly.

The real world application in design and technology has been useful here because it gives pupils a genuine reason to create a simple circuit, whereby the science knowledge is applied within a realistic and appealing context.

(Continued)

Many student teachers have been noted to lack confidence in this area. Once we have made some simple three-wire circuits to power torches and cars, this anxiety is replaced by relief and a desire to share this new knowledge. Zara may have found it helpful to consider the science curriculum requirements more closely, aligning these alongside her intended design and technology activities (as seen in Table 4.3) before teaching the lesson, to reassure herself and therefore appear more confident, as her apprehension was evident at times during the lesson.

These first two lessons offered a good combination of investigative and disassembly work as pupils tinkered with the circuits and considered how to fix them. The direct teaching and modelling of circuit-making and tool use was a good example of what the National Curriculum calls 'technical knowledge', to ensure that pupils have the level of skills and knowledge necessary to build the model before they design it. In my experience, these sorts of activities are essential to successful design and technology projects. In the remaining lessons, the pupils built a simple chassis for their battery-powered cars (lesson three), produced a design for the finished product (lesson four) and made their cars (lessons four and five). At the end of the unit of work, Zara commented that 'The children really enjoyed and felt motivated by this personalised project. There were no issues with behaviour, due to the pitching of the lessons and the engaging nature of the activities'.

DRAW ON LOCAL EXPERTISE TO SUPPORT THE REAL WORLD APPLICATIONS SELECTED

As identified earlier, the teacher's own subject knowledge is a significant factor in the effectiveness of the teaching; there can be no substitute for ensuring that yours is as secure as possible, in relation to the aspects of design and technology that you are teaching and in relation to the relevant aspects of any linked subjects. However, particularly when using real world applications, you could draw on local expertise where possible. Not only does this potentially offer additional knowledge, understanding and skills to support the pupils, it can add to the authenticity of the real world application being presented. This could range from a single person or small business, to a thriving local industry; indeed, some larger employers may already have education programmes in place which you could draw on. Where possible, in engaging with external expertise, seek to challenge possible stereotypes. This might also be an important consideration when identifying appropriate real world applications.

You may also find support from some national large companies, from useful resources made available on their websites to the opportunity to borrow materials on loan. For example, the James Dyson Foundation offers all primary schools the opportunity to borrow a 'Design Process Box' for a period of six weeks, at no charge (including delivery and collection, so the location of your school is not important).

RESPONSE TO CRITICAL TASK 4.1

Reflecting on your own experiences of design and technology

You were asked to reflect on your own experiences of being a learner in design and technology lessons during your time at primary school. Your own memories may match those of many student teachers, in that you may recall drawing designs and making products out of wood, card and reclaimed materials. Remember, though, that effective teaching of design and technology also involves evaluation and the development of technical knowledge. Remember also that the curriculum (DfE, 2013: 181–2) requires pupils to work with textiles and ingredients, as well as with construction materials. In fact, the National Curriculum for design and technology includes a distinct programme of study for cooking and nutrition (DfE, 2013: 183) for Key Stage 1 and for Key Stage 2, which needs to be addressed through each school's long-term plan for design and technology.

APPLICATION OF THE PEDAGOGIC FOCUS TO OTHER SUBJECTS

We have considered how to make effective use of real world applications to support and contextualise pupils' learning in design and technology. The use of real world applications can also be applied to other subjects in the primary curriculum. As geography should 'inspire in pupils a curiosity and fascination about the world and its people' (DfE, 2013: 184), it seems logical that we should seek to use real world applications, wherever possible, within our teaching of geography. Combining geographical skills and fieldwork with our teaching of the required knowledge and understanding is one meaningful way of applying geographical learning to the real world. Study of the local area, at both key stages, also offers the opportunity to engage with geography in a meaningful and authentic manner. As in design and technology, the selection of appropriate real world applications will be important, as will seeking to challenge possible stereotypes.

In the same way that using real world applications in design and technology can remind us that one of the fundamental principles of design and technology is that it is about creating a product that does something for someone, using real world applications in computing can provide valuable, authentic contexts for developing pupils' programming skills. At both key stages, pupils are required to create and debug programmes; creating these for a real world application will likely motivate and support pupils in identifying meaning from something that could otherwise appear potentially abstract.

SUMMARY FOR THIS CHAPTER

In this chapter, we have explored some key principles involved in teaching design and technology effectively. We have identified the potential value of using real world applications to contextualise learning in design and technology. We have explored the importance of selecting real world applications that are familiar and/or interesting for pupils, as well as considered the value of exploiting meaningful links to other curriculum areas and of drawing upon external expertise where possible.

When teaching design and technology, do:

- engage pupils in evaluation activities, through disassembly and tinkering
- use focused tasks and demonstrations effectively to teach the technical knowledge that pupils will need before they engage in designing and making
- use your own work to model ideas and to explain the methods you used to identify a problem or to tackle a task
- model and use technical language and subject-specific terms accurately at each stage of the 'evaluate, develop technical knowledge, design and make' sequence.

When using real world applications as a context for teaching design and technology, do:

- select contexts that are familiar and/or stimulating and which enable you to address the curriculum requirements for design and technology
- consider meaningful links to other curriculum subjects, ensuring that your own subject knowledge is secure in all aspects, not just in design and technology
- draw on local expertise, seeking to avoid stereotypes where possible.

FURTHER READING

As mentioned at the beginning of this chapter, design and technology does not have a deep tradition of research pedagogy in the way that some other subjects do. However, there are some useful books that explore the subject in a practical and appropriate manner. The following sources may, therefore, be helpful in further developing your knowledge and understanding of effective pedagogy.

Flinn, E. and Patel, S. (2016) *The really useful primary design and technology book*. Abingdon: Routledge.

This text manages to live up to its title claim, with ideas that are achievable and authentic to the subject.

Hope, G. (2018) *Mastering primary design and technology*. London: Bloomsbury.

Gill Hope has long been a prominent, passionate advocate for teaching design and technology. This latest text provides a comprehensive discussion of the subject and its origins, aims and relevance to pupils.

Sparke, P. (2009) *The genius of design*. London: Quadrille Publishing Ltd.

This text provides a fantastic reminder of the wonderful designers, from William Morris to Jony Ive, whose products have changed the way we live.

REFERENCES

Department for Education (DfE) (2013) *The national curriculum in England: key stages 1 and 2 framework document*. London: DfE.

Hope, G. (2006) *Teaching design and technology at key stages 1 and 2*. Exeter: Learning Matters.

Hope, G. (2018) *Mastering primary design and technology*. London: Bloomsbury.

Klapwijk, R. (2017) 'Creativity in design' in Benson, C. and Lawson, S. (eds.) *Teaching design and technology creatively*. Abingdon: Routledge, pp. 51–72.

Milne, L. (2017) 'Children learning outside the classroom' in Benson, C. and Lawson, S. (eds.) *Teaching design and technology creatively*. Abingdon: Routledge, pp. 146–58.

Newton, D. (2005) *Teaching design and technology*. London: Paul Chapman Publishing.

Ofsted (2012) 'Ofsted's subject professional development materials: design and technology: a training resource for teachers of design and technology in primary schools' [PowerPoint presentation]. Available at: https://dera.ioe.ac.uk/16456/7/Design%20and%20technology%20professional%20development%20materials%20for%20primary%20schools_Redacted.pdf (Accessed: 23 April 2019).

5

ENGLISH

DEVELOPING CHILDREN'S ABILITY TO FORM, ARTICULATE AND JUSTIFY OPINIONS

RACHEL EPERJESI AND TRACEY WIRE

OBJECTIVES

- To explore the distinctive nature of primary English.
- To consider how teachers can develop children's skills in forming, articulating and justifying their opinions in primary English.
- To reflect on opportunities to develop and apply these skills in some other subjects within the primary curriculum.

In this chapter, we explore the distinctive nature of primary English and consider its pivotal position within the primary curriculum. We consider some key principles for teaching English effectively. We then examine the role of the teacher in enabling children to develop the important skills of forming, articulating and justifying their opinions and consider some of the challenges teachers might encounter in doing so. The chapter concludes with some consideration of ways in which these skills can be developed and applied in other curriculum subjects.

WHAT IS DISTINCTIVE ABOUT TEACHING AND LEARNING IN ENGLISH?

The importance of English within primary schools cannot be overestimated, with the DfE (2013: 13) stating that English 'has a pre-eminent place in education and in society'. Additionally, English is 'the medium for teaching' (DfE, 2013: 10) all other subjects, with pupils using their spoken language, reading and writing skills to access the full curriculum.

In 2008, the National Literacy Trust's (Dugdale and Clark, 2008) *Literacy changes lives* report presented evidence suggesting that higher levels of literacy are associated with improved happiness and success. Ten years later, the Trust's new report, *Literacy and life expectancy* (Gilbert et al., 2018), considered evidence that poor literacy outcomes have a negative correlation with life expectancy, socioeconomic factors and health. While recognising that these relationships are not straightforward, in that correlation does not necessarily equate to causation, their findings support the emphasis placed upon English within the National Curriculum and beyond.

While the strategies and approaches you might use in your teaching of English are beyond the scope of a single chapter, below we consider some key principles that underpin effective learning and teaching in English.

THE JOURNEY FROM READING TO WRITING

One effective approach is to plan and teach genre-based units, taking children on a journey from reading to writing, building on a foundation of spoken language. For example, a unit might focus on the genre of persuasion or on the genre of traditional tales. As with any subject, the starting point for planning should be to identify what children need to learn by the end of the unit of work.

A good way into any genre is to begin with a reading phase, so that children become immersed in the genre and familiar with its specific structure, features, purpose and so on. This addresses aspects of the Reading strand of the National

Curriculum, purposefully and in context, while also supporting children to develop a 'toolbox' of the knowledge, understanding and skills needed to write effectively within the genre.

Children then need opportunities to orally explore ideas, vocabulary, specific language features and so on. Whether or not you follow the particular approaches outlined in *Talk for writing* (Department for Children, Schools and Families (DCSF), 2008), and whatever the genre, we suggest a spoken language phase should precede any writing phase; Myhill and Jones (2009: 265) claim that 'the principle ... that an appropriate pedagogy for writing should include planned opportunities for talk is well researched and well understood'. This approach enables aspects of the Spoken Language strand of the National Curriculum to be addressed and prepares pupils for writing by giving them the opportunity to experiment and refine their ideas before committing pen(cil) to paper.

When taught well, these phases build upon each other, developing children as readers, speakers, listeners and writers. Each phase can also provide an opportunity for children to focus on SPAG (spelling, punctuation and grammar) in context, which Myhill et al.'s (2012) research has shown to be more effective than teaching grammar in discrete sessions.

INSPIRING A LOVE OF LITERATURE

The simple view of reading (Gough and Turner, 1986) proposes that there are two strands to reading: word recognition (decoding) and language comprehension. However, the reality is that teaching children to read is complex and multi-faceted.

Alongside teaching children how to read, teachers have a responsibility to inspire a love of literature. This is supported within the aims of the National Curriculum (DfE, 2013: 13), to 'ensure that all pupils ... develop the habit of reading widely and often, for both pleasure and information'. Within genre-based units of work, it is important that the reading phase provides opportunities for children to engage deeply with whole texts, rather than endless extracts.

Cremin et al.'s (2008, 2009) research into 'teachers as readers' identified the pivotal role that teachers play in developing reading for pleasure (RfP). Teachers must develop their own knowledge of children's literature and other texts, and of children's reading experiences and practices, to select texts that engage and inspire children. They should also present themselves as readers.

This research (2009) also established 'RfP pedagogy', comprising four key elements: reading aloud to children (sharing a book for the sheer enjoyment of it); establishing social reading environments; providing time and space for independent reading; and facilitating opportunities for children to engage in informal 'booktalk' with each other, including making book recommendations.

TALK AS A FOUNDATION FOR LEARNING

Talk is used as a medium for learning right across the curriculum, and is unique in relation to English, in that the development of spoken language forms part of the National Curriculum. Thus it follows that, in addition to providing ample opportunities for children to engage in meaningful talk to support the development of reading and writing skills, teachers must explicitly teach speaking and listening skills. As with all subjects, this is built upon assessment of existing skills and identifying next steps; it is too easy to assume that 'children are talking all the time' and so they will make progress simply by doing more of it.

Taking a genre-based approach to planning and teaching units of work provides opportunities for explicitly teaching speaking and listening skills. Spoken language provides 'a bridge' between the reading and writing phases; rather than rushing from one to the other, take time to linger in the spoken language phase. This provides opportunities for children to explore their ideas orally and to practise the skills and techniques they will use in their writing.

WRITING: RAISING THE BAR

Writing attainment often lags behind reading attainment, at least when measured in statutory assessment. There are many possible explanations for this gap, not least the possibility that the assessment is flawed; nonetheless, we need to aim to raise attainment in writing, whether in an attempt to 'close the gap' or simply to have maximum impact on learners.

Writing is complex, even for accomplished writers. The compositional aspects (what do I want to say and how do I want to say it?) and the transcriptional aspects (spelling, handwriting, punctuation, etc.) compete and the writer draws on a wide range of knowledge and skills.

CRITICAL TASK 5.1

Completing a piece of writing

- Write a persuasive text to encourage tourists to visit Tintagel Castle.
- You have ten minutes to produce at least one side of A4.

We are fairly sure that you did not actually attempt the task above. The real task is to consider how you felt when faced with that activity. Were you confident to make a start immediately? Did it cause any anxiety? If so, why?

Now reflect on the implications for teaching writing to children.

A key driver for the genre-based approach is to build up to writing, enabling children to develop the necessary knowledge (of the genre and of the context) and skills to write effectively in the genre. Producing a written outcome at the end of a unit of work is not a test, nor is it designed to 'trip the child up'; instead, the process should be scaffolded through earlier sessions in the unit of work.

The following factors all contribute to raising attainment in writing:

- securing your own knowledge of the structure and specific features of the genre
- sharing good quality examples in the genre
- writing for a purpose and audience
- engaging in talk before writing
- engaging in experiential learning, providing a context for writing
- writing in response to a range of stimuli, including cross-curricular themes
- linking to children's interests
- separating presentation from composition; children can then focus on editing and redrafting, before producing a 'tidy' and error-free final version
- scaffolding writing through shared and guided work, providing supporting resources (such as working wall displays, success criteria, appropriate writing frames), collaborative work and so on
- identifying the steps to learning: first establish your expectations, then plan a 'learning journey' from the starting point to your expectations.

PEDAGOGIC FOCUS FOR THIS CHAPTER: DEVELOPING CHILDREN'S ABILITY TO FORM, ARTICULATE AND JUSTIFY OPINIONS

In the following, we have chosen poetry as a context to explore the value of developing children's ability to form, articulate and justify their opinions through exploratory talk. We are aware that, for some teachers, 'poetry is a subject they would quite readily hide in a box at the back of the literacy cupboard and forget all about' (Dyer, 2017: 151); yet poetry holds huge potential for learning and forms part of the National Curriculum. We therefore seek to raise the profile of poetry; what follows, though, could be equally applied to any aspect of English.

WHY IS IT IMPORTANT TO DEVELOP CHILDREN'S SKILLS IN FORMING, ARTICULATING AND JUSTIFYING OPINIONS?

The National Curriculum requirements for spoken language state that 'Pupils should be taught to: . . . articulate and justify answers, arguments and opinions' (DfE, 2013: 17). In doing so, it is likely that other spoken language requirements will be addressed, for they might 'consider and evaluate different viewpoints, attending to and building on the contributions of others' or 'participate in discussions, presentations ... and debates'. While these are skills that are certainly important for English, Mercer and Mannion (2018) claim that improved spoken language skills have an impact on attainment across the curriculum and on long-term academic study, social development, emotional well-being and employability.

Opinions can be as simple as making a non-verbal choice (e.g. a baby choosing a toy), to deciding as a family which movie to watch, right through to situations that require us to provide a detailed and articulate response regarding what we think about something and why (e.g. seeking to convince an interview panel why you are the best person for the job).

DEVELOPING EXPLORATORY TALK IN THE CLASSROOM

Consider the importance of spoken language in the development of thinking. Often opinion is developed, as well as articulated and justified, through talk. Not all talk, however, is equally productive. Wegerif and Mercer (1997) classified and defined types of talk; these have been summarised by Rojas-Drummond et al. (2006: 85):

- Cumulative talk: in which speakers build positively but uncritically on what the other has said.
- Disputational talk: characterised by disagreement and individualised decision-making.
- Exploratory talk: in which partners engage critically but constructively with each other's ideas.

Each of these provides an opportunity for children to actively engage in 'social modes of thinking' (Wegerif and Mercer, 1997: 53), but it is exploratory talk that provides the richest opportunities for children to develop their own opinions in collaboration with others. In the early stages of formulating, articulating and justifying their opinions, when engaged in exploratory talk, children's utterances are likely to be 'hesitant and incomplete' (Barnes, 2008: 5). Teachers must encourage children to engage in this kind of 'messy' talk, valuing it as part of an important process of developing and clarifying ideas and opinions, as well as spoken language skills. Equally, teachers should model this form of speech and development of thinking, making the process transparent to help children to develop their spoken language skills.

The need to justify is a key element of exploratory talk. This might not come naturally to all children, so teachers can support this element by modelling the use of sentence stems (e.g. 'I think ... because ...'), asking questions (e.g. 'Why do you think that?', 'Can you explain a little more?') and providing prompts (e.g. 'Try to convince me'). In the case of poetry, children should justify their opinions with reference to the linguistic features of the poems (e.g. use of rhyme, vocabulary, use of simile or metaphor).

Clearly, children will only be able to do this if they have been taught about these features. Again, teachers may need to support this by asking questions, such as 'What is it about the poem/the verse/the line that led you to that?' or 'Are there any particular words or phrases that made you think that?'. 'Good' poetry, as with other forms of literature, should evoke an emotional response; that still needs to be justified, and the justifications should be rooted in the same evidence as a discussion about other aspects of the poem. By calling upon these features and experiences, pupils provide a solid foundation for the opinions they express.

Children (and adults) will have differences in opinion; these need to be acknowledged and valued, with teachers explicitly promoting and respecting difference. This is important when discussing all forms of literature; none of us can be certain of the author's true intentions/meaning. Reassuring children that 'there are no right or wrong answers' or that 'this is just my idea and we don't know if it matches the author's or not' should encourage children to contribute, particularly if the teacher then praises and/or thanks them for sharing their idea, without 'judging its accuracy'. In our experience, 'Thank you for sharing your interesting idea' is much more likely to encourage children to share their opinion, than 'well done, that's a good idea'. Explicitly seeking differences in opinion (e.g. 'Does anyone have a different idea/think something different?') is also helpful, not only in encouraging children to contribute, but also as it is likely to prompt further justification.

CREATING A 'TALK-RICH' ENVIRONMENT

CRITICAL TASK 5.2

What is a 'talk-rich' environment?

Think about your own experiences in the classroom, as a pupil, student and teacher. Would you describe them as 'talk-rich'? What do you think this means?

A classroom full of talk is not necessarily what we would describe as talk-rich. Talk should be purposeful, enabling pupils to develop and articulate their reasoning. Speaking to communicate is an integral part of most children's lives before they begin their schooling. This does not mean that talk is easy; we still need to work hard to ensure that children develop their spoken language skills. To develop a talk-rich environment, pupils should be taught the skills of both speaking *and* listening (Mercer and Mannion, 2018). In their everyday dealings with pupils and in planned interactions, adults need to: model well-structured, coherent speech; introduce pupils to a broad and vibrant vocabulary (both verbal and written); model and promote active listening and responding; and help children to understand the conventions of conversation and discussion, such as taking turns, making eye contact and avoiding interrupting.

Children need to have something meaningful to talk about. Teachers should identify purposeful foci for talk that are engaging and, as with selecting texts, connect with children's personal interests. When seeking to raise levels of attainment in both spoken language and thinking, teachers need to challenge and inspire children to engage in exploratory talk, both with the teacher and with other children.

COLLABORATIVE WORK

CRITICAL TASK 5.3

Planning for collaborative talk-based learning

What might teachers need to consider when planning for collaborative, talk-based learning?

To promote exploratory talk in the classroom, teachers must plan for children to work in groups and speak their thoughts in an open and extended way, so that they are able to socially construct meaning. Only with careful guidance and opportunities to practise will working collaboratively enable children to develop their opinions, moving from cumulative and disputational talk to rich exploratory talk. By enabling this kind of talking and 'thinking together' (Rojas-Drummond at al., 2006: 91), children should be able to develop, justify and present their opinions effectively. Indeed, it is often the case that it is only through speaking their thoughts aloud that pupils begin to interrogate their own ideas at a deeper level; the act of speaking itself engages the individual in actively developing and questioning their own thoughts. However, it is only within the context of a talk-rich environment, and well-planned and resourced lessons, that children can develop the skills and confidence they need in order to take risks in the development of their thinking and its expression.

This approach can present challenges, particularly for inexperienced teachers. Pupils new to this approach frequently find themselves unsure of the 'rules'. This can feel threatening both for teachers accustomed to controlling every aspect of the learning environment and for those pupils who consistently look to their teacher for direction. The teacher might take a 'little and often' approach, with well-structured tasks and tightly focused teacher questioning and prompts for thinking. Initially, pupils are likely to be highly dependent on their teacher to set the parameters of an activity, model how to work collaboratively and drive the learning forward. An incremental, scaffolded approach should support pupils to relearn the rules of classroom engagement, to move away from directing every utterance through their teacher to a position where they engage in meaningful dialogue with their peers directly. As children become increasingly familiar and comfortable with this approach, they should become more independent, self-directed and confident to take risks with their own learning.

Group membership and size are important. Carefully considering children's spoken language skills before placing them in a group is essential. Match the size of the group to the task you are setting. As a general rule, the bigger the group, the harder it is to manage in terms of both learning and behaviour, so begin with talk partners. Even when children move on to working in small groups, the use of talk partners within the group can help support the development of spoken language and reasoning. Giving individual pupils specific roles within the group can also facilitate productive collaboration.

The physical environment also plays a part. Think about the layout of your classroom. Would it be best to reconfigure your classroom on a permanent basis or do you need to move chairs and tables to suit particular activities? It is very difficult, for example, to engage in meaningful dialogue if you cannot see the people you are talking to; eye contact and facial expressions are important cues that can guide our responses. Working in a circle means that children can see one another.

Establish rules and routines for talk. Children must listen to others in order to respond effectively to what they say; teaching children to actively listen is an essential starting point for 'talk rules'. Making eye contact, being respectful and turn-taking are all basic features of quality interaction and should be made explicit so that they become characteristic of all classroom talk (not just that planned by the teacher). These features of high-quality collaborative talk are the same whether children are taking part in a mathematics reasoning activity, circle time or discussing poetry, and should be reinforced.

It is easy to become narrowly focused on classroom outcomes but, through moving pupils to independence in their use of spoken language and promoting their ability to reason and problem-solve as part of a group, it is important to remember that pupils are learning skills that will serve them well throughout their lives.

CASE STUDY 5.1

In this example, Harriet, an undergraduate primary student teacher in her second year of training, is undertaking a session with a group of Year 2 pupils who have been assessed as working at greater depth in reading. She is seeking to

(Continued)

develop the children's skills in developing, sharing and justifying their opinions. She shares the poem 'Winter' (Nicholls, 1987) with the group, then initiates a discussion. Short extracts from the whole transcript are presented below. Before reading the transcript, you should read the poem; this can be easily located on the internet, including on The Poetry Archive website.

Harriet: So we're just going to talk about the poem; you can just talk to me and tell me what you think about it. There are no wrong or right answers; you just tell me what you think.

[Harriet reads the poem to the group.]

Harriet: What do you think it's about? *[2 second pause]* Belle, what do you think it's about?

Belle: Um … winter?

Harriet: Why do you think winter?

Belle: Because you kept saying things about winter.

Harriet: Anything else that made you think it was about winter? Did anyone think it was about something different?

Toby: There were icicles on his lips.

Harriet: Why did icicles make you think of winter?

Toby: Because icicles are always hanging when it's really cold in winter.

[Other children are asked, in turn, whether it makes them think of winter and why. After they have all responded, Harriet reads the poem again and the children join in spontaneously.]

Harriet: Are there any words in there that you're not sure about? Do you know what a limpet is?

Saira: I don't.

[Harriet provides an explanation.]

Harriet: Emily, what do you think about the poem then?

Emily: I think it's really nice and calming, and like … well, a bit of me is thinking it's turning into winter.

Harriet: So just becoming winter… ? Are there any words in there that make you think that?

Emily: Yeah … froze, frozen … and um … icicles. Winter's going through the world and making it winter.

Harriet: Interesting. Joseph, what about you? *[1.5 second pause]* Callum? Anything about the poem that tells you anything? *[2 second pause]*

Harriet: Ok, what about this bit: 'Winter crept through the whispering wood'? What's whispering?

Saira: Animals?

Harriet: You can't be wrong. It's your idea. Anyone else?

Joseph: The trees.

Harriet: Why might the trees be whispering?

Joseph: 'Cos when it's cold it might be windy and the trees make noises.

[Harriet reads from another section of the poem and asks the children what they think of it.]

Emily: The limpets are stuck with ice, like cracks or something.

Harriet: Nice. What makes you think that?

Emily: Because … well, when you get a frost bite, you know, it's um, it's like the frost is kind of nipping you and my car, it had loads of little frost bites on it and it had sealed the door closed. My dad had to pull it really, really hard to get it undone.

Harriet: So you're using what you already know, what you have already seen and comparing it to the limpet on the stones. Amazing.

Student teacher evaluation: Harriet identified that the children were 'quite good at explaining themselves' and that it was 'really nice that they drew on their own thoughts and experiences'. When we commented positively on Harriet's use of questioning to draw out justification, she replied, 'Well, I don't want them to think that what they say doesn't matter. So we've been doing a lot of "what do you think, what's your idea, it might not be the same as everyone else's". So I do want them to know that'. She continued, 'I don't want to give my opinions too much. I didn't want to shape their opinions. So I didn't know whether I should model giving my ideas so they could see … or … I don't know. It's about them'.

Expert critique: In feeding back to Harriet, there was much to be positive about. From the outset, she was clear that differences in opinion were

(Continued)

welcome and that there were 'no wrong answers'. As well as eliciting children's opinions, she used questioning to draw out justification based on evidence from the poem. She also ensured that the children understood the vocabulary to aid their comprehension of the poem. When responding to Emily, she summarised and praised the approach Emily had taken, to make the thinking process clear to all children in the group. We encouraged Harriet to thank the children for their contributions more frequently and to try to praise the process, rather than the opinion itself. For example, she might say, 'Well done for using the poem to explain why you think that so clearly', rather than 'Good idea', which suggests that, despite what the teacher says about 'no wrong answers', it might be the 'right' answer.

The poem was well chosen. It was challenging, but not so challenging that the children were unable to access it at all (not least because they all had some experience of winter). This enabled children to demonstrate sophisticated comprehension skills. After considering the whole poem, Harriet broke it down into manageable chunks (one verse or even one line at a time), to ensure the children were sharing and justifying more focused opinions, drawing on specific aspects from that section of the poem.

We noted that the children tended to only interact with Harriet (rather than each other), one at a time, and some only when asked to do so. We encouraged Harriet to give children more time to talk in small groups, before engaging in a whole group discussion. The intention was for children to have the chance to use exploratory talk to begin to form an opinion, before being asked to share it more widely. We hoped that it would also encourage the children to work more collaboratively, with less reliance on Harriet to lead the discussion.

Harriet asked whether she should model giving her ideas and was encouraged to do so, as long as she remembered to make it clear that they were just her ideas, so the children's ideas might be different. We also suggested that she could take a 'some people think that … and other people think … ' approach, if she was concerned her own views might 'lead' the children too much.

CASE STUDY 5.2

In this example, we return to observe Harriet leading a similar session with a different group of Year 2 pupils, following her own evaluation of the previous session and after receiving our feedback. These children are mostly working at the expected standard for reading, with one (Byron) working towards the expected standard. Harriet was initially concerned about using the same poem with this group of children, as their reading attainment was lower than the previous group, but we encouraged her to try it. Short extracts from the transcript are presented below.

[Having spent some time reading the poem, Harriet asks the children to talk in pairs about the setting. After two minutes of the children talking and returning to the poem with a partner, Harriet brings the group back together.]

Harriet: Ok, lovely. So, the author, the poet, where do you think she's talking about?

Kitty: Maybe a winter forest.

Harriet: Well, have a look at the words. What about them makes you think of a forest?

Kitty: Because there's a stream.

Byron: Or a beach.

Evie: Because there's a limpet … the sand.

Byron: The sand and the rocks.

[Later the children come close to an understanding of personification, a concept they have not yet encountered.]

Harriet: Thank you for sharing your ideas. I like that you're really thinking about it. None of us really know, do we? I don't really know. So these are all our ideas and these are really interesting ideas. So, what do you think about the last bit?

[Harriet reads the final verse of the poem and gives the children the opportunity to discuss in pairs for one minute.]

Harriet: What do you think?

Byron: Look – 'his breath'. A man.

Harriet: So, we're back to talking about a man again. What about you, Lily, do you think the same or do you think something different?

Lily: I think it's a man getting frozen and stuck.

Byron: Everything's getting frozen.

(Continued)

Student teacher evaluation: Harriet noted that these children were talking as a group far more frequently than the previous group and suggested this was probably due to letting them talk in pairs at key points. She felt that this reminded the children that they 'had permission' to talk and that she wanted them to do so. She noted that Lily, who often calls out and talks over people, had not done that during this session and had listened attentively to other children, as well as making her own contributions. Harriet suggested this was partly due to Lily being interested in the discussion and partly because Lily knew she would have the opportunity to speak to a partner, so would be 'heard' and therefore did not need to compete. Harriet was pleased that the children had been willing to share different ideas, and noted that she had reinforced 'there's no wrong answers' and 'you can't be wrong' and had asked 'do you think the same or do you think something different?'. She was both surprised and pleased with the depth of the discussion, commenting, 'I didn't expect this group to get as much out of the poem as the last group, but it just shows that you shouldn't put a limit on them, just because of their own reading skills. They might understand much more if they can talk about it'. Harriet was a little concerned that this had been longer than the previous session, but noted that she now intended to let the children talk to each other more in future lessons 'as I feel their responses will be better for it'.

Expert critique: This session demonstrated that Harriet had made progress in her ability to develop children's skills in forming, articulating and justifying their opinions. All the children were much more willing to contribute and justify their opinions, having had the opportunity to form these through exploratory talk with a partner first. At times, Harriet allowed the children to take the lead; she was successful in setting up a talk-rich environment and establishing a collaborative situation. She acknowledged that the discussion was richer and deeper than with the previous group, as she had enabled them to work together to build a shared understanding through different types of talk.

We reassured Harriet that although incorporating talk might mean that you 'cover' less in a lesson, what is covered will be in far more depth, while simultaneously developing transferrable skills. A few key discussion points can be much more valuable for learning, than attempting to cover many points in a superficial way.

APPLICATION OF THE PEDAGOGIC FOCUS TO OTHER SUBJECTS

We have considered how to develop children's skills in forming, articulating and justifying their opinions in English, within the specific context of poetry. The same skills can be developed, using the same or similar approaches, in other contexts in English and in other subjects in the primary curriculum. For example, one of the aims for music in the National Curriculum (DfE, 2013: 196) is to ensure that all pupils 'listen to, review and evaluate music across a range of historical periods, genres, styles and traditions', thus providing purposeful opportunities for children to express and justify their own opinions about the music that they have listened to. Teachers can use the same approaches outlined in this chapter, such as making use of exploratory talk and providing opportunities for collaboration, to support pupils in effectively evaluating music that they have listened to. The ability to identify and communicate what they like and dislike, and why, will also support children with the compositional aspects of music, where they will need to make decisions, possibly in collaboration with others.

The Personal, Social, Health and Economic Education (PSHE) Association programme of study (2017: 3) states that one of the aims of PSHE is to 'enable [children] to communicate constructively in a variety of settings'. It goes on to outline skills and attributes that children should develop through PSHE, which include 'clarifying their values' and 'skills for employability', such as 'active listening and communication', 'team working' and 'presentation skills' (2017: 5). The approaches to teaching explored in this chapter can equally be employed in teaching PSHE, providing children with meaningful opportunities to develop, express and justify their opinions (as well as engage positively with those of others) in relation to a wide range of topics related to health and well-being, relationships and citizenship.

SUMMARY FOR THIS CHAPTER

In this chapter, we have explored some key principles involved in teaching English effectively. We have learnt that English can provide valuable and purposeful opportunities for children to develop their skills in forming, articulating and justifying their own opinions, and that the teacher plays an important role in facilitating this development. We have explored the importance of establishing a talk-rich environment, in which there are plenty of opportunities for collaborative work and in which exploratory talk is valued and modelled, as part of the thinking process.

When teaching English, do:

- plan and teach units of work in English which address all three strands: reading, spoken language and writing
- inspire a love of literature alongside the teaching of reading
- give ample opportunities for children to engage in meaningful talk which supports them in reading and writing, as well as developing their spoken language skills
- teach children the knowledge and skills needed to write effectively in a range of genres.

When developing children's skills in forming, articulating and justifying opinions, do:

- create and value a talk-rich environment
- provide opportunities for children to engage in discussion
- model and encourage the use of exploratory talk to support children in organising and communicating their thoughts
- teach children the skills needed to engage in effective collaborative work and provide opportunities for them to do so.

FURTHER READING

The following sources may be helpful in further developing your knowledge and understanding of effective pedagogy:

Medwell, J., Wray, D., Minns, H., Griffiths, V. and Coates, E. (2017) *Primary English: teaching theory and practice*. 8th edn. London: SAGE Publications.

This text explores a wide range of pedagogy for effective teaching of primary English.

Mercer, N. and Hodgkinson, S. (eds.) (2008) *Exploring talk in school*. London: SAGE Publications.

This edited text is a very useful resource for any teacher wanting to engage children in purposeful talk, both to develop their spoken language skills (such as their skills in forming, articulating and justifying their opinions) and as a tool to support and extend learning across the curriculum and beyond.

The Open University (2018) 'Research rich pedagogies. Excellence in research: inspiring creative pedagogies'. Available at: www.researchrichpedagogies.org/ (Accessed: 23 April 2019).

This useful website considers a range of research in relation to the potential implications for pedagogy. The section on 'reading for pleasure' pedagogy is particularly relevant to this chapter.

REFERENCES

Barnes, D. (2008) 'Exploratory talk for learning' in Mercer, N. and Hodgkinson, S. (eds.) *Exploring talk in school*. London: SAGE Publications, pp. 1–15.

Cremin, T., Bearne, E., Mottram, M. and Goodwin, P. (2008) 'Primary teachers as readers', *English in Education*, 42(1), pp. 8–23.

Cremin, T., Mottram, M., Collins, F., Powell, S. and Safford, K. (2009) 'Teachers as readers: building communities of readers', *Literacy*, 43(1), pp. 11–19.

Department for Children, Schools and Families (DCSF) (2008) *Talk for writing*. London: DCSF.

Department for Education (DfE) (2013) *The national curriculum in England: key stages 1 and 2 framework document*. London: DfE.

Dugdale, G. and Clark, C. (2008) *Literacy changes lives: an advocacy resource*. London: National Literacy Trust.

Dyer, H. (2017) 'Poetry' in Waugh, D., Jolliffe, W. and Allott, K. (eds.) *Primary English for trainee teachers*. 2nd edn. London: SAGE Publications, pp. 151–67.

Gilbert, L., Teravainen, A., Clark, C. and Shaw, S. (2018) *Literacy and life expectancy*. London: National Literacy Trust.

Gough, P.B. and Turner, W.E. (1986) 'Decoding, reading and reading disability', *Remedial and Special Education*, 7(1), pp. 6–10.

Mercer, N. and Mannion, J. (2018) 'Oracy across the Welsh curriculum.' Available at: http://oracycambridge.org/wp-content/uploads/2018/07/Oracy-across-the-Welsh-curriculum-July-2018.pdf (Accessed: 23 April 2019).

Myhill, D. and Jones, S. (2009) 'How talk becomes text: investigating the concept of oral rehearsal in early years' classrooms', *British Journal of Educational Studies*, 57(3), pp. 265–84.

Myhill, D., Lines, H. and Watson, A. (2012) 'Making meaning with grammar: a repertoire of possibilities', *English in Australia*, 47(3), pp. 29–38.

Nicholls, J. (1987) 'Winter', *The Poetry Archive*. Available at: www.poetryarchive.org/poem/winter (Accessed: 23 April 2019).

Ofsted (2007) *Poetry in schools: a survey of practice 2006/07*. London: Ofsted.

Personal, Social and Health Education (PSHE) Association (2017) *PSHE education programme of study (key stages 1–5)*. Available at: www.pshe-association.org.uk/system/files/PSHE%20Education%20Programme%20of%20Study%20%28Key%20stage%201-5%29%20Jan%202017_2.pdf (Accessed: 23 April 2019).

Rojas-Drummond, S., Mazón, N., Fernández, M. and Wegerif, R. (2006) 'Explicit reasoning, creativity and co-construction in primary school children's collaborative activities', *Thinking Skills and Creativity*, 1(2), pp. 84–94.

Wegerif, R. and Mercer, N., (1997) 'A dialogical framework for researching peer talk', *Language and Education Library*, 12, pp. 49–64.

6

GEOGRAPHY

USING PRACTICAL APPROACHES TO PROMOTE ENGAGEMENT

JOANNA RIGG

OBJECTIVES

- To explore the distinctive nature of primary geography.
- To consider how teachers can make effective use of practical approaches to promote engagement with learning about our world.
- To reflect on the application of practical approaches to promote engagement in some of the other subjects within the primary curriculum.

In this chapter, we will explore the nature of primary geography, identifying the ways in which it is distinctive from other curriculum subjects and considering what it has to offer children as part of their primary education. We will consider some key principles for teaching geography effectively. We will then consider how a range of practical approaches can be used to promote engagement with learning about our world, as well as some of the challenges that teachers may face in using such approaches. The chapter will conclude with some consideration of ways in which these approaches can be applied in other curriculum subjects.

WHAT IS DISTINCTIVE ABOUT GEOGRAPHY, AND TEACHING AND LEARNING IN GEOGRAPHY?

When student teachers are asked what they remember about geography at school, a common response is: 'Maps: colouring maps.' This memory encapsulates one of the difficulties that primary teachers can encounter in teaching geography; that is, understanding the nature and scope of the subject and how to teach it (Ofsted, 2011).

WHAT IS GEOGRAPHY?

A simple definition of geography is 'the study of the physical features of the earth and its atmosphere, and of human activity as it affects and is affected by these' (Oxford Dictionaries online). Alternatively, the Geographical Association (2009: 5) suggests that 'Geography underpins a lifelong "conversation" about the earth as the home of humankind'. A preferred touchstone comes from the National Curriculum (DfE, 2013: 184): 'A high-quality geography education should inspire in pupils a curiosity and fascination about the world and its people that will remain with them for the rest of their lives.'

Geography is ubiquitous, all around us, as we live our daily lives and others live theirs: it is about observing what is happening, being able to record and describe what we notice, and, by using this information and that from other experiences, suggest explanations as to why this is happening. According to Martin (2006), geography should enable children to learn to live in the world.

GEOGRAPHY'S BIG IDEAS

Geographers use key concepts to help piece together information and understand the world around us. These help us 'to understand how the world works, what we do in and to it, and what the effect of natural and human actions are and might be' (Catling and Willy, 2018: 35). At the heart of geographical learning are *enquiry skills*, around which are other big ideas or key concepts: place, space, scale, change, diversity, human and natural (adapted from Catling and Willy, 2018: 35). These concepts overlap and are inter-related. It is likely that most people have everyday understanding of these ideas, but it is also important to recognise the specific geographical meanings, which will be drawn on as we teach children about places and people. These concepts are summarised in Table 6.1.

Table 6.1 Key concepts in geography

Geography's key concepts and ideas
Geographical enquiry and skills. Geographical enquiry can be described as the processes and skills used in raising questions, gathering information, making sense of information, answering questions and communicating this to others (Roberts, 2003). Enquirers will use and develop skills from across the curriculum. 'Graphicacy' is a key element: this encompasses the visual skills used to gather, interpret and explain evidence, such as making and interpreting maps, diagrams, graphs, sketches, photographs, aerial photos and 3D representations. These may be in 'traditional' forms or may use digital technology.
Place: a sense of place, with similarities and differences. A place can be defined as an area with particular characteristics, the combination of which will be unique to that place; geographers often call this a 'sense of place'. Places will be both similar to and different from one another, so these aspects should be discussed, in relation to particular characteristics, with a focus on details rather than making generalisations.
Space: location and pattern. Space relates to where features and places are located and the relationship to other features and places. Patterns in features and places can be used to explain the processes that have formed or changed them.
Scale: local to global. This can be thought of as the 'zoom lens' of geography and enables learners to make links at a range of scales (local, regional, national and international) and to relate their knowledge of process at one scale to help understand how this relates at a different scale.
Change: connections and environmental impact. This relates to change over time and in space: relationships between features, places, people and processes will often mean that a change in a particular location, time or process will not be 'contained' but will have impacts elsewhere; one change in an environment will often produce subsequent changes. The physical and human worlds we live in are the result of a succession of such changes; any environment will have been shaped by previous events and decisions. Once we comprehend this process, we can understand that current natural events and human actions, and the interaction of the two, will form our future worlds. Alongside this understanding, we hope to instil in pupils a sense of stewardship (responsibility to those who will follow).
Diversity: awe and wonder. Children should develop an understanding that our world is infinitely varied and diverse, and appreciate and wonder at the richness of our world, both physical and human. Children should understand diversity not only throughout the world, but also within a particular place, including the people and places with which they are most familiar. This awareness is intimately linked to an understanding that people or places will be both similar and different at the same time. They will share characteristics and also have differences between them.
Human and natural: features and processes. The human world relates to the structures and processes, social and concrete, constructed by people as they live, including features and processes such as home, work, consumption and leisure. The natural world (often called physical geography) encompasses land, water, air and ecological systems and associated landscapes. It is important to understand that both worlds contribute to the characteristics of a particular place and to recognise the processes that produce and change them. Teaching should include elements of both worlds and the inter-relationship between them. (Do not spend energy on trying to classify features as human or physical, as this is surprisingly complex: e.g. a planted tree is part of both the human and natural world.)

GEOGRAPHY IN THE PRIMARY YEARS

It is important to note that there is significant overlap between the key concepts presented in Table 6.1. Effective teaching will not focus on one concept in isolation but combine several 'big ideas'. Children should make progress in knowledge, skills and understanding within each lesson and sequence of learning (Geographical Association, 2014). Teaching will enable children to develop and use their skills to find out about specific features, people and processes in order to build a sense of place. Geographers also seek to understand the changes and patterns of these features and processes at a range of scales, in order to establish underlying explanations for what is happening. Many of the skills developed will be shared with other areas of the curriculum. However, the focus provided by a framework of 'location and pattern' emphasises fieldwork skills and graphicacy: using images, diagrams and maps to gather, make sense of and communicate evidence and conclusions.

CRITICAL TASK 6.1

Generating geographical questions

Think about your local area. Identify a geographical question that children might investigate. It should be of interest to children of the age you are thinking about and it will reflect the characteristics of the place. Here are some examples:

- Where could we go for a teddy bears' picnic?
- We have been asked to write a leaflet for the local estate agent to tell people about our area. What should we include in the leaflet?
- Where does the water in our stream/river come from and where does it go?

Look at the key concepts of geography: which would be involved in this enquiry? How does it relate to the National Curriculum? Identify the knowledge, skills and understanding that could be developed through exploring your local area.

SUBJECT KNOWLEDGE AND CURRICULUM DESIGN

It has been established that geographical learning is hindered when schools give insufficient or irregular time to teaching (Catling and Willy, 2018; Ofsted and Spielman, 2017). Geography is often taught in combination with other subjects; this offers many potential advantages, but can also lead to surface learning and a lack of progress. Long- and medium-term plans should identify where and how geography is regularly taught (this may be in a cross-curricular context through themes or topics). There is considerable choice within the National Curriculum, so teachers can choose material that is topical or relevant to their children and should ensure that there is sufficient time devoted to geography to allow deep learning to be achieved, in which children make progress in geographical knowledge, skills and understanding (Catling and Willy, 2018; Ofsted and Spielman, 2018).

Many writers emphasise the impact of a teacher's own understanding of geography on children's learning (Catling and Willy, 2018; Ofsted and Spielman, 2018). Teachers need to make sure they have good subject knowledge. The Geographical Association *In the Know* documents, available to purchase through its website, are a good starting point.

CHARACTERISTICS OF EFFECTIVE TEACHING

A starting point for teaching geography to young children should be to encourage them to notice, describe and understand the world that they are living in, moving on to the 'everyday' (Martin, 2006) and 'living' geographies of others (Geographical Association, 2009), both in their place and elsewhere. The primary teacher should start from children's experience, but then deepen and broaden it, to enable children to develop a 'different view' (Geographical Association, 2009) of both their immediate surroundings and the wider world. The integrated acquisition and development of knowledge, skills and understanding are fundamental to this learning. Each component is needed to support the development of the other.

Meanwhile, teaching also needs to inspire curiosity about the world, to prompt children to wonder, 'That's interesting, what's going on? Why is that happening?'. These simple but leading questions constitute the basis of enquiry and effective learning of geography.

Catling and Willy (2018: 9–15) draw on inspection reports to outline the characteristics of effective teaching as:

- Purposeful: children have a reason for the learning, that is relevant to them and provokes curiosity.
- Problem orientated: children's work is not limited to description but involves analysis, evaluation and possible implications or solutions to topical questions.
- Enquiry-based: children do the finding out and draw on a range of evidence to reach conclusions.
- Co-operative: they learn with and from each other to contribute to investigations.
- Promoting active engagement with the world: this should be topical and may be through engaging with visitors, fieldwork or virtual fieldwork and communicating with others at a distance.
- Using high-quality, accurate resources: this may be through first-hand experience of the world outside the classroom and a range of secondary sources such as images, maps, newspapers, artefacts and a wide range of information technology.

PEDAGOGIC FOCUS FOR THIS CHAPTER: USING PRACTICAL APPROACHES TO PROMOTE ENGAGEMENT

Learning about the world as it is – 'the real world' – is the core of geography. We need a range of strategies to promote the gathering of evidence about places, so children know what is going on and understand it. Each approach should enable children to do the finding out to:

- notice
- describe
- explain
- look to the future.

Our central resource in geographical learning should always be the world as it is: the real world. We will consider a range of practical strategies to enable children to engage with the real world in your geography teaching.

ENQUIRY

Enquiry is a central approach in this engagement. This does not mean the teacher abdicates responsibility for the learning, but helps children to structure their finding out. Roberts (2003) suggests a possible framework for approaching enquiry, in which there is strong potential for engaging with the real world.

Table 6.2 Stages of enquiry, adapted from Roberts (2003)

Stage of enquiry	What is involved	Note
1. Creating a need to know	Inspiring curiosity, posing a problem, raising questions.	This may result in an overarching question for the enquiry.
Example: The headteacher writes to the class saying she has some money to improve the school playground. Question: What do the children think should be changed?		
2. Gathering data	This may be qualitative or quantitative.	Stages 2 and 3 may happen several times. Analysing the information may raise further questions or the need for more data gathering and subsequent making sense.
Example: Children go into the playground, take digital photos and identify features they would like to improve.		
3. Making sense of the information	Organising the data. Making links between the information gathered. Using it to answer questions.	This may involve activities such as listing, ranking, sorting, classifying, presenting data as charts or graphs, Venn diagrams, matrix diagrams, map-making, model-making.

Stage of enquiry	What is involved	Note
Example: Children annotate photos with problems, draw and annotate a possible solution, and group similar ideas together. They draw up a class list.		
4. Communication of what has been found out	Often this involves an end product that will be viewed by others. This may be linked to the original 'creating a need to know'.	Examples include: story, poetry, persuasive letter, report, explanation, instructions, leaflet, a poster, map, model, display, presentation, video, animation, song, picture, sculpture, textile.
Example: Write letters to the headteacher. Make a class video in the playground outlining problems and suggesting solutions. Meet with headteacher to discuss.		
5. Reflection on learning	Considering the security of findings. How good was the evidence? What might we do differently? What further finding out could we do?	This can be done with all ages with greater sophistication.
Example: Consider places that were missed or things we didn't think about. Headteacher replies telling the children what action is going to be taken and does it.		

Many student teachers, when presented with this approach, ask how this fits with the National Curriculum and whether Ofsted will allow this. Do not worry: there is a close relationship between this framework and the skills outlined in the National Curriculum for geography and, indeed, the requirements of other subjects, such as English and mathematics. Ofsted reports for geography (Ofsted 2008, 2011) and other subjects, for example religious education (Ofsted, 2013), emphasise the positive impact on pupil learning of an enquiry approach.

CRITICAL TASK 6.2

Structuring collaborative enquiry

In Critical task 6.1, you identified an overarching question that children might answer, relevant to the key concepts of geography. This would be the start of a class enquiry about an aspect of your local area.

Now, consider the next steps in a learning sequence related to each part of Roberts' (2003) enquiry framework:

- Creating the need to know: activities to raise the question.
- Gathering data: activities to seek evidence.

(Continued)

- Making sense: activities to sort and analyse evidence.
- Communication of what has been found out: answering the question, suggesting solutions, expressing a reasoned viewpoint.
- Reflecting on learning: is there anything we could add or do better?

Table 6.2 gives you a brief example of an enquiry that follows this framework. As you decide on activities, look for opportunities to include Catling and Willy's (2018) characteristics of effective practice, especially the recommendation that children should have the opportunity to work collaboratively. Each child in the class should participate in each stage of the enquiry, but groups or individuals may focus on different aspects of data gathering or making sense as they seek the evidence that will allow them to suggest an answer to the question. Indeed, children may reach different conclusions or suggested solutions to the question posed. In the example in Table 6.2, children might focus on different parts of the playground when gathering information, annotating photographs and suggesting changes. Each group might then put forward ideas and priorities to suggest to the headteacher, or the class might combine evidence to propose a joint improvement scheme. Collaboration allows each child's contribution to be important and provides a need to communicate with each other throughout the process, constantly developing skills.

FIELDWORK

Fieldwork is the process of gathering data in a particular place. It is an essential part of any geographical education and a requirement at both Key Stages 1 and 2 of the National Curriculum (DfE, 2013). The name 'fieldwork' misleads some students: you do not need to be in a field wearing welly boots, but simply in the real world finding out what is going on. Indeed, some fieldwork will be done inside where much human activity takes place. Fieldwork is more than an educational visit, as it should sit within an enquiry framework, most commonly as part of data gathering. The data gathered about a place in fieldwork is not random, but specific to a particular question. Fieldwork needs to be followed up by making sense of this information, alongside that from other sources, to allow children to form a reasoned response to the original question. Occasionally a field visit might be used to create an awareness of a particular issue (e.g. parking outside the school), but subsequent data gathering in the field would also be needed.

Fieldwork may take place in the school grounds, the local area or further afield. Wherever it takes place, a risk assessment should be completed to identify and minimise any potential risks. Children should be part of this process so they learn about potential dangers and how to keep themselves safe. The Geographical Association website (see the Further reading section) has some useful examples of how teachers have done this.

In fieldwork, teachers will need to design activities that will help children to notice and describe. The activity should focus on heightening children's awareness of what is around them, encouraging pupils to use all their senses; it should guide them to see, describe or measure the features or processes that are the object of the learning. For example, in a class enquiry trying to establish what colour clouds produce rain, a pair of children could go outside, note how heavy the rain is and match the particular shade of white, grey or black of the cloud to a range of colours on a paint chart. Information technology resources may be used to help this process, through taking photos, recording conversations or taking measurements.

CASE STUDY 6.1

In this example, Sumaya and Greg, two undergraduate student teachers, use a fieldwork trail on the school grounds to teach grid references and map-work skills to a class of Year 4 children. The teaching starts with a class discussion about when it might be important to pinpoint locations using room numbers, addresses or postcodes, such as when ensuring that an ambulance gets to the right place to help a patient. This leads to identifying the problem of describing how to find a particular place if there are no buildings, so the idea of grid references is introduced. This creates a 'need to know', providing a reason for learning related to the real world.

Sumaya and Greg start with a map of the UK, with letter grid squares, and gradually zoom in to the location of the children's school, at each stage adding further digits to the grid reference. Children practise giving and finding grid references for particular features near the school.

Prior to the lesson, Sumaya and Greg have prepared maps of the school grounds, using *Digimaps for schools*. Children use these, working in groups of three, to solve the problem of tracking down a 'biscuit thief' by following a trail around the school grounds, with clues at various points. Sumaya and Greg have thought carefully to make the task of following the route and identifying locations progressively harder as children become more confident. Through this fieldwork, children are gathering data that enables them to solve their problem and present their solution on their return to the classroom.

(Continued)

Student teacher evaluation: Sumaya and Greg felt that it was particularly beneficial to involve children with maps of their own local area and their own school, as this engaged them and helped them to relate their learning about map-reading to a meaningful context. The children also responded well to the 'biscuit thief' storyline and were motivated to solve the problem. The children did well with orientating the map, identifying key local landmarks and finding them on the map; as they progressed through the activity, their understanding and ability to justify their location and explain to others where they were, using features on the map and linking them to their location, rapidly improved. As such, the children were able to make links between the abstract (the maps) and the real world. Sumaya and Greg wondered if it would be useful to progress to some independent work to assess the children's learning.

Expert critique: Sumaya and Greg did well in establishing a clear 'need to know' to guide the work in this lesson and this proved motivating for the children. The children were supported with the skills required for carrying out the enquiry and encouraged to co-operate in their groups and develop their questioning and problem-solving skills. Specific geographical vocabulary was modelled by the student teachers and adopted by the children in their discussions. In their reflections, the student teachers correctly noted that the most significant learning occurred when children were outside, getting on with the task and linking the abstract map to the real world. The student teachers also understood that, as children develop their skills, the teacher needs to step back and allow children to work independently.

Fieldwork will not always be possible. We may not be able to travel to a distant place, the context may be too dangerous, we may not be able to observe the details of a process because it is happening too fast or too slowly, or we may just need another viewpoint or additional evidence. In these circumstances we will need to use other strategies to engage with the real world and gather data. We will consider some of these more briefly as the principles involved are similar to those considered in this discussion of fieldwork.

VIRTUAL FIELDWORK

Technology can help us to engage with a distant or dangerous place that we cannot visit. Teachers may use film or video to enable children to 'visit' a place. There is a danger of learners being passive, so clips should be short and chosen for a particular purpose. As in fieldwork, children should seek answers to particular questions and specific tasks should be given to provide a focus and ensure children are actively engaged with the material that is presented. Film is also able to speed up or slow down processes that we might find difficult to observe in the real world. More powerfully, this video or time-lapse photography may be material the children have taken or set up themselves as part of fieldwork.

There is now a range of applications that will enable the children to 'see' a distant place in real time, such as webcams and communication apps on smartphones or tablet devices. These can also be used in combination with links to particular people so children can talk to others, or video message or email if time differences make talking difficult. They can then ask for specific evidence or information and be actively engaged with someone in a distant place. These applications are often used to good effect with twinned schools (see the British Council link in the Further reading section for more information) or with personal links of the teacher or class members.

Another approach enabling children to gather information at a distance is using internet-based applications, such as Google Earth or Street View, to zoom in or out of places and to navigate their way around. These have the advantage over still photos as children are able to be active in deciding where they are looking for evidence. *Digimaps for schools* is an excellent digital mapping programme suitable for primary-aged children which enables them to move between maps at a range of scales, using historical maps and aerial views. It also enables children to actively map by adding information and photos to base maps, as well as use a range of measuring tools. Children need to be aware that, as with filmed material, this is not 'live' information and so may already have changed.

Children may gather live information using the internet. For example, they could plan journeys using transport timetables, plan where and what they are going to eat, where they might visit or shop. One student teacher on placement gave children one million pounds to 'spend' in Mumbai to address their misconception that the population of India was entirely rural and poor, and children explored ways in which they could spend such a sum of money.

CASE STUDY 6.2

In this example, Lee, a final-year undergraduate student teacher, is teaching a sequence of lessons about the River Nile. The class has already spent several weeks considering the 'Gift of The Nile' to the Ancient Egyptians and Lee now poses the question: 'Is the River Nile still important in Egypt?'. Travelling to Egypt for fieldwork is not an option, so Lee models how Google Earth can be used to search for evidence and to help raise further questions. He demonstrates how

(Continued)

to follow the course of the River Nile, occasionally 'zooming in' to particular spots to check key geographical ideas, such as which way the water flows (mountains to the sea), where the river starts (the source), where rivers join (the confluence of the White and Blue Niles), where it flows into the sea (the mouth), and which countries it flows through (not just Egypt), identifying major cities along its course and where most people live. Lee had identified, in advance, particular features that he thought the children might notice and raise further questions about, such as the 'circular fields' created by centre pivot irrigation systems, and had created a simple model to help children understand how these systems function. In the lesson, the children are supported to use Google Earth themselves, in pairs, and record their questions, observations and learning by adding sticky notes to a large-scale map on display, so that relevant information is placed near its location.

Student teacher evaluation: Lee was pleased that the children were engaged, curious and focused. Once into the paired work, they engaged with very little adult input because they wanted to find out more, and independently identified features such as cities, buildings and farming areas. They made links and developed enquiry skills; for example, while discussing farming areas, they identified straight lines as canals that transport water to the farms further from the Nile. Lee was pleased with the way in which the children collected, recorded and contributed information as the lesson progressed. The pre-prepared model of centre pivot irrigation and how this formed circular crop fields seemed to help all the children to understand the relationship to the circles seen on Google Earth. On reflection, Lee wondered whether the children could have had more time to explore using Google Earth, as they were captivated by this and were very focused on making observations and raising questions.

Expert critique: This case study illustrates that, even when fieldwork is not feasible, technology can enable children to engage with the real world using virtual approaches. It also demonstrates that, once an enquiry is underway, subsidiary questions, raised by the children, will often emerge. In this case, modelling, images and maps were used to explore issues that were raised. Lee was successful in structuring the enquiry so it was not simply descriptive, but children identified a range of features and deepened their understanding. The children were supported to make sense of what they were finding out, by adding information to their large-scale map. In reflecting on this lesson, Lee has learnt to trust the children more; when given well-focused opportunities to engage in geographical enquiry, the children's curiosity and intellect will generate some stimulating learning.

VISITORS

If we cannot get to a place we may be able to arrange for someone who has lived in or visited that place to come to school to share their experiences with us. This again enables learners to take an active part in gathering data through asking questions and looking at evidence alongside a more knowledgeable other. For example, a visitor who has climbed Mount Everest and brings in equipment, photos or film clips, tells their story and answers questions may be a powerful source of data in a study of mountain environments.

MODELLING

This term covers a range of activities where, following experience, we recreate the real world in some way to develop further understanding. This is another way of speeding up, slowing down or zooming in on processes in order to understand them. Additionally, we might change a particular variable to see what happens. So, for example, we might simulate rainfall on a range of materials to see how much water is absorbed, recreating the storage of rainfall in different types of ground. We might keep on adding water until the material is saturated and children notice the water running on the surface, mimicking surface run-off or a flash flood.

APPLICATION OF THE PEDAGOGIC FOCUS TO OTHER SUBJECTS

We have considered the use of practical approaches to promote meaningful learning in geography and the same approaches can be utilised across the primary curriculum. For example, in science, practical work can enable children to gather their own evidence to inform their conceptual understanding and their appreciation of the scientific method. Practical work is central to 'working scientifically' and offers great opportunities for children to develop higher order thinking skills, through being critical of their own approach to setting up enquiries, the validity and reliability of their results and the relevance of their conclusions. In some cases, this may challenge long-held alternative conceptions; active involvement through practical work, rather than through passive transmission, enables children to be far more receptive to modifying these alternative conceptions.

'Learning a foreign language ... provides an opening to other cultures' (DfE, 2013: 193). In many cases, fieldwork (by visiting another country) is unlikely to be realistic, but the use of virtual fieldwork and visitors can certainly have a positive impact on children's learning in primary languages. For example, webcams and communication apps might be used to set up 'oral pen pals' in another country. A visitor may share traditional stories and songs in the foreign language, while also modelling accurate pronunciation and intonation, as the children seek to join in with familiar or repeated phrases.

SUMMARY FOR THIS CHAPTER

In this chapter, we have considered the central role that enquiry holds in children's learning in geography, and the importance of children accessing and understanding 'big ideas' about the natural and human worlds and how these relate to each other. We have identified the potential of geography to develop children's active engagement with the world and with important issues at both local and international levels. We have explored the importance of taking practical approaches to support children's learning in geography and to ensure that their learning is rooted in exploring the real world.

When teaching geography, do:

- teach the big ideas in geography, related to specific places and people
- plan for collaborative enquiry: children observe, describe, organise, explain and look to the future
- plan purposeful learning experiences that engage children both with their immediate world and the wider world.

When using practical approaches to promote engagement, do:

- support children to work through each stage of an enquiry
- plan fieldwork for children to gather data
- additionally, or alternatively, use virtual fieldwork, visitors and modelling
- plan activities in each approach that align with specific learning objectives.

FURTHER READING

The following texts may be helpful in further developing your understanding of effective teaching and learning in geography and exploring how to engage children with practical approaches to learning.

British Council (2019) 'Connecting classrooms through global learning'. Available at: https://connecting-classrooms.britishcouncil.org/ (Accessed: 23 April 2019).

The British Council offers a range of valuable resources, including support with finding an international partner school. This can be very useful when undertaking research and virtual fieldwork, to understand human and physical geography across the world.

Pike, S. (2016) *Learning primary geography: ideas and inspiration for the classroom*. Abingdon: Routledge.

This explores a wide variety of geographical learning through illustrated case studies of children's learning from a range of schools and classrooms. It demonstrates the fantastic work all children can do in primary geography and explains how and why creative approaches such as enquiry learning, learning outside the classroom and using imaginative resources work so well in primary geography.

The Geographical Association (www.geography.org.uk)

The Geographical Association website is the best source of up-to-date reading and support materials for teaching primary geography. Here you can download journal articles from *Primary Geography*; these are often accounts from teachers of work they have undertaken with children. It also offers online continuing professional development, such as 'Critical thinking for achievement'.

REFERENCES

Catling, S. and Willy, T. (2018) *Understanding and teaching primary geography*. London: SAGE Publications.

Department for Education (DfE) (2013) *The national curriculum in England: key stages 1 and 2 framework document*. London: DfE.

Geographical Association (2009) 'A different view: a manifesto from the Geographical Association'. Available at: www.geography.org.uk/write/MediaUploads/Support%20and%20guidance/GA_ADVBookletFULL.pdf (Accessed: 23 April 2019).

Geographical Association (2014) 'An assessment and progression framework for geography'. Available at: www.geography.org.uk/write/MediaUploads/Teacher%20education/GA_Assessment_4pp_flyer-3.pdf (Accessed: 23 April 2019).

Martin, F. (2006) *Teaching geography in primary schools: learning to live in the world*. Cambridge: Chris Kington Publishing.

Ofsted (2008) 'Geography in schools: changing practice'. Available at www.geography.org.uk/download/ofsted%20report%20good%20practice%20in%20schools%20-%20changing%20practice%202008.pdf (Accessed: 23 April 2019).

Ofsted (2011) 'Geography: learning to make a world of difference'. Available at: www.gov.uk/government/publications/geography-learning-to-make-a-world-of-difference (Accessed: 23 April 2019).

Ofsted (2013) 'Religious education: realising the potential'. Available at: www.gov.uk/government/publications/religious-education-realising-the-potential (Accessed: 23 April 2019).

Ofsted and Spielman, A. (2017) 'HMCI's commentary: recent primary and secondary curriculum research', 11 October. Available at: www.gov.uk/government/speeches/hmcis-commentary-october-2017 (Accessed: 23 April 2019).

Ofsted and Spielman, A. (2018) 'HMCI's commentary: curriculum and the new education inspection framework', 18 September. Available at: www.gov.uk/government/speeches/hmci-commentary-curriculum-and-the-new-education-inspection-framework (Accessed: 23 April 2019).

Oxford Dictionaries Online. Available at: https://en.oxforddictionaries.com/definition/geography (Accessed: 23 April 2019).

Roberts, M. (2003) *Learning through enquiry: making sense of geography in the key stage 3 classroom*. Sheffield: Geographical Association.

7

HISTORY

DEVELOPING CHILDREN'S HIGHER ORDER THINKING THROUGH HISTORICAL ENQUIRY

KATE THOMSON AND TRACEY WIRE

OBJECTIVES

- To explore the distinctive nature of primary history.
- To consider how teachers can develop children's higher order thinking skills in primary history.
- To reflect on opportunities to develop and apply these skills in some other subjects within the primary curriculum.

In this chapter, we discuss the distinctive nature of primary history and its place in the curriculum. We then go on to explore some of the ways that teachers can develop children's higher order thinking skills within the context of enquiry-based, knowledge-rich learning. To conclude, we consider how some of the strategies and approaches used to develop children's higher order thinking through enquiry in history might be employed in other areas of the curriculum.

WHAT IS DISTINCTIVE ABOUT TEACHING AND LEARNING IN HISTORY?

The purpose of the history curriculum is to 'help pupils gain a coherent knowledge and understanding of Britain's past and that of the wider world' (DfE, 2013: 188). Not only should children *know* about the past, they should also develop an *understanding* of concepts such as chronology, similarity and difference, and change and continuity. In order to develop knowledge and understanding, children should be taught to deploy a range of historical skills. In the programmes of study, teachers are reminded that their role is to 'equip pupils to ask perceptive questions, think critically, weigh evidence, sift arguments and develop perspective and judgement' (DfE, 2013: 188). 'Learning history', therefore, involves an equal emphasis on historical knowledge, conceptual understanding and skills.

History has value in its own right, but also in terms of its wider learning potential. History often leads cross-curricular topics in primary schools, and provides opportunities for developing an understanding of broader themes such as identity, citizenship, culture and community. There are meaningful and natural connections to be fostered between learning in history and learning in other National Curriculum subjects, particularly English. To engage in the study of history, children need to use and apply key skills such as speaking and listening, reading and writing as part of the enquiry process.

DEVELOPING CHILDREN AS HISTORIANS

Historians investigate the past by interrogating the traces that have been left behind. Therefore, the study of history, at any level, necessitates engagement with historical sources. As teachers, it is important to plan opportunities for children to behave like historians. By asking and answering questions and interrogating historical source materials, children learn to understand the methods of historical enquiry and, in turn, develop a knowledge and understanding of the past. It is in this way that children can also develop an understanding of the distinctive nature of history and teachers can 'raise the bar' in terms of children's progress.

KNOWLEDGE-RICH TEACHING

Active learning is often seen as learning that has a skills focus. However, it is important to recognise the importance of historical knowledge. This knowledge underpins progression in skills and so should be taught explicitly. While children can learn a great deal through independent source-led enquiries, there will always come a point where it is helpful to work collaboratively with peers or with the support of an adult.

'Knowing' about the past might involve knowing about a significant individual, an event, or knowing about the characteristic features of a period. It is very easy to underestimate young children's capacity for learning historical knowledge.

Children can learn about the past in a variety of ways, such as through storytelling, by engaging in book or internet research or simply through skilful teacher exposition. The most effective knowledge-rich teaching often happens as part of an interactive source-based enquiry, when a teacher 'drip feeds' pupils with knowledge that enables them to interpret or make sense of the sources they are analysing. For example, when studying a picture source the teacher might explain when the picture was produced and who produced it, and model some key vocabulary to describe elements of the image. Rather than giving a long and dense knowledge-rich input at the beginning of the activity, this is more effective when responding to children's utterances during the enquiry.

Knowledge-rich teaching is important as it provides children with the building blocks they need to engage in higher order thinking and reach higher levels of attainment. We often refer to 'enabling knowledge', knowledge that is given to children early in a lesson or a sequence of work, which enables them to go on to engage in more sophisticated thinking.

CRITICAL TASK 7.1

Knowledge needed in relation to the Great Fire of London

Consider the knowledge that children need to answer the question, 'Why did the Great Fire of London spread so quickly and destroy so much of the city?'.

For children to be able to answer the question in Critical task 7.1 effectively, they need to have both contextual knowledge and specific knowledge. In terms of contextual knowledge, it would be helpful for children to know what London was like in 1666: which building materials were used, how close together the buildings were, as well as the types of buildings in London at that time. They would also need to have specific knowledge of the weather at the time, how people responded to the fire and how attempts were made to stop the fire. Children also need foundational knowledge of how materials behave and fire travels; it is easy to assume they already have this, but it is important to ensure this is the case. For example, you might need to explain to children how much water is needed to extinguish a house fire.

The implication, of course, is that primary teachers need to be knowledgeable themselves in order to be able to take an active role in imparting knowledge to their pupils (Coe et al., 2014; Maddison, 2014). They also need to have sufficient knowledge to enable them to select *what* to teach. Judgements about aspects of a topic that are most significant and most engaging should be informed by teachers' knowledge of the 'big picture'.

SETTING IN-DEPTH LEARNING WITHIN A BROADER CONTEXT

You might feel overwhelmed by the idea that you need to know everything about world history, and understandably so. However, remember that the curriculum is flexible, which means that not every subject needs to be taught in the same amount of detail. For example, in one term you might teach a short unit on local history and a six-week unit on Ancient Egypt. Not all units need to be the same length, nor do all topics need to be covered in the same depth. Likewise, it is helpful to consider that some aspects of a unit might need to be studied in depth, while others might benefit from a 'lighter touch' and be addressed as part of an overview. Skilful teachers use this approach to avoid superficial learning and ensure that they integrate the teaching of knowledge, concepts and skills.

In any unit of work there should always be a balance of 'overview' and 'depth' lessons (Maddison, 2014). Overview lessons examine the 'big picture' or context. Depth lessons are more tightly focused. For example, at Key Stage 1, a class might be learning about Rosa Parks and the Montgomery Bus Boycott. Depth lessons would cover these particular events and people, while overview lessons would need to examine the broader social context of the USA in the 1950s (the North–South divide, Jim Crow laws and the beginnings of the civil rights movement). Children can only understand why Rosa Parks' actions were significant if they also understand that African Americans were discriminated against in law at this time.

At Key Stage 2, you could provide context within a unit of work on the Romans by constructing a timeline showing the duration of this period and its relationship to the Iron Age and Anglo Saxon period. This will help to establish a chronological framework. Depth lessons might then consist of source-based enquiries using archaeological evidence to explore sites, events, people and the way of life. For example, in a series of lessons you might examine the Roman fortress site at

Caerleon, Boudicca's rebellion, and life in towns through an examination of Verulamium (Roman St Albans). You would then draw upon these depth studies to help pupils assess the 'impact' of the Romans on Britain in an overview lesson (DfE, 2013: 190).

In the following section, we explain how to maximise children's learning by integrating the teaching of knowledge, concepts and historical skills within an enquiry-based approach that promotes higher order thinking.

PEDAGOGIC FOCUS FOR THIS CHAPTER: DEVELOPING CHILDREN'S HIGHER ORDER THINKING THROUGH HISTORICAL ENQUIRY

In order to develop children as historians, we need to engage them in challenging enquiries which have the potential to promote learning. With this in mind, we often hear teachers talk about developing children's 'higher order thinking skills'. Teachers seem to think they will know these when they see them, but if asked to define what they mean they are likely to find this very challenging. This comes as no surprise: after all, it has been the subject of much debate in academic circles (for example see Brookhart, 2010; Lewis and Smith, 1993; Miri et al., 2007). While we do not claim to have a definitive answer to the question, perhaps it would be useful to set out what we mean when we refer to higher order thinking skills within the context of teaching primary history.

We often see Bloom's Taxonomy (see Chapter 14) employed in schools and teachers referring to the top two or three skills as being higher order. However, Bloom's Taxonomy is only one among many models. We propose taking a practical approach to this problem and, like Brookhart (2010), intend to focus on developing children's ability to do the following:

- transfer knowledge: apply existing knowledge to new situations
- think critically: not to take information at face value, but to analyse and evaluate it (this means consider whether information is 'true', biased, fake and so on)
- problem-solve: this means that children need to answer questions that do not simply require recall of information; to arrive at a solution or a range of possible solutions.

You are probably already thinking that there is a lot of overlap here. You might also be pondering the idea that these skills are not just useful in history, or even just in the classroom. You would be correct and it is for this very reason that explicitly teaching higher order thinking skills is so important. Without these skills, children cannot make good progress in any subject and cannot effectively make their way in a world that requires them to be 'thinking citizens'.

ENQUIRY-BASED APPROACHES TO HISTORY

In order for children to develop as historians, we need to take an enquiry-based approach to teaching, particularly in our depth studies. Historical enquiry offers many opportunities to develop pupils' ability to engage in higher order thinking. Children need many and varied opportunities to work with a range of challenging historical sources, such as pictures, artefacts, buildings, oral and written sources. In selecting appropriate resources, teachers should consider:

- the learning focus (knowledge, concepts, skills)
- the nature of the unit of work
- level of challenge
- children's interests
- quality of sources.

CRITICAL TASK 7.2

Identifying sources

Identify the types of primary sources you might use when planning to teach a unit of work about the Romans in Britain. Compare these with the types of sources you might use when teaching children about people's experience of World War II in the local area.

When selecting your sources, prioritise those that have potential to encourage children to apply their existing knowledge of the past and their own lives to new situations, to analyse and evaluate sources and to solve complex historical problems. Teachers who manage the use of sources really well, link them together to scaffold children's thinking and learning. They select just a few high-quality sources (those with lots of learning potential) with clear connections. They inspire curiosity by presenting a mystery to be solved. They ask children to 'do less, better'.

MAKING SOURCES ACCESSIBLE

One way of encouraging higher order thinking is to engage pupils with enquiries based on challenging primary sources. Primary sources are those produced at the time being studied, for example contemporaneously written first-hand accounts, newspapers, images, buildings and artefacts. Sometimes the level of challenge is determined by the type of source: for instance, written sources are likely to be more challenging than artefacts. It is important to remember that some artefacts are easier to interpret than others. If we consider written sources, we need to think about the length, complexity of the language, handwriting and so on, and recognise that these could be barriers to learning. The role of the teacher is to overcome these barriers and make these challenging sources accessible. In this way the teacher opens up the possibility of children being able to engage in higher order thinking,

You might employ a number of strategies for making sources accessible:

- providing opportunities for children to handle artefacts
- teaching young children how to 'read' pictures, for example by using viewfinders, by playing 'I spy', by looking, naming and describing
- explicitly teaching subject-specific vocabulary
- reading written sources aloud
- using extracts from written sources, or drawing attention to parts of a picture or artefact
- providing transcripts of 'difficult to decipher' written sources
- asking focused questions that support children to find information and make deductions and inferences
- using a complex source alongside a more accessible source

In effect, what you are doing here is breaking down the analysis into small, manageable steps. This inclusive approach enables you to have an impact on all children's quality of thinking.

THE ROLE OF TALK FOR THINKING

Although it is sometimes appropriate for children to work quietly, or even in silence, this is not a very productive way to develop their higher order thinking skills. As part of a historical enquiry, it is important that children are provided with opportunities to talk with each other and with the teacher in order to develop their thinking. Sometimes children can be given the space to discuss and explore among themselves, given time to revisit their existing knowledge, to share this with others and to make links to a new context. On other occasions, that talk might take place with a teacher. Teacher talk is only effective in this situation if it is enabling; by this, we mean it helps to move children's learning forward.

If we are setting a challenging task, and using challenging sources, for example, we should provide opportunities for children to engage in productive talk, perhaps through paired or group work, in order to help develop their thinking and enable them to solve problems collaboratively. Not everything about a task should be difficult and challenging, otherwise children are faced with too many barriers and are likely to fail at the first hurdle, no matter how hard they try and how hard they work.

CASE STUDY 7.1

In this example, Jameela, an undergraduate primary student teacher in her third year of training, is working with a Year 6 class. Her aim is to explore the experience of prisoners held at Gloucester Gaol in the early 1850s, as part of a local study. Children are engaged in a source-based enquiry using written records from the county archives. The lesson begins with an investigation of the gaol register of prisoners and a study of the experiences of one prisoner. Jameela wants to help pupils to access the challenging handwritten document and develop pupils' higher order thinking skills, to apply their existing knowledge to a new situation in order to speculate and to engage in problem-solving. She is keen to set high expectations from the outset and encourage children to 'take risks'.

Jameela: We are going to look at evidence from the past and try and work out what it means. I want you to take risks and have a go … sometimes it helps to say things out loud to work out what you think.

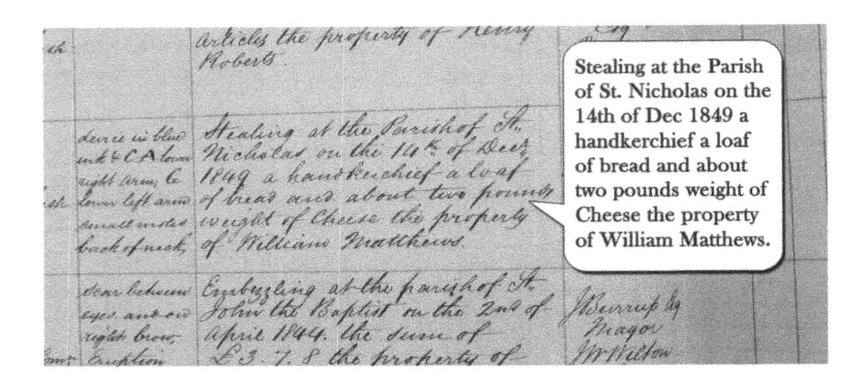

Figure 7.1 Gloucester Archives (2013). Extract from Gloucester Gaol Register (1850)

Jameela: Where did the crime take place?

Isaac: The Parish of St Nicholas.

Jameela: What is meant by the Parish of St Nicholas?

Joshua: Is it something to do with Father Christmas?

David: It *is* December.

Student evaluation: When considering this short extract of the transcript, Jameela began by stating, 'I think it was a good idea to encourage the children to take risks at the beginning. It meant that they felt able to make a "good guess" based on the evidence'. She noted that, 'The children were eager to contribute to the discussion'. However, she worried that, 'Some of their answers were a bit silly at times and it was difficult to know how to respond to get them back on track'.

Expert critique: There is clear evidence here that the children have responded well to Jameela's invitation to 'take risks'. This encouraged the children to engage in higher order thinking without the fear of making a mistake.

The children's responses reveal much about their historical thinking. Although Jameela described the responses as 'a bit silly', both Joshua and David have engaged in reasoning that is supported by evidence and is informed by previous knowledge and experience. When asked to interpret the phrase 'In the Parish of St Nicholas', they have identified previous occasions when they have heard this vocabulary and applied this knowledge in a new, unfamiliar context. This is a useful generic strategy that should be praised by the teacher. The children are not 'off track' here, but actually engaged in sophisticated, reasoned thinking.

This example also raises some interesting questions about the relationship between historical knowledge and skills. The children are unable to make more accurate deductions because they simply do not know enough. 'Parish' is the crucial word in this source extract; if the children had understood this term, they would have been able to draw more accurate conclusions about the location of the crime. There are implications here, then, for the student teacher. Pupils need to be given knowledge in order to make sense of unfamiliar source materials. In this case, Jameela might have gone on to explain this key term or shown the children a map featuring the location of the crime and the proximity to the church of St Nicholas. This would have enabled the children to go further in solving the problem.

At the end of the extract, Joshua and David begin to engage in cumulative talk, where one child builds positively but uncritically on the statement of the other (Barnes, 2008). Joshua makes a deduction ('Is it something to do with Father Christmas?'), then David returns to the source to gather more information and uses this to add weight to Joshua's initial proposition ('It *is* December'). This talk might have been more productive and the children might have been able to develop their thinking further if Jameela had provided them with the opportunity to talk to one another before responding to her initial question.

Teachers sometimes worry about the need to gather a multitude of primary sources in order to engage in an enquiry-based approach to teaching in history. However, as Case study 7.1 demonstrates, the skilful choice and use of a single, short extract has the potential to promote productive discussion and complex thinking. The teacher's role here is to introduce children to the source and to establish an environment where children can develop their thinking through talk. As can be seen in Case study 7.2, the teacher might develop these principles further by inviting children to draw upon a greater body of knowledge to support deduction and inference.

CASE STUDY 7.2

Later in this lesson, Jameela encourages the children to solve a problem related to the primary source. She wants them to decide where and how the theft had occurred; she begins by exploring the language contained in the source.

Jameela: How much do you think 2 lbs of cheese is? What might it look like? Show me with your hands.

[A variety of children's responses indicate that they are having difficulty in interpreting imperial measurements. Jameela had anticipated this. She shows the children a 2 lb block of cheese and a loaf of bread, wrapped in a spotted handkerchief. Next, she asks the children to make some inferences about the detailed nature and location of the crime.]

Jameela: Option number 1: William Matthews was carrying the bread and cheese. The thief was a 'pickpocket'. Option number 2: William Matthews was a shopkeeper. The bread, cheese and handkerchief were on sale in the shop. The thief was a 'shoplifter'. Option number 3: William Matthews owned a house in Gloucester. The thief broke into the house to steal the items. I'd like you to weigh up the evidence. Which of these options is more likely? Talk to your partner and solve the problem together.

[Jameela gives the children one minute to talk to their partners before bringing the class back together.]

Jameela: So, what do you think?

Olivia: The bread and cheese were too big to carry in William Matthews' pocket. The thief wasn't a pickpocket.

David: I disagree … William Matthews was taking the cheese to someone's house. He had it in the handkerchief over his shoulder; I saw it in Shakespeare.

Connie: One shop wouldn't have sold all three things. They didn't have supermarkets then.

Sarah: I think he stole the bread and cheese from a house. He took the handkerchief to carry them. He wanted to hide the things he'd stolen.

Student evaluation: Jameela recognised that the children were 'using their own experiences' to help them respond to her questions. She was also surprised as she 'didn't know that Connie knew that there were different types of shops in Victorian times'. She also recognised that the use of the resources (the bread and cheese) alongside her invitation to select an option worked well. Jameela commented that the paired discussion had worked well and that children were keen to share their thinking and explain their ideas to the whole class.

Expert critique: All four responses demonstrated the transfer of knowledge and problem-solving, characteristics of higher order thinking identified by Brookhart (2010). The children were able to test the hypotheses by referring to the source-based evidence and their prior knowledge and understanding. Showing the children the bread, cheese and handkerchief was clearly influential, as knowledge about the size of the stolen items informed the deductions the children made. This new knowledge was accessible to all the children in the class. When presenting their opinions, the children also drew upon their individual knowledge base: David knew that handkerchiefs were sometimes used to carry goods because he saw it 'in Shakespeare' and Connie knew that 'they didn't have supermarkets then'; indeed, her response suggests she might have knowledge of specialist shops in Victorian times, such as bakers, grocers, haberdashers, etc. The children's prior knowledge enabled them to engage in sophisticated thinking.

When planning a source-based enquiry it is useful for teachers to anticipate the aspects of the source that children might find challenging and plan opportunities to provide 'enabling knowledge'. This example also illustrates the value of scaffolding enquiries, so that pupils are 'freed up' to focus on the demanding materials, thereby providing high-challenge but low-threat learning opportunities. The student teacher facilitated higher order thinking by structuring the activity so that pupils went straight into tasks with a higher cognitive demand: evaluating the evidence, reasoning and justifying opinions. She asked carefully constructed, well-timed questions in order to support the children's thinking and move them on in their learning. For example, the

(Continued)

question 'Which of these options is more likely?' was effective because it required the children to work sequentially through a number of steps: to consider each option in turn; review the evidence related to each option; compare and evaluate before discussing with a partner and making a judgement. Jameela made this complex task accessible to all the children in the way that she selected and introduced resources. Importantly, she also 'inspired curiosity' by encouraging children to become invested in solving a mystery (DfE, 2013: 188).

This enquiry worked well because the children did not have to work from scratch, but rather to engage in critical thinking and evaluate the three hypotheses they were given (Brookhart, 2010). They were given time to think; their paired talk provided a 'safe space' to explore and develop their points of view, and to receive feedback from a peer. In this instance, some were already engaging in what Barnes (2008) categorises as 'exploratory talk', coming together to constructively engage with one another's ideas. They needed to return to the evidence in order to justify their thinking and solve the problem. This then continued once Jameela brought the class back together. The children responded to one another's ideas rather than taking turns to answer Jameela.

APPLICATION OF THE PEDAGOGIC FOCUS TO OTHER SUBJECTS

In this chapter, we have considered how to develop children's higher order thinking as part of a historical enquiry. You could also use some of the strategies suggested to develop children's higher order thinking through an enquiry-based approach in other subjects in the primary curriculum. For example, within PSHE, children should develop a number of skills and attributes, including the ability to formulate questions and to analyse and assess the 'validity and reliability of information' (PSHE Association, 2017: 6). It is important that children have the opportunity to interrogate critically challenging issues. This context provides a valuable opportunity to engage children in enquiry-based learning, with an emphasis on the development of higher order thinking. The use of exploratory talk and of targeted questioning will be particularly valuable strategies to support children in considering these challenging issues.

An enquiry-based approach can also be used effectively to develop children's higher order thinking in computing. In order to address the National Curriculum requirements relating to writing and debugging programs (DfE, 2013), children will certainly need to apply their existing knowledge and think critically in order to problem-solve. As outlined in Chapter 3, paired programming can be a very effective approach, and this would also enable children to engage in talk for thinking, by discussing potential solutions with their partner.

RESPONSE TO CRITICAL TASK 7.2

Identifying sources

Earlier in the chapter, we asked you to identify the types of primary sources you might use when planning to teach units of work about the Romans in Britain and World War II in the local area.

The key is to select a few really useful sources that promote higher order thinking as part of your depth study. These will in part be determined by the nature of the unit and the availability of the sources from the period. When studying the Romans in Britain, use archaeological evidence to study named sites, for example Chedworth Roman Villa. When studying World War II there is the opportunity to use the full range of sources (e.g. photographs, maps, oral histories, newspapers, sites).

SUMMARY FOR THIS CHAPTER

In this chapter, we have explored some aspects of the distinctive nature of primary history. We have considered the importance of having high, but realistic, expectations of children's learning. We expect children to be able to apply existing knowledge to new situations, to think critically and to solve problems. The teacher has a crucial role to play in selecting appropriate sources, making them accessible and providing children with opportunities to develop and to share their thinking through talk. Through an enquiry-based approach to teaching, using high-quality primary sources, history can provide valuable and purposeful opportunities for children to develop their higher order thinking.

When teaching history, do:

- take an enquiry-based approach to teaching and learning
- use primary sources to develop children's higher order thinking
- begin from a position of high levels of teacher subject knowledge
- plan opportunities for in-depth learning within a broader context.

When developing children's higher order thinking, do:

- employ a 'talk for thinking' approach
- teach children the knowledge and vocabulary to enable them to articulate their thinking
- make some aspects of a task easy to 'free-up' children to engage in higher order thinking (provide high-challenge, low-threat learning opportunities)
- ask targeted questions that trigger higher order thinking.

FURTHER READING

Cooper, H. (ed.) (2018) *Teaching history creatively*. 2nd edn. Abingdon: Routledge.

This edited text is useful for those wishing to develop creative approaches to the use of primary sources in order to enhance pupils' thinking.

Doull, K., Russell, C. and Hales, A. (2019) *Mastering primary history*. London: Bloomsbury.

Using examples from the classroom and drawing upon academic research, this text is helpful for those hoping to develop a thorough understanding of the requirements of the National Curriculum for history, approaches to teaching and effective assessment.

Mercer, N. and Hodgkinson, S. (eds.) (2008) *Exploring talk in school*. London: SAGE Publications.

This text is a valuable resource for those seeking to improve the use of talk in the classroom, including ways in which talk might be used to develop children's thinking skills.

REFERENCES

Barnes, D. (2008) 'Exploratory talk for learning' in Mercer, N. and Hodgkinson, S. (eds.) *Exploring talk in school*. London: SAGE Publications, pp. 1–15.

Brookhart, S.M. (2010) *Assessing higher order thinking skills in your classroom*. Alexandria, VA: ASCD.

Coe, R., Aloisi, C., Hoggins, S. and Major, L.E. (2014) 'What makes good teaching? Review of the underpinning research'. Available at: www.suttontrust.com/wp-content/uploads/2014/10/What-makes-great-teaching-FINAL-4.11.14-1.pdf (Accessed: 23 April 2019).

Department for Education (DfE) (2013) *The national curriculum in England: key stages 1 and 2 framework document*. London: DfE.

Gloucester Archives (2013) 'Take one prisoner' [PowerPoint presentation]. Available at: www.gloucestershire.gov.uk/archives/learning-for-all/key-stage-2/take-one/take-one-prisoner-online-resource/ (Accessed: 23 April 2019).

Lewis, A. and Smith, D. (1993) 'Defining higher order thinking', *Theory into Practice*, 32(3), pp. 131–37.

Maddison, M. (2014) 'The national curriculum for history from September 2014: the view from Ofsted', *Primary History* (Spring), 66, pp. 4–7.

Miri, B., David, B. and Uri, Z. (2007) 'Purposely teaching for the promotion of higher-order thinking skills: a case of critical thinking', *Research in Science Education*, 37(4), pp. 353–69.

PSHE Association (2017) 'PSHE education programme of study (key stages 1–5)'. Available at: www.pshe-association.org.uk/system/files/PSHE%20Education%20Programme%20of%20Study%20%28Key%20stage%201-5%29%20Jan%202017_2.pdf (Accessed: 23 April 2019).

8

LANGUAGES

CREATING PURPOSEFUL COMMUNICATION THROUGH MEANINGFUL CONTEXT

CATHY BURCH

OBJECTIVES

- To explore the distinctive nature of primary languages.
- To consider how utilising meaningful contexts can promote purposeful communication in primary languages.
- To reflect on opportunities to utilise meaningful contexts to promote purposeful communication in some other subjects within the primary curriculum.

In this chapter, we will explore the nature of primary languages, identify the ways in which it is distinctive from other curriculum subjects and consider how teachers can develop independent language learners of the future, capable of communicating in a foreign language. We will consider ways in which meaningful contexts can be utilised to promote progress through the teaching of relevant language. We will conclude the chapter by looking at how utilising meaningful contexts can support effective learning in other curriculum subjects.

WHAT IS DISTINCTIVE ABOUT TEACHING AND LEARNING IN PRIMARY LANGUAGES?

Teaching a foreign language can be one of the most rewarding experiences for a primary school teacher and is an excellent contribution to the provision of a 'curriculum which is balanced and broadly based' (DfE, 2013: 5). Languages became part of the statutory curriculum at Key Stage 2 in 2014, but many schools have been teaching a foreign language for several years. The National Curriculum for languages (DfE, 2013) stipulates that any ancient or modern foreign language (MFL) may be taught at Key Stage 2. Research shows that about three-quarters of primary schools teach French (Tinsley and Board, 2017), with Spanish the second most popular at around twenty-five per cent. The curriculum is mainly skills-based, focusing heavily on the four language skills of listening, speaking, reading and writing, with a clearly stated emphasis on practical comprehension and communication:

> It should enable pupils to understand and communicate ideas, facts and feelings in speech and writing, focused on familiar and routine matters, using their knowledge of phonology, grammatical structures and vocabulary (DfE, 2013: 194).

There is very little reference to specific topics or vocabulary areas to be covered, except brief specific references to, for example, 'familiar and routine matters' (DfE, 2013: 194), opinions and describing people, places and things. Despite this, most primary language teachers still tend to cover a typical 'MFL playlist' (Horton, 2018) of name, age, birthday, family, pets, school subjects and clock times. Although these are worthy topics to cover, they do not necessarily lend themselves to practical communication and there is no limit to the list of topics from which to choose.

What is particularly distinctive about the teaching of languages relates to how a foreign language is learnt and how it is retained in one's memory, relating to characteristics of the learner and their language-learning environment (Lightbown and Spada, 2006).

THE PRIMARY LANGUAGES LEARNER

There is much debate over the best age to introduce a foreign language, in terms of how well children pick up good pronunciation skills and how motivated they are to learn (Jones and Coffey, 2013). Although research shows that some schools in England begin teaching primary languages in Key Stage 1 (Tinsley and Board, 2017), this is not part of the National Curriculum and so the vast majority of pupils start Key Stage 2 with no knowledge of a foreign language at all. In contrast, by this stage children will have already gained a good understanding in many other subjects included in the curriculum at Key Stage 1 and are fluent communicators in their own language.

Unlike the majority of their foreign peers, children in the UK are exposed to very little foreign language in everyday life; according to Crystal (2003), English is a global language of popular culture worldwide, for example in broadcasting, cinema and popular music. Therefore, for primary school children living in the UK, the classroom is likely to be the most significant source of foreign language for them. Accessing language through audio-visual resources, such as foreign language songs and clips from the internet or published schemes of work, increases the amount of spoken language to which the children are exposed. These materials can allow children to gain an understanding of the sounds of the language they are learning, including its pronunciation, intonation and flow, and enable teachers to share native speakers speaking or singing in the target language. Pupils see 'real' people, including other children, speaking the target language; this stimulates their curiosity and provides valuable insight into intercultural understanding, as well as providing native-level spoken language input. Children may also benefit from being able to see written language around them in the form of classroom displays, labels and children's work in the foreign language.

TEACH, PRACTISE, REVISIT AND REAPPLY

Regular language practice is vital if children are to gain confidence in speaking a language and for them to make progress. Paired or small-group activities work well for this, as they provide a less stressful situation for a beginner than speaking in front of the whole class. These may be integrated into highly enjoyable activities such as games, role-plays or surveys, but, importantly, they maximise talk time for all children and enable the teacher to listen and assess progress. Language structures and vocabulary have to be frequently practised and revisited if they are to be retained in a child's working memory, so it is important to regularly review what they already know on a regular basis, as what has been taught in a discrete lesson may be almost entirely forgotten within a day or two. However, different teaching strategies need to be used in order to sustain children's engagement and to extend their understanding.

Equally important is reapplying or 'recycling' of prior learning, and using the same language in different contexts to build on children's understanding of how the language works. For example, if the pupils are able to state their opinions on one subject (e.g. food items), this prior knowledge could then be reapplied to state opinions on a different topic (e.g. sports or hobbies). According to neuroscientific research, teachers should make explicit links to prior knowledge, as this connection-making process is still developing in children (Howard-Jones et al., 2018).

At first, your class may not understand simple phrases such as 'I like' or classroom instructions such as 'listen' in a foreign language. Adding a clear gesture or action when you introduce the word will help them to be able to guess, understand and reinforce a word's meaning. Research suggests that gestures enhance memorisation in language learning, due to the retrieval cues and richer memory traces that they provide (Porter, 2012), so add gestures to the language you use wherever possible, and encourage children to use them too. Checking pupils understand what a word means in their native language is an essential part of language teaching and helps children to make those all-important connections between languages.

It is thought that words need to be repeated sixteen times before they are retained in the working memory, so say the words and get the children to echo you several times; for example, in funny voices (loud, quiet, squeaky…). The more quality language the children are exposed to, the better the understanding children will gain of that language as a result.

ERROR CORRECTION

The language learning environment also needs to be one in which children are gaining confidence in their language ability, where they feel motivated to learn and use that language. This kind of environment may be achieved through the use of lots of praise (in the target language), positive gestures (thumbs up, big smile, etc.), and so forth. Pupils should feel encouraged to speak in a foreign language, even if they make errors; like children beginning to learn how to use their first language, mistakes are inevitable, but errors in a second language demonstrate a willingness to experiment and take risks, which will help towards the National Curriculum's goal of communication. Corrections should be made sensitively, in order to keep children's enthusiasm and confidence intact. One way of doing so when working with the whole class is to feed back on persistent errors in a general way rather than singling out individuals and their errors, and correcting only those errors linked to the key focus of the lesson.

THE PRIMARY LANGUAGES TEACHER

As their primary school class teacher, you will act as a key role model in the lives of those young children you teach. As such, you will be able to engage them in learning about different languages and cultures through your attitude and approach to language teaching and learning. Even if you do not feel very confident in your language knowledge and skill, it is important that you approach your teaching of the subject with visible confidence and enthusiasm, and commit yourself to developing your knowledge further.

In order to use high-quality target language with their class, teachers need to have sufficient language knowledge and confidence. As Jones and Coffey (2013: 13) point out, the teacher is, after all, the 'most essential resource by far' available in the primary languages classroom. It may be reassuring for less confident language speakers to hear that this language should be fairly simple, repetitive and clear. Resources such as the *ALL Connect KS2 Language Co-ordinator's Handbook* are readily available and have many useful phrases to get you started, including common simple instructions and praise phrases. There is also an array of language teaching resources and ideas easily accessible, both published schemes of work and online resources, for example on the website of the Association for Language Learning. You can also check how to pronounce individual words and common phrases using a good pronunciation website such as www.forvo.com. Better still, familiarise yourself with the basic phonics, and teach this to the children in your class; an understanding of the basic phonics of a foreign language will improve children's understanding in the four language skills of speaking, listening, reading and writing.

PEDAGOGIC FOCUS FOR THIS CHAPTER: PURPOSEFUL COMMUNICATION THROUGH MEANINGFUL CONTEXTS

As we have seen earlier in this chapter, language needs to be revisited repeatedly and in different contexts if it is to be remembered, so the choice of vocabulary that we select for children to learn is paramount. If we want them to understand and respond to a foreign language, we need to teach children those phrases that we use on a regular basis. Many primary language teachers encourage the use of the target foreign language as much as possible outside their discrete language lessons, in order to increase the children's use of the foreign language.

CRITICAL TASK 8.1

Frequently used phrases

Think through all the phrases you frequently say to other people you meet (pupils and staff), just as a natural part of your day. These might include greetings

(Continued)

such as 'Hello. How are you?', expressions of gratitude such as 'please' and 'thank you', and farewells such as 'goodbye'. Note these down and start to introduce these phrases in your chosen language as part of your day.

Next, think of instructions, praise and phrases that you typically use in class every day. It is important that this is a list of language that *you* use, so do not skip this part of the process. Note these down in a list as shown in Table 8.1 in the left-hand column. Next, take the time to note down or find out the translations for these phrases in your chosen target language. You may need some help with this: a great source of useful information is the *ALL Connect KS2 Language Co-ordinator's Handbook*. If you have looked up any phrases, make sure that you know how to pronounce them by using a pronunciation website and note any comments you need to in the final column of Table 8.1. Last, but not least, practise saying these phrases aloud, at the same time as practising a gesture for that phrase.

Table 8.1 Frequently-used phrases

English phrases I often use in class	Target language translation	How is this pronounced?
e.g. Listen!		
5, 4, 3, 2, 1...		

After you have made this list, keep it with you while you teach so you can check that you have all the phrases you will need when you begin teaching a foreign language. Add any extra phrases you need to your list.

USING YOUR CLASSROOM AS A CONTEXT FOR MEANINGFUL COMMUNICATION

Children spend at least thirty hours a week at school, so your classroom provides an excellent 'real' context in which children may learn valuable and meaningful aspects of a target language. The everyday routines and activities of this dynamic learning environment can become vehicles in which to support children's understanding of key words and phrases and provide a context in which they might begin to practise and develop their own use of the language. The children in your class may be overwhelmed if you try to introduce 'too much' language all at once. Similarly, 'too little' might be a waste of time, as the children will easily forget what has been taught. 'Just right' in this case would be the use of the target language on a regular basis (at least every day): the important thing is that the language should relate to real aspects of the daily life of the classroom.

CASE STUDY 8.1

In this example, Chris, an undergraduate student teacher in the second year of training, has been reflecting on how he went about introducing French during a placement with a lower Key Stage 2 class who had never learnt languages before. Chris' intention was to introduce meaningful interactions with the children in his new class in a foreign language, on top of his discrete language lessons, as he believed that this would create an environment in which language learning was encouraged and enhanced.

Student teacher evaluation: Chris explained that he started by observing the class teacher's routines, then thought about how that could be adapted to fit in with using French. For example, the class teacher would sometimes saying 'Speaking!' and the children would reply 'Listening!' and so Chris translated those phrases into French. He explained this to the children and gave them examples; once they understood, he repeated the phrases regularly over time. He explained: 'That was my approach with everything: I saw the systems in use and adapted them to fit in with the French language. I started with the register and started at a basic level to build their confidence up, beginning with how to say "hello". Then I had a French lesson where I went through some basic greetings like, "How are you?" and the response options, and then I added this in as part of the register. By the end of the placement it had become much more of a natural conversation: it had taken it from just a single phrase to more of an authentic communication between people.'

Chris then introduced French language into ordering dinners, in which the children had a choice of red, green and yellow lunches. He taught the children the names of the colours, and then the 'magic' phrase, 'I would like… ', which he put on display, with the question and a thought bubble next to the dinner menu. To start with, many of the children just said the colour but, over time, Chris encouraged them to include the magic phrase, too. If they got that, he would encourage them to use 'please' and 'thank you'. Chris commented: 'I found

(Continued)

that, if you modelled the language a lot, the children were able to use it themselves naturally. So I would use the modelled language during the discrete lessons but also throughout the day.'

Chris aimed to make the language purposeful by embedding it in routines: communicating for a purpose had a positive impact on the children's enthusiasm for learning languages. They replied naturally in the French language and developed their vocabulary over time. Chris noted: 'By the end of the placement, they really enjoyed learning languages. I have realised it is important not just to do it in that half-an-hour lesson each week. Having the language all the time in the classroom makes all the difference because it's not strange to them any more: it's familiar to them.'

Expert critique: Here, Chris is taking the first steps to introducing the foreign language into the everyday routines of the classroom. He has chosen to begin with key classroom language that the children meet every day. Acting as their class teacher, Chris sees the children every day and this enables him to revisit and therefore reinforce that language on a daily basis. At this stage, the children are not only responding to his classroom instructions, but are also beginning to initiate speech in that language. The fact that this language is limited is completely in keeping with the level of vocabulary knowledge the children have at this early stage. Chris is encouraging the children to extend that speech by using the 'magic' phrase, 'I would like'. At this stage, some children may not be ready to use much, if any, of the language themselves, but all the children are responding to classroom instructions, and some are beginning to use the language in either single words or complete phrases. Next, Chris could think about how the content of his discrete language lessons might continue to extend the children's use of the foreign language on a regular basis. Possibilities might include learning to count to thirty. Once this has been mastered, children can use their position in the register to respond accordingly, and this can become a real test of speed, with the children working together to 'beat the clock'. It is also extremely useful transferable knowledge, needed, for example, when stating the date, birthdays or age, and can be used in physical education lessons when counting repetitions or scoring.

PLANNING THE CONTENT OF YOUR DISCRETE LANGUAGE LESSONS

The average length of a Key Stage 2 language lesson is typically thirty to forty-five minutes each week (Tinsley and Board, 2017), although research has found that an hour's lesson per week generates faster progress (Graham et al., 2017). Within a lesson, the number of new words that children might typically learn is between five and ten (Bauckham, 2016), depending on how easy these words are to learn (cognates are often easier to learn as they are recognisable from English, and children may struggle to learn longer words or phrases). Therefore, it is worth taking a moment to consider which vocabulary would be most useful for children to learn first, in terms of how often it would be used in a way that is relevant in their everyday lives. Language structures are often useful phrases we can learn to communicate in a foreign language. These commonly contain a verb, for example, 'I have' or 'There is'. Once children are taught how to formulate a corresponding question ('Do you have … ?'), then simple conversations may be achieved on myriad topics, from pets to classroom objects through to family members.

CASE STUDY 8.2

Jenny is a PGCE student teacher working on placement with a class of children who have had some language lessons on a fairly regular basis for the last two years. She is reflecting on how much language the children are using, and how she has encouraged this through what she has taught them during language lessons, but also through regular revisiting each day outside those discrete language lessons.

Student evaluation: Jenny wanted to teach the children the phrase 'Can I … ?', so taught this in context with the sentence, 'Can I go to the toilet?'. They quickly adopted and used this phrase, without prompting. The children had already learnt the phrase 'I would like', so Jenny asked the children to write letters to Father Christmas, using that phrase, and they learnt how to say the presents they would like for Christmas.

Jenny was pleased to see the way that the children were experimenting and developing in their use of language. She noted: 'They were playing with the language, trying to use what they knew to communicate in the language. For example, one boy could not remember the French for "Can I go to the toilet?", but he came up with "Je voudrais … aux toilettes", showing he had remembered the phrases for "I would like" and "to the toilet". They were willing to give it a go like that, which is great. I tried to respond quickly to them when they spoke in French, to make sure they knew they were understood. They are accepting of language learning, and that encourages them to try out more language.'

(Continued)

Expert critique: Jenny picks up on several important ideas here. First, in terms of the language she is teaching, she is recycling and reusing phrases the children already know, such as 'I would like', and applying them to other topics of conversation. In doing so, she is revisiting the phrase and reinforcing its meaning in the children's memory, but also showing the children that they can use existing knowledge to help them communicate new ideas, an essential learning point for any foreign language speaker. In her later example, the boy tries to use the phrases he knows to communicate in this way, making connections between the language he already knows with what he wants to communicate. Mindful of the children's confidence and motivation to try to communicate in a foreign language, Jenny purposefully responds quickly and positively. In this way, their confidence and motivation are maintained, and they are much more likely to 'risk' speaking French spontaneously in the future.

SEIZE OPPORTUNITIES

Children are naturally inquisitive creatures and, given the right encouragement, their enthusiasm for language learning is high and highly infectious. Responding to the children's interest in language learning is crucial. Find out about the children's activities and interests outside school and share with them some of the key vocabulary about these. For example, identify and teach a few key words that might help them to talk about how they spend their weekends or their holidays. In particular, invite the children to raise their own questions about the vocabulary that they would like to learn, then support them in finding out what the key words and phrases might be and develop their confidence in pronunciation.

CASE STUDY 8.3

In this example, Fiona, a School Direct PGCE student teacher, reflects on how she has responded to the children's interest in foreign language.

Student teacher evaluation: Fiona said: 'We are grabbing opportunities as they arise: for example, the children suggested that we sang "Happy Birthday" in French rather than English, so I double-checked the language and went with it. Giving the children exposure to foreign languages early on means that they have already had a positive experience of language learning: we are fostering that positive attitude, the desire to know more. They pick up on the attitudes towards language learning of those around them, and they are not afraid to try using the language at that age. They feel good about themselves that they can speak in a foreign language (or in some cases, two). I am not explicitly teaching everything, but I am "surrounding" the children with language learning, so that they can soak up more and more.'

Expert critique: Whether it is the words for 'packed lunch', the words to the song 'Happy Birthday', or learning how to say the type of pet they have, these children are keen to learn more. Fiona is being responsive to the children's interest in language and encouraging this learning. At this young age, children are indeed like sponges 'soaking up' language: as teachers, our job is to make sure that we provide them with an environment rich in the foreign language. To do this, we must ensure that we double-check the language we are teaching is correct, as this student teacher quite rightly did. Never be afraid to speak to other language teachers or co-ordinators to check your pronunciation or consult a pronunciation website if you are unsure. Another way of tailoring learning to children's individual interests is to give them strategies to begin to find out for themselves. For example, you could teach them how to use a bilingual school dictionary. If you have also taught them the phonics of the foreign language, they will be able to sound out the words they find and, in doing so, begin to develop key skills in autonomous language learning, which will promote and enhance their learning for years to come.

APPLICATION OF THE PEDAGOGIC FOCUS TO OTHER SUBJECTS

We have considered ways in which purposeful communication can be developed within languages through the utilisation of meaningful contexts, and this is an approach that can be exploited across the curriculum. For example, in religious education, a visit to a local place of worship can be a great stimulus for rich and genuine conversations about key aspects of a particular faith and their significance in the lives of followers of that faith. Key vocabulary can be explored with the children, both before and after the trip, so that they are able to talk knowledgeably and sensitively about the artefacts, people and places that they encounter.

In music, opportunities for children to meet with and talk to professional and amateur musicians can extend their subject-specific vocabulary, as key words can be used in context and with meaning. Children can also be encouraged to use subject-specific vocabulary to talk about the music they listen to or perform outside of school music lessons, in order to further contextualise their learning. Where possible, peripatetic music teachers should be informed about the vocabulary children have been introduced to through music lessons in class, so that they can reinforce and extend the use of this through their own lessons.

SUMMARY FOR THIS CHAPTER

In this chapter, we have explored the principles of effective teaching in primary languages and the importance of teachers developing their own knowledge and confidence and providing children with many opportunities to experience and experiment with language, in both formal and informal ways. We have explored the importance of utilising real contexts for using language in meaningful ways.

When teaching primary languages, do:

- expose children to the target language repeatedly and gradually, in a way that they are able to access and understand
- encourage children to use and practise the target language, even if they make mistakes
- check and reinforce your subject knowledge so that you are providing a simple, but highly accurate level of foreign language.

When promoting purposeful communication within meaningful contexts, do:

- identify the 'everyday' language used in your classroom
- use the everyday environment of your classroom as a context for meaningful communication
- seize opportunities to harness the children's interest in learning the language they use in real life.

FURTHER READING

The following sources may be helpful in further developing your knowledge and understanding of effective primary languages practice.

ALL Connect (2016) *ALL Connect KS2 language co-ordinator's handbook.* https://allconnectblog.files.wordpress.com/2016/01/all-connect-ks2-languages-coordinator-handbook1.pdf

This handbook is a valuable resource in relation to all aspects of language teaching and learning and includes a particularly helpful list of commonly used classroom phrases in French, Spanish and German. The handbook, together with many other valuable resources and ideas, can be found on the Association for Language Learning website: www.all-languages.org.uk

The Research in Primary Languages website: www.ripl.uk

This website provides a good range of research into primary languages, including easily accessed one-page summaries of recent research findings related to teaching and learning in languages.

For more information and guidance on foreign language phonics, in French, German or Spanish, look at www.rachelhawkes.com and, for French, www.cavelanguages.co.uk

REFERENCES

Bauckham, I. (2016) 'Modern foreign languages pedagogy review: a review of modern foreign languages teaching practice in key stage 3 and key stage 4'. Teaching Schools Council. Available at: https://tscouncil.org.uk/wp-content/uploads/2016/12/MFL-Pedagogy-Review-Report-2.pdf (Accessed: 23 April 2019).

Crystal, D. (2003) *English as a global language*. 2nd edn. Cambridge: Cambridge University Press.

Department for Education (DfE) (2013) *The national curriculum in England: key stages 1 and 2 framework document*. London: DfE.

Graham, S., Courtney, L., Marinis, T. and Tonkyn, A. (2017) 'Early language learning: the impact of teaching and teacher factors', *Language Learning: A Journal of Research in Language Studies*, 67(4), pp. 922–58. doi: https://doi.org/10.1111/lang.12251

Horton, G. (2018) 'The building blocks of language learning' [lecture at NALA 2018 conference 'Building Horizons']. Stratford, 29–30 June.

Howard-Jones, P., Ioannou, K., Bailey, R., Prior, J., Yau, S.H. and Jay, T. (2018) 'Applying the science of learning in the classroom'. *Impact*, 2. Available at: https://impact.chartered.college/article/howard-jones-applying-science-learning-classroom/ (Accessed: 23 April 2019).

Jones, J. and Coffey, S. (2013) *Modern foreign languages 5–11: a guide for teachers*. 2nd edn. Abingdon: Routledge.

Lightbown P.M. and Spada, N. (2006) *How languages are learned*. 3rd edn. Oxford: Oxford University Press.

Porter, A. (2012) 'A helping hand with language learning: teaching French vocabulary with gesture', *The Language Learning Journal*, 44(2), pp. 236–56. doi: 10.1080/09571736.2012.750681

Tinsley, T. and Board, K. (2017) *Language Trends 2016/7: language teaching in primary and secondary schools in England: survey report*. British Council. Available at: www.britishcouncil.org/sites/default/files/language_trends_survey_2017_0.pdf (Accessed: 23 April 2019).

9

MATHEMATICS

PROMOTING TALK TO DEVELOP REASONING

RUTH HOLLIER, EMMA HOWELL AND JACKIE MCNEIL

OBJECTIVES

- To explore the nature of mathematical reasoning and its central place in learning mathematics.
- To consider how teachers can effectively promote children's talk to develop mathematical reasoning.
- To reflect on how talk can be used to develop reasoning and support developing understanding across the primary curriculum.

In this chapter, we will engage with research and learning theories to explore the nature of mathematical reasoning, identify the significance of reasoning in developing conceptual understanding in primary mathematics and consider the importance of purposeful talk in furthering reasoning skills. We will examine how teachers can promote talk and engage children in purposeful dialogue that is effective in deepening their understanding of key mathematical concepts through reasoning. We will conclude by considering how developing children's mathematical reasoning also supports children in developing critical thinking skills. We also consider how strategies to promote talk can be applied effectively to support reasoning in some other subjects.

WHAT IS THE NATURE OF MATHEMATICAL REASONING AND WHERE DOES IT 'FIT' IN RELATION TO MATHEMATICS?

Reasoning is fundamental to being mathematical: you cannot do mathematics without reasoning. Without reasoning, you are merely recalling facts or using procedures without a deep understanding of the mathematics involved. There is a difference between using mathematics functionally (knowing what to do to find an answer or solution) and being a mathematician, which involves understanding why that works. Moreover, research by Nunes et al. (2009: 1) showed that 'mathematical reasoning, even more so than children's knowledge of arithmetic, is important for children's later achievement in mathematics'. That is why this chapter is about teaching mathematics, viewed through the lens of developing children's reasoning.

Ofsted (2008) highlights the importance of children understanding and making sense of mathematics so that they can use it independently. You may be familiar with situations where children are able to calculate correctly, but when faced with a worded problem, are unable to extract the mathematics from the context and so are unable to solve the problem itself. Reasoning enables children to discover the structure of the underlying mathematical problems and make decisions about which calculations to apply.

You may remember a time in school when you learnt mathematics facts such as times tables 'off by heart' and 'rules' for calculating. Student teachers often tell us that they found mathematics at school impenetrable because it was about learning 'how' to do mathematics, rather than understanding the concepts involved. They link this to feelings of anxiety and the need to be 'right'. Reasoning enables you to understand the 'why', and this, according to Haylock and Manning (2019: 6), is fundamental to effective teaching: 'One of the ways for children to learn and understand much of the mathematics in the primary school curriculum is for a teacher who understands it to explain it to them.'

In the National Curriculum (DfE, 2013), reasoning is specifically identified as one of three main aims, alongside developing fluency in the fundamentals of mathematics and problem-solving. However, the NRICH primary team (2014a) suggests that 'reasoning could be thought of as the "glue" which helps mathematics make sense'.

These three aims are interconnected and, as such, should not be seen as separate elements or taught separately. When designing and teaching mathematics lessons, you will need to remember that, although the programmes of study are organised into what looks like separate content areas, the three aims should be embedded across your teaching for all children. The National Curriculum (DfE, 2013: 99) goes on to state that, 'Pupils should make rich connections across mathematical ideas to develop fluency, mathematical reasoning and competence in solving increasingly sophisticated problems'.

Making these rich connections requires reasoning processes that children need to learn and that need to be modelled by the teacher.

REASONING ABOUT MATHEMATICAL STRUCTURES

Mathematical reasoning includes thinking systematically so that it is possible to notice patterns and structures; this means reasoning about what changes and what stays the same when considering different examples, and using this understanding to identify mathematical structures and relationships and to generalise about them.

For example, in this pattern, children could be asked to notice what is the same and what is different about odd and even numbers.

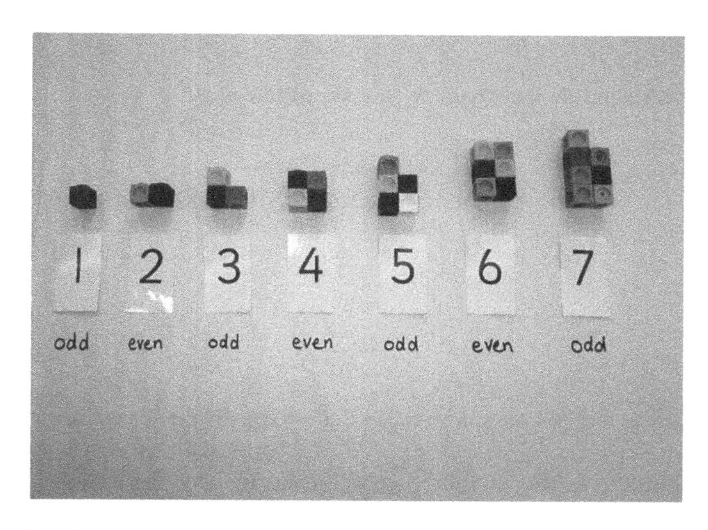

Figure 9.1 Odd and even numbers in concrete and abstract form

A mathematical structure can be thought of as the 'shape' of the mathematics beneath the numbers. For example, consider this question:

> 750 tickets for 'Cinderella' at the Grand Theatre have been sold. The show is about to start. 690 people are seated already. How many more people are yet to arrive?

On the surface this looks like an addition calculation, as it uses the words 'How many more'. In working this out mentally, you might count on to find out how many to add to equal 750:

690 + ? = 750

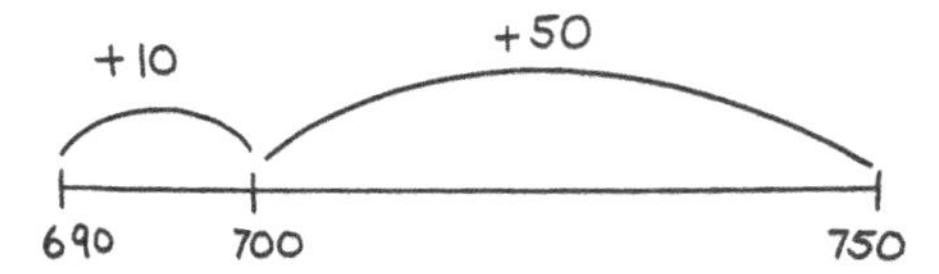

Figure 9.2 Number line: counting on to find the difference

You might also take away 690 from 750, thus:

750 – 690 = ?

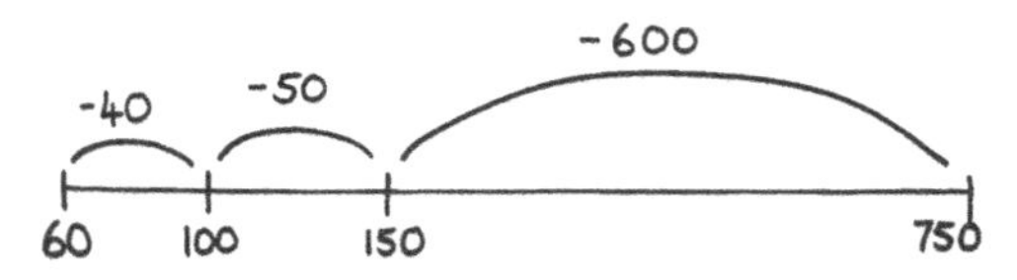

Figure 9.3 Number line: counting back to find the difference

However, if using a written calculation method, you would need to use a subtraction algorithm. That is because this example relates to the subtraction structure related to finding the difference, described by Haylock (2019) as the inverse of addition.

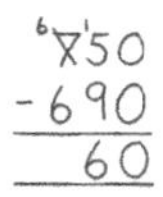

750
-690
60

Figure 9.4 Columnar method for subtraction: finding the difference using an algorithm

Reasoning enables children to see beyond the numbers and words and understand the structure of the mathematics. Having this 'number sense' enables them to select appropriate strategies and 'tools' to solve the problem.

REASONING ABOUT RELATIONS

'I've got more than you!'

Young children reason from an early age about number, without attaching an actual number value. That is because they are reasoning about quantities and the relations between values rather than engaging in arithmetic (Nunes et al., 2009).

Often, teachers focus on helping children learn number facts. There is no getting away from the reality that mathematics is made up of terminology, symbols and basic facts such as number names, addition and multiplication facts and the 'equals' sign, to name a few. Children do need to know these, but they also need to develop their understanding of relations such as 'more', 'less' and 'the same' which help them to reason about these facts. Here we have a paradox: learning facts in isolation will not mean you can do mathematics, yet you cannot do mathematics without knowing some facts. Reasoning helps children to make this link, to develop number sense and understand relations. If you are interested in reading more about developing children's understanding of the relationships between numbers and areas of mathematics, we recommend Skemp's (1989) work on instrumental and relational understanding.

REASONING AND PROBLEM-SOLVING

When you start problem-solving, the first question you ask is, 'How do I solve this problem?'. This is when reasoning begins. What happens next depends on what type of problem you are faced with.

The National Curriculum (DfE, 2013) suggests a difference between routine and non-routine problems. A routine problem would be one that has one straightforward, predetermined pathway and a set of calculations that lead to a specific solution. In a routine problem, children need to use reasoning to detect the underlying structure of the mathematics and decide which calculation strategy to use. You could think of these as the traditional 'I bought three sweets … ' kind of worded problems.

A non-routine problem involves children in creative thinking and decision-making from the start. It does not have a set path, or even a set starting point, but involves children in reasoning their own route through the problem-solving process, selecting the most appropriate strategies to reach an outcome, over which they have some determination. In this way, children follow a line of enquiry, asking 'what if?' then deciding on appropriate next steps to find out. These non-routine problems can present a range of solutions or just one; they encourage children to be curious and imaginative yet logical, and require them to use their reasoning to determine the pathway for themselves through conjecture, hypothesis and systematic investigation.

Here is a good example of such a problem:

Take any three consecutive numbers.

Add them together to find the total.

What do you notice?

Try again with different sets of three consecutive numbers.

What do you notice? What's the same? What's different?

Can you find a rule?

Similar problems are available at www.nrich.org.uk

Getting stuck and making mistakes are a natural, inherent part of problem-solving. A problem is not a problem unless you have been stuck at some point and, without mistakes, we cannot know what will and will not work. Mason et al. (2010: ix) suggest that 'mathematical thinking is provoked by contradiction, tension and surprise', so getting stuck is a *requirement*. As a teacher, you need to be able to create these conditions for children.

This means that to solve problems effectively, children need to develop resilience and a positive attitude (Boaler, 2013). You will need to value and celebrate the mistakes made along the way, encouraging trial and improvement as an expected part of learning. You will need to encourage children to persevere in their thinking, to pursue their line of enquiry. This will mean being prepared to discuss 'what to do when you're stuck', such as trying a different way, taking a break or working collaboratively to find other ideas on how to proceed. Mathematical reasoning enables children to overcome their difficulties, but they need to be resilient too.

REASONING AS PART OF MATHEMATICAL DEVELOPMENT: A SENSE OF PROGRESSION

For young learners, and when learners meet new concepts, reasoning simply involves describing what you see or do. From this, reasoning develops into explaining why you did what you did or offering some ideas as to why things might be as they appear. The next stage is to become convincing in this explanation. Beyond that, reasoning involves justifying the chain of ideas, using words like 'because' and including examples to support points. At this stage of reasoning, mathematical communication needs to become more elegant and succinct. Proving a watertight argument is the final, most complex stage of reasoning. This, even at primary level, involves children in thinking about mathematical proof, relating to generalised patterns and structures. This progression, suggested by the NRICH primary team (2014b), associates the development of mathematical thinking with the ability to communicate about thinking in a 'clear, succinct and logical manner'.

So, developing reasoning involves providing children with opportunities to explore the higher order skills like justifying and proving, rather than simply describing. This is not easily done, as it cannot be explicitly taught in the way that calculation methods can be taught. It takes time, as children need to think, explore and share strategies and to experience mathematical thinking being modelled by the teacher. All this requires teachers to have deep and secure subject knowledge, to be familiar with their own reasoning processes.

PEDAGOGIC FOCUS FOR THIS CHAPTER: PROMOTING TALK TO DEVELOP REASONING

Talk is one of the easiest ways for most people to communicate their ideas. As a teacher, being able to talk articulately about mathematical ideas is a most important skill, which enables you to explain the mathematics clearly to the children and for the children to share their thinking in return. For really young children, or some pupils with special educational needs and disabiities (SEND), there may be other ways to communicate, such as using concrete apparatus, drawings or symbols, which are as valid as talk in revealing children's reasoning. Even if children are limited in their own dialogue, they can still develop their reasoning through listening to the talk of others.

Talk, in the form of dialogue, does more than merely pass knowledge from one person to another. The emphasis in this chapter is on children engaging in dialogue with one another and developing their reasoning though talking together. In 'real life', mathematicians work in communities of learning, not in isolation. Purposeful talk enables children to refine and adapt their understanding, and meaningful mathematical dialogue can help children to build vocabulary and strategies for sharing ideas.

Askew (2016) suggests that the back and forth exchanges of talk in the form of dialogue is how 'knowing' comes about. This suggests there is a distinction between having some superficial knowledge about mathematics and really 'knowing' and deeply understanding mathematics. However, in order for this to be effective, talk needs to involve listening as well as speaking, requiring children to develop social skills along with the subject-specific vocabulary and terminology that makes up the language of mathematics.

Talk alone is not enough for children to really understand mathematics, though, for what would children talk about? Bruner (1966) argues that physical experiences are vitally important to the development of understanding, forming the core of enactive learning, the first of three modes of representation he proposed. Manipulating physical objects supports children in creating mental images of mathematics, which enables them to 'read meaning into the artefacts' (Askew, 2016: 132) to unlock the concept. Pictures and images are useful to aid memory (Liebeck, 1984) but, according to social constructivist learning theory, all learning is centrally concerned with interaction with others. Learning mathematics is inseparable from the use and development of language alongside concrete and pictorial models and images that help make sense of abstract ideas.

It is suggested in the National Curriculum (DfE, 2013: 100) that the 'quality and variety of language that pupils hear and speak' are crucial to developing reasoning and talking mathematically. This is not as simple as just getting children to talk 'about mathematics'; as Askew (2016: 156) says, there is a 'difference between talking about Italian and talking Italian'. He goes on to suggest that we need to give children something 'mathematically worthwhile' to talk about (2016: 156).

In the following sections, we will explore ways to do this and ways in which to manage mathematical talk and develop children's reasoning. It is worth remembering that you can only be successful in this if your own subject knowledge is secure enough for *you* to be able to reason mathematically and make connections, and if you have established a positive classroom ethos where everyone feels confident to share their thinking.

USE RESOURCES AND REPRESENTATIONS SELECTIVELY

It is important to use concrete apparatus (e.g. counters on a ten frame) or visual representations (e.g. pictures, such as pairs of socks or images like a number line or bar model) in your lessons for children to talk about. This can help them develop their reasoning and enable them to clarify their thinking and illustrate ideas that they might find hard to express in words. These are most effective when used alongside each other and linked to number symbols, signs and specific vocabulary.

Do not make the mistake of thinking resources like these are only for younger children. All children can benefit from using these routinely, and any conversation about mathematics in the classroom should be supported by representations, to make sure children can 'see' the mathematics and understand the structure.

Carefully selected resources can represent concepts and be used to support understanding; they are not just for adding fun, as a 'side dish', and their use needs to be carefully modelled. When choosing resources and representations, think carefully about how well they are matched to the concept or method you are teaching. For example, a number line might be very useful for children to think about division as 'grouping'. They could easily count how many 'groups' or 'jumps' of 4 are in 32. However, this would not be as useful if they were thinking about division as 'sharing' 32 between 4.

CRITICAL TASK 9.1

Using resources and representations

Equivalent fractions, decimals and percentages: if you are exploring the links between ¾, 0.75 and 75%, how might you use:

- a circle or a square pictorial representation?
- dienes base ten equipment or counters?
- a number line or a hundred square?
- a combination of these?

Consider which would be most useful to model and help children talk about their understanding of equivalents.

How might your teaching be different in each case? How might the dialogue between children differ, given different resources? What vocabulary might be used?

BE AN ACTIVE LISTENER: RESIST THE URGE TO FILL SILENCES

Carefully managed whole-class talk can enable children to become a community of mathematicians. This goes beyond listing answers and describing methods. It means children share strategies, listen to and learn from others, clarify their own thoughts and reason deeply about the mathematics they are studying. As a teacher, your role in this is to listen actively, to value children's responses and to help children explore and communicate their reasoning.

It is very easy to fall into the trap of dominating the talk in the classroom. There is an urge to avoid silence; we sometimes think that silence is unproductive. However, silences can be hugely valuable for thinking time in mathematics and it is not always useful to emphasise the speed of reasoning or calculating. You need to allow children time for reflection and, in doing so, you become the listener, the prompter, the guide, rather than the leader of the talk. So, avoid putting words into the mouths of children by quickly saying 'Did you mean … ?' and giving a correct response if they hesitate or if their response is not quite correct.

BEWARE OF CONTROLLING THE DISCUSSION IN ORDER TO GET TO A PREDETERMINED END

Teachers do need to facilitate classroom talk, but rather than looking for predetermined answers, you should give children space to explore and develop their mathematical thinking (Bagnall, 2011). Do not be afraid to explore children's reasoning along lines of enquiry that may seem to go 'off script'. Be prepared to bring the focus back to the key learning point. Good, open dialogue between teacher and children has to be based on strong subject knowledge, so you can feel confident to go along with children's thinking along lines of enquiry where you do not necessarily know the answer. Sometimes, this might involve unpicking children's errors and making it into a learning opportunity.

CASE STUDY 9.1

In this example, Maya, an undergraduate primary student teacher, is working with Year 5 on rounding decimal numbers to the nearest tenth. Following her teaching input, a small group of children identify that they are not yet confident enough to work independently. Maya is providing further teaching support for this small group, seated on the carpet, using the board for her teaching. The children have individual whiteboards to display responses.

[Maya writes 7.53 on the board, displayed for all children.]

Maya: Let's round 7.53 to the nearest tenth. Write your answer on your whiteboard.

[Silence, less than a minute, while the children work.]

Maya: Show me your whiteboards.

[Charlotte has written 7.6 on her board.]

Maya: Charlotte, why did you put 6 … ?

Charlotte: Umm . . .

Maya: Did you look at this (*pointing to the 3*)?

[Short pause, three seconds.]

Maya: OK. What did anyone else put?

Ben: I put 7.5

Maya: Yes, well done, that's right.

[Maya moves on to her next question.]

Student teacher evaluation: In reflecting on the lesson, Maya felt that the pace of the lesson was good because she had kept the discussion moving on. In her view, the children had been able to share their answers. She considered she had made good use of formative assessment because she could see who had got the answer right and who had not by looking at responses on individual whiteboards. She thought she had been able to address Charlotte's mistake by sharing Ben's answer.

Expert critique: It may have been helpful to show a number line, like the one in Figure 9.5, on the board. This would have enabled the children to see that 7.53 is closer to 7.5 than 7.6, supported their reasoning and given them something to refer to when talking. The visual image might have helped structure the reasoning and filled in any 'gaps' in the children's ability to verbalise ideas.

Figure 9.5 Number line representation to support rounding

When Charlotte could not explain, Maya 'rushed to fill the silence' to keep the pace of the discussion moving and to avoid going 'off script'. This limited Charlotte's 'thinking time' and opportunity to reason about her original answer and potentially self-correct. There was no way of knowing whether Charlotte's incorrect answer was simply an error or due to a lack of understanding (misconception).

When Ben gave the correct answer, Maya praised him and missed an opportunity for him to talk through his reasoning. Rather than simply accepting the right answer, Maya could have used his response as a teaching point to help Charlotte, and other children, develop their own reasoning and understanding. In this example, Ben's answer could have been the beginning of a shared journey to deeper understanding of the concept.

ASK THE RIGHT QUESTIONS

Closed questions such as 'what is 20 + 30?' do have a place; children need to recall mathematical facts and calculate correct answers. However, the answer is only the beginning. Children need to reflect on their reasoning, the decisions taken and their understanding. As well as asking 'what is the answer?', questions like 'how did you do it?' and 'why did you do it in that way?' open up the discussion and challenge children to explain their reasoning further.

Keep an open mind about children's possible responses to questions like this. If you have a fixed idea in your head and prompt children towards that direction, you limit children's opportunity for reasoning and, by skipping to 'your' answer or method, they avoid the grappling process of reasoning.

CASE STUDY 9.2

In this example, Josef, a PGCE primary student teacher, is leading an early-morning mathematics practice task in which his Year 2 children are working through a range of arithmetic problems using pencil and paper. Children have access to a range of concrete resources including counters and cubes, though most choose not to use them. When reviewing the answers as a whole class, Josef noticed that many children were stuck on this problem: 'What is ¼ of 20?'.

Josef: What's ¼ of 20?

Hari: It's 5

Josef: How did you work it out?

Hari: I added 1 and 4

Josef: Did you? That's interesting. Let's go through it together. How do we find a quarter of a number? We don't need to add, we *sh*...

[Little response from the class.]

Josef: We 'share'. We need to share 20 between 4.

[Having directed to them to share, most children used counters or jottings to divide 20 into four equal groups, and then counted one of these groups to reach a correct answer of 5.]

Student teacher evaluation: Josef's initial evaluation of this interaction was that he had led the children's thinking well. When Hari gave the correct answer, Josef asked an appropriate follow-up question: 'How did you work it out?'. He believed this was a good opportunity to model the mathematics to all children, making connections between the written fraction and the practical sharing into four equal parts. He acknowledged that he had not really addressed Hari's incorrect thinking about adding the numerator and denominator and that he had simply moved on to prompt them to use the correct method. Josef was pleased that most children had then been able to reach the correct answer.

Expert critique: Even though Hari showed a misconception when explaining how he had reached his correct answer, this would have been a useful point for Josef to ask a more probing question such as 'why did you work it out in that way?' and to give children the opportunity to talk to a partner about their own strategies. This might have prompted Hari to review his thinking and enabled the rest of the class to share in the process. Josef could also have asked Hari to try using the same strategy on another question (e.g. ¼ of 12) where adding the numerator and denominator would not work.

It is clear from this transcript that Josef had a fixed idea in his mind of the responses he wanted from his question, 'How do we find a quarter of a number?'. The question itself could have elicited a wide range of responses but, when Josef suggests the word they need to provide him with begins with 'sh…', he is signalling that only one answer will do. Therefore, the children are limited in their responses because they know that Josef is looking for a specific answer and are not able to talk about their reasoning in their own words.

SUPPORT CHILDREN TO COMMUNICATE

Before the lesson, consider what mathematical vocabulary children might need in order to communicate their thinking, and make sure you model that for them. Make sure they can see working walls from where they are sitting to remind them of prior learning and key ideas. Some teachers like to use sentence starters to help children verbalise ideas.

Give children access to concrete apparatus or mini-whiteboards during discussion, so they can build or draw their reasoning. This also enables you to see what is in their heads, even if you cannot listen to each child's verbal response or if they find it difficult to explain in words.

Giving time for children to rehearse and explore their reasoning with a partner can help them to clarify their thoughts and alleviate anxiety about being put on the spot in front of the whole class. To encourage them to become good listeners, actively thinking about their partner's ideas, it is useful to ask them to feed back on their partner's reasoning, rather than their own. A partner can also be a valuable support when children inevitably 'get stuck'.

REITERATE, REPHRASE, REPROPOSE

Children cannot be part of a community of mathematicians if they cannot hear or understand what other children are saying in discussion. If children speak quietly, you should check others can hear and, if needed, repeat what they have said. If they are quite wordy or vague in their responses, you can rephrase it more concisely to include correct vocabulary and support other children in understanding. Sometimes simply repeating back (reproposing) what children have said can prompt further reasoning or explanation.

USE MATHEMATICAL 'TALK TASKS'

To promote reasoning and deep understanding of mathematics, Boaler (2014) suggests we should set tasks that have the 'space within them' for learning. She suggests these should be open tasks that are challenging and cause children to struggle, experience cognitive conflict and make mistakes. Tasks need to be carefully selected to ensure that they offer opportunities for reasoning rather than finding answers. Working on such tasks with a partner or in a group should lead children to talk purposefully and in depth about their reasoning and understanding of concepts. This might also lead on to a wider discussion as a class, sharing findings and possibly uncovering misconceptions.

To ensure tasks are accessible and that children are supported to tackle them, your teaching needs to be well aligned to the tasks so that you have modelled the mathematics you want children to use in the task.

Here are some starting points for collaborative talk activities that can be adapted to fit any mathematics topic.

Anti-examples (misconceptions). Explore common misconceptions by giving children provocative questions or statements to discuss. A good example is 'Do bigger sized coins have greater value?' or, phrased as a statement, 'A 2p coin is worth more than a 5p coin. Do you agree?'. Concept cartoons (Keogh et al., 2008) provide a range of ideas for this. They provide scenarios where cartoon children explain their ideas about mathematics, which include misconceptions for children to explore. This provides less confident children with a 'safety net' as none of the 'wrong' ideas are their own.

Sometimes, always or never true. This approach can also be used to uncover misconceptions and explore key concepts, such as in the following example:

> 'A square is a rectangle ... sometimes, always or never true?'

The key is to insist that children explain their answers, either to each other or to the whole class.

Odd one out. Choose a set of mathematical facts or images for children to talk about. For example, show children some shapes (square, rectangle, parallelogram and rhombus) and ask them to explain which is the 'odd one out', and why.

In any set, each item could be the odd one out. This activity requires children to justify their choice, reason about their existing knowledge and explore connections. Children can be creative in their thinking to justify less 'obvious' choices.

Collaborative puzzles or problems. Opportunities for children to work together in groups or pairs on the same problem will mean they are able to talk about and justify their approaches, strategies and solutions. This 'community' approach can be supportive for children who are reluctant to share ideas in a wider forum. It also enables children to learn from each other and refine the way they communicate ideas. As a teacher, you need to make sure the tasks you set are accessible to everyone in the group, but have enough scope to provide challenge. Useful resources are available from NRICH (https://nrich.maths.org) and in a range of publications from the ATM (Association of Teachers of Mathematics, www.atm.org.uk).

'Big paper' working. This is a great way for children to record their collaborative ideas. Some schools with smooth tables allow for working with wipeable whiteboard pens, but big paper can possibly be displayed on a working wall or shared for whole-class discussion (see Figure 9.6).

Figure 9.6 Big paper collaborative working

Making connections. A practical task many teachers commonly use is to divide a piece of paper into sections where the mathematical question or focus is displayed in the middle. In each section, children are encouraged to find different ways to solve or represent it: visually, in numbers, in words using a story, or in a different way of their own choosing (see Figure 9.7).

This could be a paired or group activity, working collaboratively on big paper, or children could do it independently on A4 or in workbooks, to rehearse their reasoning before sharing. Talking about it helps children make connections between different ways of representing the same ideas.

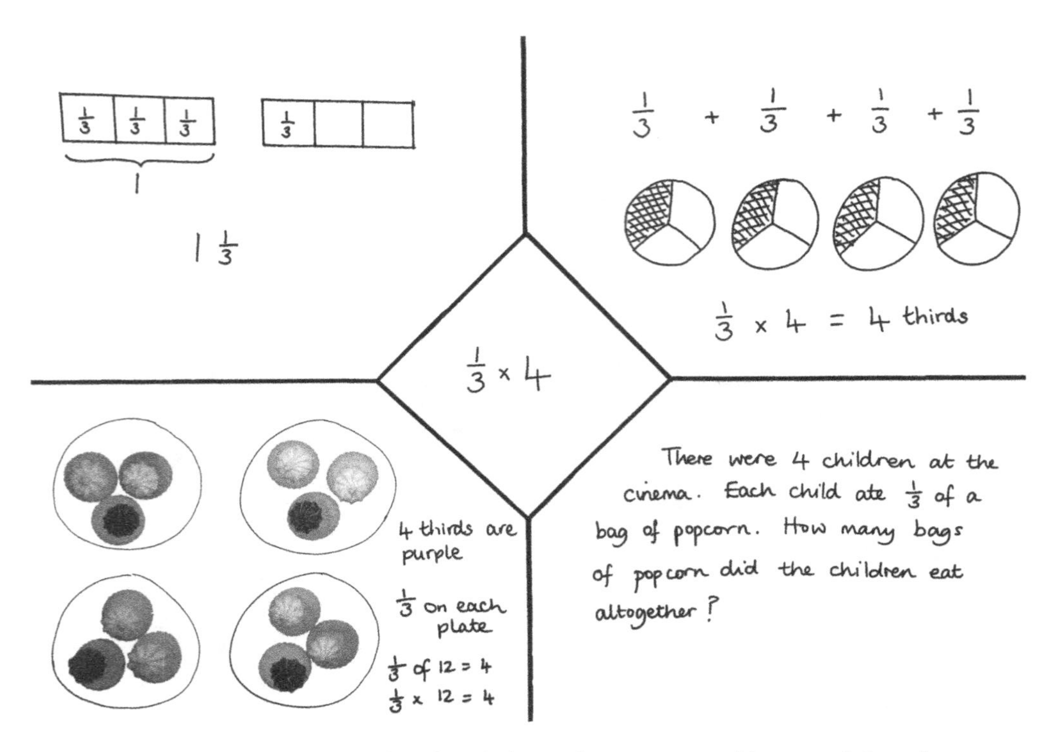

Figure 9.7 Multiply proper fractions by whole numbers, supported by materials and diagrams

What is the same? What is different? What do you notice? Building these questions into your teaching, along with carefully selected examples, is a powerful way of helping children look for and talk about patterns and key features of mathematical concepts.

Consider this example:

$10 \times 3 = 30$

$100 \times 3 = 300$

What is the same? What is different? What do you notice?

When thinking about which examples to use in your lessons, you may like to read more about variation theory (Askew, 2016), which suggests that making very small, deliberate changes when sequencing examples can help children notice specific details and avoid mechanical repetition.

Pattern sniffing: what do you notice? Investigating sequences can generate in-depth discussion. This might involve sequences of any kind, for example shapes or numbers. The example in Figure 9.8 has accompanying prompts, which support children's reasoning but also help them start to ask their own questions.

Figure 9.8 Pattern sniffing: what do you notice about this triangle sequence?

Draw the next 3 in the sequence.

Draw the 12th in the sequence.

True or false? The 15th will be △.

How do you know?

'Pattern sniffing' activities like these encourage children to look for and reason about patterns and relationships in other aspects of mathematics.

What mathematics can you see? Exploring pictures and photographs from everyday environments to look for patterns and links to mathematics can generate in-depth talk and reasoning, as can creating pictures to match number facts.

CRITICAL TASK 9.2

Selecting 'talk task' approaches

Consider the case studies in this chapter. How might Maya or Josef have used any of these 'talk task' approaches to promote children's talk and reasoning in their lessons?

APPLICATION OF THE PEDAGOGIC FOCUS TO OTHER SUBJECTS

Though we have discussed ways to promote talk for developing *mathematical* reasoning in this chapter, the skills involved in reasoning and communicating your thinking are the same no matter what the subject. Whether they are discussing division or Diwali, children still need to think about what they already know, make connections, use the correct terminology, communicate ideas in a sensible and logical way and justify their thinking or opinions. It is no surprise that many of the teaching strategies outlined in this chapter can be applied across the curriculum. Consider, for example, how you might use some of the 'talk task' starting points mentioned earlier to promote discussion about similarities and differences in patterns when teaching a science topic, like properties and changes of materials (DfE, 2013: 169).

Religious education offers valuable opportunities to explore and consider beliefs and opinions, which may differ from your own, in an open and respectful manner. Therefore, just as in mathematics, it is important to give children time to think; be an active listener and beware of having a predetermined outcome in mind or of trying to control children's responses. Regardless of the subject matter, being effective in promoting talk for reasoning requires secure subject knowledge and a willingness to explore children's ideas rather than transmitting your own.

SUMMARY FOR THIS CHAPTER

In this chapter, we have emphasised that reasoning underpins all aspects of mathematics so it should be embedded in all aspects of mathematics teaching and learning. We have explored how reasoning leads to a better understanding of mathematical relations, structures and problem-solving. The focus has been on the pedagogical importance of talk in developing reasoning and on strategies for teachers to deploy which promote this in the classroom every day.

As teachers, we need to remember the importance of modelling how to communicate mathematically and ask probing questions to unpick children's reasoning. In mathematics, we should let children's answers be the beginning and focus our talk around the journey of learning, as well as the destination. We should avoid dominating the discussion and be prepared to stray 'off script' to create a community of mathematicians who are willing to ask and answer questions. Children need to enjoy grappling with the reasoning and see being stuck as a positive part of learning in mathematics.

For you to be effective in promoting talk for developing mathematical reasoning, you need to become confident in talking about your own reasoning, through secure subject knowledge and an awareness of the range of common misconceptions. You also need to gain experience of solving problems on your own and with others, and of discussing and communicating mathematical ideas.

When teaching mathematical reasoning, do:

- make reasoning a fundamental part of every mathematics lesson
- ensure you understand the concepts yourself so you can make mathematical structures clear for children
- help children make connections and understand relations between mathematical ideas
- model your thought process out loud for children in every lesson in order to promote mathematical thinking
- help children to see 'getting stuck' as a positive experience.

When promoting talk to develop children's mathematical reasoning, do:

- recognise the importance of talk in developing reasoning
- use resources and representations selectively
- be an active listener and resist the urge to fill the silence
- ask the right questions at the right time
- use mathematical 'talk tasks' regularly.

FURTHER READING

The following sources may be helpful in further developing your knowledge and understanding of effective pedagogy.

Askew, M. (2016) *Transforming primary mathematics*. Abingdon: Routledge.

This is a helpful book, which discusses how theories and cutting-edge research in the field relate to practice, enabling teachers to reflect on how they teach mathematics. There are also clear, practical approaches to help you make mathematics 'welcoming, engaging, inclusive and successful'.

Haylock, D. with Manning, R. (2019) *Mathematics explained for primary teachers*. 6th edn. London: SAGE Publications.

This book makes concepts simple and helps you gain confidence and a personal understanding of the structure and principles of what you will be teaching to primary children. It is in line with current National Curriculum programmes of study and is consistent with the current emphasis on teaching for mastery.

The University of Cambridge's NRICH website (https://nrich.maths.org/)

NRICH provides thousands of free online mathematics resources for children aged 3 to 18. This includes a range of rich activities with a focus on developing problem-solving and encouraging exploration and discussion. Alongside this, you will find many useful articles and research reports from experts at the University of Cambridge and beyond to support your further professional learning.

REFERENCES

Askew, M. (2016) *Transforming primary mathematics*. Abingdon: Routledge.

Bagnall, B. (2011) 'What's all the talking about?' Available at: https://nrich.maths.org/6662 (Accessed: 23 April 2019).

Boaler, J. (2013) 'Ability and mathematics: the mindset revolution that is reshaping education', *Forum*, *55*(1). Available at: www.youcubed.org/wp-content/uploads/14_Boaler_FORUM_55_1_web.pdf (Accessed: 23 April 2019).

Boaler, J. (2014) 'The mathematics of hope: moving from performance to learning in mathematics classrooms'. Available at: www.youcubed.org/resource/growth-mindset/ (Accessed: 23 April 2019).

Bruner, J.S. (1966) *Toward a theory of instruction*. Cambridge, MA: Belknap Press.

Department for Education (DfE) (2013) *The national curriculum in England: key stages 1 and 2 framework document*. London: DfE.

Haylock, D. with Manning, R. (2019) *Mathematics explained for primary teachers*. 6th edn. London: SAGE Publications.

Keogh, B., Dabell, J. and Naylor, S. (2008) *Concept cartoons in mathematics education*. Stafford: Millgate House.

Liebeck, P. (1984) *How children learn mathematics*. London: Penguin.

Mason, J., Burton, L. and Stacey, K. (2010) *Thinking mathematically*. 2nd edn. London: Pearson.

NRICH (2014a) 'Reasoning: identifying opportunities'. Available at https://nrich.maths.org/10990 (Accessed: 23 April 2019).

NRICH (2014b) 'Reasoning: the journey from novice to expert'. Available at: https://nrich.maths.org/11336 (Accessed: 23 April 2019).

Nunes, T., Bryant, P., Sylva, K. and Barros, R. (2009) 'Development of maths capabilities and confidence in primary schools'. *Research Brief DCSF-RR118*. London: DCSF.

Ofsted (2008) *Mathematics: understanding the score*. London: Ofsted.

Skemp, R. (1989) *Mathematics in the primary school*. Abingdon: Routledge.

10

MUSIC

DEVELOPING COLLABORATIVE SKILLS

COLIN FORSTER

OBJECTIVES

- To explore the distinctive nature of primary music.
- To consider how teachers can help children develop collaborative skills within primary music.
- To reflect on the application of developing collaborative skills in relation to some other subjects within the primary curriculum.

In this chapter, we will explore the nature of primary music, identify the ways in which it is distinctive from other curriculum subjects and consider what it has to offer children, both as a part of their primary education and their wider life. We will also examine ways in which children can be supported to develop collaborative skills through music. We will conclude the chapter with some consideration of ways in which collaborative skills can be developed in some other curriculum subjects.

WHAT IS DISTINCTIVE ABOUT TEACHING AND LEARNING IN MUSIC?

Do you ever hear a piece of music on the radio that vividly reminds you of a time in your life, a particular experience or a specific person? Have you ever been to a wedding or funeral where *no* music was played? Have you ever heard a piece of music that 'moved' you emotionally? Do you ever play particular pieces of music to match your mood or to influence a change in your mood?

Music, it seems, is part of being human: in ways that are hard to define, music enriches our lives, stimulates our psyches and touches our deepest emotions, as noted by Swanwick (1999: 20): 'It is because of its non-literalness, because of its non-explicit but profoundly suggestive nature that music has such power to move us.' Music heightens our awareness of our present, connects us to our past and gives us skills and confidence for our future.

Music, then, is so much more than a 'curriculum subject', even though it has been included in every version of the National Curriculum since its inception in 1988 and, in the latest version, music is still seen as an important aspect of a child's rounded education. It should enable children to develop their appreciation of a wide range of music, to understand how music is created and to develop their own musical proficiency.

According to the National Curriculum (DfE, 2013: 196), 'Music is a universal language that embodies one of the highest forms of creativity'. Enabling children to learn the 'language' of music gives them access to all sorts of life-enhancing opportunities and experiences. Singing as part of a choir or playing an instrument as part of an orchestra or band gives an extraordinary feeling of being connected to others and being part of something that is bigger than oneself. Having musical proficiency enables young people to move almost anywhere in the world and easily get involved in music groups and activities: the ability to play an instrument is like having an intercultural passport.

However, we need to be aware that children's 'music capital' (the sum of all their musical experience and competence) is significantly related to socioeconomic issues and is likely to be very varied across the school population. For example, while some children are fortunate to come from 'musical homes' or to receive private instrument tuition during their formative years, many are not, as the costs are prohibitive for many families (Musicians' Union, 2018). It is in this context that the primary school teacher should seek to redress the balance and support all children in learning the universal language of music.

CRITICAL TASK 10.1

The inter-related dimensions of music

The National Curriculum for music refers to the following inter-related dimensions of music. Suggest a suitable definition for each one.

Table 10.1 The inter-related dimensions of music

Dimension	Definition
pitch	
duration	
dynamics	
tempo	
timbre	
texture	
structure	

OFFERING RICH MUSICAL EXPERIENCES

Primary music should offer children opportunities to experience a wide range of high-quality experiences, in order to broaden their familiarity with musical genres, provoke their curiosity and raise their expectations. Invite local artists (choirs, soloists, brass groups, string quartets, rock groups, etc.), both established and up-and-coming, professional and amateur, to perform for your class and to talk about their instruments and their experiences of music. Seek cheap opportunities to take your class to see musicians perform in local venues. Experiencing live music is great for inspiring children, and talking to performers about their own learning can help children to see that even great musicians started as complete beginners. This is an important point to emphasise, as children may see skilled musicians performing and think that they have some inherent 'talent', something that they, themselves, could never aspire to; but all musicians started as non-musicians and, through hard work and perseverance, developed their musical skills.

BECOMING MUSICAL: DOING MUSIC

Listening to live music and hearing from musicians of all kinds is an important aspect of children's musical education, but it is important that they also have meaningful opportunities to start becoming musical themselves. This involves 'doing' real music: listening analytically, singing as part of an ensemble (group), experimenting, composing, and creating or reading informal and formal musical notation.

Aim to provide children with opportunities to listen to a wide range of music, both purely for pleasure and for analysing the musical features of the work. Draw on music from a range of genres (for example, jazz, classical, electronic dance music) and do not be afraid to challenge them and yourself by listening to music that is outside your normal comfort zones. Ideally, listen to the same piece several times. As Holt (1992) notes, this enables the listener to become familiar with the 'shape' of the music and to listen for particular features of the piece, such as the various instruments that feature prominently at different points or the changes in tempo (speed) and volume that change the mood or feel of the piece.

Singing is an essential part of a primary school child's education and an inclusive and accessible aspect of 'doing music'. Having all children sing the same song 'in unison' (singing the same tune) is a good starting point but do aim to get children singing different parts and harmonies, so that they can feel embedded within the music and make a contribution to a musical moment that is bigger than themselves. The experience of singing as part of an ensemble is enriching and, according to some researchers, there is some evidence to suggest that it has a positive impact on mental well-being. Clift (2012: 114) draws on a number of research studies to identify a range of potential benefits, including that singing can be 'mood enhancing' and can 'bring people together to create a sense of group identity, social support and friendship'. Acquah (2016: 7) found, in a survey of students engaged in regular singing in a group, that 'participants indicated how the mixed chorus released their tension and relieved them of sadness because it usually uplifted them spiritually'.

It is important to give children time to experiment with music. Every instrument, including the voice, can be played in a number of different ways, and it is good to give children time to explore the variety of notes, tones and sounds that can be produced and utilised to create different aural images. Children will also want to explore ways in which sounds from different instruments can be combined to create a musical effect.

Experimentation is the mother of composition, which is about creating new, original pieces of music. This is an important aspect of 'doing music' and gives children the opportunity to use their musical knowledge creatively. It can sometimes be a challenge to get started on the process, so one way to support children in creating their own compositions is to give them a mental picture to try to recreate musically. This can be done by asking the children to look closely at a picture of a particular scene (for example, a city street, a small village beside a river, a building site or a tropical rainforest) and inviting them to suggest particular sounds that they might hear and to think about how these might be recreated using music. They can then choose appropriate instruments and work in small groups to create short performances that might help someone who had not seen the original picture to imagine what it might look like.

Children should be encouraged to create their own ways to make a written or pictorial record of their compositions; this will be a kind of informal shorthand that easily helps them to remember quickly, when they come to do a performance, the key aspects of their composition. This informal approach to recording their musical ideas could lead, quite naturally, to a discussion about the benefits for musicians of sharing a standard approach to scribing music, so that one player can easily 'read' what another has 'written'. This would be a good point to introduce some simple elements of standard musical notation, which is used to show the length and pitch of each note. This may seem daunting if you have not read music before, but the good news about musical notation is that, once you understand a few basics, it is a good deal more logical than reading English. For example, a note on the second line in the treble clef is always a 'G' (unlike all of the different ways in which the letter 'G' might be used in English, in words such as gull, gel, rough, ring, gnome …). The two main elements of reading musical notation relate to the length of the note and the pitch of the note, and there are several helpful videos on the internet to help explain the basic ideas related to reading these.

Becoming musical should include explicit opportunities for children to develop skills in listening to music, in singing together, in experimenting with a range of instruments and in understanding how musicians read and write music. These are essential parts of teaching and learning in music and, in the next section, we will explore how to aim even higher.

BE AMBITIOUS

If you are going to be ambitious with your music teaching, you will want to aim to go beyond using the hand-held percussion. There is nothing wrong with using hand-held percussion to develop a range of musical skills, but there is only so far children's musical expertise can be developed through experimenting (again) with the cabassa, agogo or vibraslap, so it is good to give children regular access to playing tuned percussion instruments, such as xylophones, hand bells or boomwhackers (colourful plastic tubes of different lengths) or other instruments, such as ukuleles, which can be relatively cheap to purchase and easy to get started with playing. Be ambitious in inviting children to start learning to play real instruments; of course, this is challenging but we should never underestimate the children's capacity for learning new musical skills.

In your plans to be ambitious about your children's musical development, be kind to yourself: you do not have to do it all yourself so look out for opportunities to draw on the expertise of others. Search for local organisations that might offer whole-class lessons in brass, ukuleles or other instruments. These might be county or local authority music teams or voluntary organisations such as brass bands.

CULTURE

It is important to consider what kind of 'musical culture' you would like your classroom to have, bearing in mind the purpose of study stated in the National Curriculum: 'a high quality music education should engage and inspire pupils to develop a love of music and their talent as musicians' (DfE, 2013: 196). Aim to embed music in your classroom in many ways and to promote joy in learning about musical pieces or skills.

CRITICAL TASK 10.2

Opportunities for music across the curriculum

Here is a list of all the National Curriculum subjects (apart from music). Suggest ways in which music could enhance the learning in each.

Table 10.2 Music across the curriculum

Curriculum subject	Opportunity for music to enhance the learning
Art and design	
Computing	
Design and technology	
English	
Geography	
History	
Languages	
Mathematics	
Physical education	
Personal, social, health and economic education	
Religious education	
Science	

A key part of the musical culture of your classroom is your own commitment to learning new musical skills. If you do not yet play an instrument, be prepared to learn to play one; this is best done alongside the children. If you have already mastered one instrument, learn another. It is very important that the children do not see you as a musician (or a non-musician) but as a learner of music, someone prepared to grapple with the challenges, frustrations and joys of learning to make music with others. Be open about the parts of learning that you find to be tricky and model a positive approach to persevering in order to make progress.

CRITICAL TASK 10.3

Mr Brown

A true story: Mr Brown taught a Year 2 class. Every day, he would play his guitar and teach the children all sorts of songs that he enjoyed, including 'Star Man' by David Bowie and other classics from his personal favourites list. Mr Brown kept his guitar in the corner of the classroom and children were allowed and encouraged to explore how it worked. One year, a curious change was observed to happen in Mr Brown's classroom: by about October, one or two of the children brought in their own small guitars each day, they learnt a chord or two and strummed along while the class sang. By Christmas, the number of guitars in the corner of the classroom swelled to about a dozen and, in January, almost every child in the class had a cheap guitar and brought it in most days to join in with the music making.

To consider: what was the key ingredient in this little musical miracle?

PEDAGOGIC FOCUS FOR THIS CHAPTER: DEVELOPING CHILDREN'S COLLABORATIVE SKILLS

Working well together is a key aspect of any successful musical ensemble, and primary music offers many good opportunities for children to develop collaborative skills that will be beneficial to them throughout their school careers and lives. It is important that we are explicit with children about the key collaborative skills that we would like them to develop and that we identify and provide good opportunities for them to do so. We also need to support children in learning how to resolve conflicts, which inevitably arise as they learn to work well together, and to model a positive approach to collaboration in our own work and relationships. We will consider these issues in more depth.

WHAT ARE COLLABORATIVE SKILLS?

Music offers great opportunities for children to develop collaborative skills, some that are quite specific to music and some that are more generic but all of which can be used to help children develop their ability to work well with others. Gillies (2003: 37) notes that 'placing students in groups and expecting them to work together will not necessarily promote co-operative working', so it is worth being clear in our own minds about what 'good collaboration' might look like in our lessons and then communicating this clearly to children, so that they understand what is expected.

An example of a music-specific collaborative skill is for a child to play or sing their part in time and in balance with others, so that their contribution to the music fits well with the rest and enhances the overall quality of the performance. Similarly, a key part of musical collaboration is *not* playing or singing, at times, so that the other voices can come to the fore. When not playing, a key collaborative skill is counting carefully so that, when the moment to join in the playing arrives, everyone is ready and the whole ensemble works effectively.

Other valuable collaborative skills that are applicable in many situations can also be learnt through music, and it is important to be explicit with children about these skills and to help them to reflect on their own progress in these areas. Listening is a key skill in discussions about compositions and children should be encouraged to consider other people's ideas, as well as expressing their own. The real challenge comes when they hear an idea that they do not like the sound of: in this situation, children sometimes need some help in providing feedback that is about the idea rather than the person. It would be better to say, 'David, I like your idea about the shakers but I'm not sure the triangle fits with the rest of the music' rather than, 'I don't like David's idea'.

RESOLVING CONFLICTS

We have established that, in order for children to develop collaborative skills, we have to give them the opportunities to do so. This means taking some risks, relinquishing some control, and letting children get stuck in on collaborative tasks that might, at times, be socially 'messy' (not to mention noisy). Remember that the ability to resolve conflicts is part of growing up and it is important that children learn how to do this themselves, without relying on the teacher to 'sort out' every disagreement. Giving them the skills to avoid conflict in the first place by focusing their comments on ideas rather than people is a good start. It would also be helpful to equip them with some phrases that they might use if difficulties arise, such as 'I like what you're doing with the drum and I think it would fit better with the rest of the piece if it was a bit quieter', or 'Would it be OK if I tried the guiro for a moment?'.

CASE STUDY 10.1

In this example, Gordon, an undergraduate primary student teacher, is supporting Year 5 children to develop their understanding of how the valves on a cornet 'work' to change the pitch of the notes produced, in a cross-curricular lesson with links to science and design and technology. He has planned for the children to work in groups of three to look closely at both the exterior and internal features of the cornet.

At the outset of the lesson, Gordon tells the children that the aim of the task is for them to work collaboratively, in a small group, to provide a clear explanation of how the valves function to enable a cornet player to change the pitch of the note. He sets out his expectations about how each group is to work, emphasising the importance of taking turns, listening to other opinions and, at all times, taking care of the instruments. In each group of three, the children agree on one child to hold and move the cornet carefully so that all aspects of the external features can be examined and discussed, one child to carefully remove each of the valves and one child to ensure that these are placed carefully (in order and the right way round) on a piece of paper, to enable observation and analysis of the internal features of the cornet.

Student teacher evaluation: Gordon felt that, on the whole, the children collaborated well, with every group coming up with a good explanation of how the valves change the flow of air through the instrument. Only one group managed to muddle up the valves so that the cornet was (temporarily) unplayable and most made some good sketches of the features of the instruments.

Expert critique: Gordon established his expectations well in relation to both care of the instruments and the children's collaborative skills and they responded well to this, with very good discussions developing about the shape, structure and function of the cornet valves. In future lessons, Gordon could explore making the specific collaborative skills to be utilised in the lesson more explicit to the children and seek their help in identifying some success criteria by which they might judge their own collaborative skills.

CLIMATE: MODEL COLLABORATION

In addition to the aspects of developing children's collaborative skills that we have so far considered, it is also important for a great music teacher to think about the working climate that they want to create in their classroom and identify ways in which they could model a collaborative approach. For example, this might involve working closely with teaching assistants and other adults in the classroom or joining one of the children's groups to work with them on their musical composition.

CASE STUDY 10.2

In this example, Katy, a primary PGCE student, is working with Year 2 children to use a range of tuned and percussion instruments to create a 'sounds of the riverbank' musical tableau. After an introduction to help the children imagine sitting by a river on a summer day, she begins the practical work by organising the class into groups of five children. Each child is invited, in turn, to choose a musical instrument that they think might help them to create the tableau and the groups are given fifteen minutes to prepare a thirty to sixty-second performance.

Student teacher evaluation: Katy was generally pleased with the way in which the children worked together to create their short performances; although, on reflection, she wondered whether the collaboration might have been more effective had the groups had a maximum number of four children. She also wondered whether it might have been beneficial to give the children time to discuss ideas in their groups before choosing their instruments.

Expert critique: Katy is right to think that smaller groups may have worked more effectively for this task. In order to give the best opportunity for children to collaborate in this context, groups of three or four would have made it easier for the children to share ideas and experiment with sounds. It would also have been valuable for the children to be able to 'spill out' of the classroom into various areas to enable them to work in quieter spaces; this would have supported a collaborative approach, as it would have been easier for them to discuss ideas and experiment with the instruments.

RESPONSE TO CRITICAL TASK 10.1

The inter-related dimensions of music

We asked you to suggest a suitable definition for each of the inter-related dimensions of music referred to in the National Curriculum for music. Here are our suggestions.

Table 10.3 The inter-related dimensions of music: revisited

Dimension	Definition
pitch	Used to describe how low or high a note is
duration	Length (in time) – long and short
dynamics	Used to describe how loud or soft a note is
tempo	Speed – fast and slow
timbre	Different characteristics of sounds
texture	Different ways sounds are combined/layered
structure	Different ways sounds are organised

RESPONSE TO CRITICAL TASK 10.2

Opportunities for music across the curriculum

In this task, we asked you to consider ways in which music could be utilised to enhance learning across the curriculum. Here are some of our suggestions.

Table 10.4 Music across the curriculum

Current subject	Opportunity to enhance the learning
Art and design	Listen to appropriate or relevant music when creating artworks.
Computing	Create and edit music using technology.
Design and technology	Disassemble a musical instrument. For example, taking the front off the school piano is a magical moment, as, for many children, they see the workings of the instrument for the first time.
English	Listen to a classical piece of music, for example 'Mars' from the *Planets Suite*, and write some words and phrases that could be used in a poem.
Geography	Listen to music from the region of the world being studied, such as Bolivian music in a Key Stage 2 focus on a South American region.
History	Explore music that was significant to people or individuals in the period of history being studied.
Languages	Learn nursery rhymes and songs in French or Spanish.
Mathematics	Ask children to create a rap to help them remember multiplication facts or specific vocabulary.

(Continued)

Table 10.4 (Continued)

Current subject	Opportunity to enhance the learning
Physical education	Use music from around the world, including current popular music in the United Kingdom, to provide the soundtrack to dance and gymnastic presentations.
Personal, social, health and economic education	Invite children to share music that is important to them and explain why.
Religious education	Explore the way music is included in religious rituals in various faiths.
Science	Explore how pitch and volume change on a number of instruments, such as a guitar, piano, trombone or pipe organ.

RESPONSE TO CRITICAL TASK 10.3

Mr Brown

We asked you to consider what the key ingredient was in the little musical miracle that Mr Brown worked with his class. We think it might be defined as 'gentle inspiration'. By sharing his own enthusiasm for music in a very natural way, and embedding it into the life of his class, Mr Brown was an influential model for the children and an inspiration to them in starting their own musical journeys.

APPLICATION OF THE PEDAGOGIC FOCUS TO OTHER SUBJECTS

We have considered the importance of developing children's collaborative skills in music and these are important personal skills that children should develop and utilise across all other subjects in the primary curriculum. For example, in science it is important that children work well together to engage in scientific enquiry to plan and carry out practical activities. The collaborative skills of listening and agreeing or disagreeing with a point rather than a person should be emphasised, particularly when discussing different ideas about how to undertake an enquiry or when interpreting results.

In physical education, the teacher's role is significant in providing carefully judged guidance in paired and small group collaborations in, for example, dance or gymnastics. It is important that the teacher watches and listens carefully to the children's collaborations and allows sufficient time and space for children to discuss their thoughts, feelings, problems and solutions, before making well-judged and supportive interventions through non-judgemental yet provocative observations. The teacher might also model collaboration by working with a partner of their own or by joining one of the small groups.

SUMMARY FOR THIS CHAPTER

In this chapter, we have explored the power of primary music to support children's development as intelligent and creative individuals, who can listen critically to music, experiment with musical ideas, create their own compositions and begin to speak, read and write the 'language' of music. We have learnt that teachers of music should aim to be ambitious in their plans for children's musical development and be explicit with children about the collaborative skills that they are developing through working with others. Above all, the teacher of music should aim to model a positive approach to their own learning of music and aim not to dominate the learning experience.

When teaching music, do:

- engage children with a wide range of musical experiences
- give children many opportunities to work musically
- take an ambitious approach to their music development
- foster a culture of musical enjoyment and learning.

When developing children's collaborative skills, do:

- be explicit about the skills you expect children to demonstrate
- plan opportunities for developing these skills
- support children in resolving difficulties themselves
- model a collaborative approach yourself.

FURTHER READING 

The following texts may be helpful in further developing your understanding of effective teaching and learning in music and exploring the complex issue of developing collaborative skills.

Cain, T. and Cursley, J. (2017) *Teaching music differently: case studies of inspiring pedagogies.* Abingdon: Routledge.

This book provides a range of examples to provoke thinking about teaching and learning in music.

Crozier, R. (2016) *Learning a musical instrument: a guide for adult learners.* Marlborough: Hale.

This helpful book is useful for exploring the benefits, challenges and opportunities of learning to play a musical instrument as an adult.

Nickol, P. (2008) *Learning to read music: how to make sense of those mysterious symbols and bring music alive*. 3rd edn. Oxford: How To Books.

This valuable book provides a clear and accessible guide to reading music, from first principles to more advanced aspects.

REFERENCES

Acquah, E.O. (2016) 'Choral singing and wellbeing: findings from a survey of the mixed-chorus experience from music students of the University of Education Winneba, Ghana', *Legon Journal of the Humanities*, 27(2), pp. 1–13.

Clift, S. (2012) 'Singing, wellbeing, and health' in MacDonald, R., Kreutz, G. and Mitchell, L. (eds.) *Music, health, and wellbeing*. Oxford: Oxford University Press, pp. 113–24.

Department for Education (DfE) (2013) *The national curriculum in England: key stages 1 and 2 framework document*. London: DfE.

Gillies, R.M. (2003) 'Structuring co-operative learning experiences in primary school' in Gillies, R.M. and Ashman, A.F. (eds.) *Co-operative learning: the social and intellectual outcomes of learning in groups*. Abingdon: RoutledgeFalmer, pp. 36–53.

Holt, J. (1992) *Never too late*. Ticknall: Lighthouse Books.

Musicians' Union (2018) 'MU makes a splash as music education disparity highlighted', *The Musician* (Winter).

Swanwick, K. (1999) *Teaching music musically*. Abingdon: Routledge.

11

PHYSICAL EDUCATION

MEETING INDIVIDUAL AND DIVERSE NEEDS

BARBARA BROWN

OBJECTIVES

- To explore the distinctive nature of physical education and the principles of effective teaching in this subject.
- To consider how to engage in inclusive practice in physical education.
- To reflect on the application of the principles of inclusive practice in relation to some other subjects in the primary curriculum.

In this chapter, we will explore the distinctive nature of physical education and some principles of effective teaching in this subject. We will examine the principles of inclusive practice and how to enable children to access physical education within a shared teaching and learning ethos and a culture of high expectations related to pupil progress. We will conclude the chapter with some consideration of ways in which inclusive practice can be embedded across the curriculum.

WHAT IS DISTINCTIVE ABOUT TEACHING AND LEARNING IN PHYSICAL EDUCATION?

Physical education is a National Curriculum foundation subject that should provide children with the opportunity to know and understand how to move and improve in terms of their physical development, across a range of contexts. The purpose is to enable children to become physically educated, in order that they can become lifelong movers in a range of movement pursuits, from participating for enjoyment to developing the knowledge, understanding and skilfulness required to work at performance standard (Harris, 2018).

Currently, in the United Kingdom, there is an emphasis on increasing the activity levels of children, to seek to combat their sedentary lifestyles at home and in school, compounded by an unhealthy diet that is high in fat, sugar and salt, as many children are 'hard wired' into sedentary lifestyles and diet by the age of seven years. Physical education has an important role to play in helping children develop positive habits in relation to their personal health, but lessons should achieve much more than just 'getting children active'. The body is the tool in physical education and lessons should provide the highest degree of movement learning opportunities that are possible in the available time.

THE DEVELOPMENT OF PHYSICALLY LITERATE CHILDREN

Physical education should provide appropriate opportunities for children to become 'physically literate' (Maude, 2001). Physical literacy is a way of understanding movement competence: it is a range of movement responses that develop through engaging in learning situations, from simple to complex, related to play, curricular or extracurricular movement learning contexts. A skilful, experienced mover develops an ongoing, rich 'movement vocabulary' that enables them to be 'physically articulate' in increasingly open, complex and challenging learning situations. Progression in movement skill development is strongly influenced by appropriate opportunities to learn how to move, through trial and error and with the guidance of significant others. Children should experience an increasing range of appropriate movement learning opportunities, in order to develop a rich movement vocabulary, with an increasing level of skilfulness that will enable them to solve problems and challenges in increasingly complex situations in athletics, dance, games, gymnastics, outdoor and adventurous activities, play, and swimming and water safety. An easy way of understanding physical literacy is to observe change in a child in a movement situation and the impact of increased knowing and understanding on their level of competence, including skilfulness.

CRITICAL TASK 11.1

Developing physical literacy

In this example, what steps might the teacher take next to develop the children's physical literacy?

Dan and Emily, both in Year 5, do not know how to receive and redirect a ball with control in a one-two possession play situation in hockey. They are losing control and possession due to a lack of movement through their feet, knees, bodies, arms and fingers. They are not moving their bodies to absorb the pace of the incoming ball and their bottom hand is holding the shaft of the stick too tightly to be able to send, receive and redirect the ball.

THE IMPORTANCE OF KNOWING AND UNDERSTANDING IN PHYSICAL EDUCATION

Physical education should enable children to learn how to move and how to improve in a range of contexts in order to become physically literate. In order to develop movement competence, children have to *know* and *understand* how to move and respond appropriately in a variety of movement situations. The teacher should introduce the children to the key concepts and knowledge that will enable them to make progress, as explored in the example about gymnastics in Critical task 11.2.

CRITICAL TASK 11.2

Physical literacy in gymnastics: static balance

Consider the key elements that a child would need to *know* and *understand* in order to make progress with these outcomes in gymnastics:

(Continued)

- to explore, develop and refine different points of balance
- to focus on the shape of the body, degree of stretch (through to fingers and toes), focus with the eyes (on either fingers or toes) and line of the body in the tuck, pike and straddle shapes
- to move slowly into and out of each shape
- to focus the body on being strong throughout each balance.

UTILISING A LAYERED APPROACH

Physical education is not just about 'playing games', but about providing children with opportunities to develop their knowledge, understanding and skills related to various sports so that, when they do play a game, they are equipped to engage positively.

It is valuable to identify the 'foundational' knowledge and skills that are the building blocks for any activity within physical education.

For example, in hockey, a starting point could be, through modelling, to enable the children to move in different directions while holding a stick in their fingers, on both the open (with the open face of the stick foremost) and closed sides of the body (with the closed face of the stick foremost). The top left hand controls the shaft of the stick through a secure finger grasp and the bottom right hand controls the face by a light grasp of the fingers, which allows the face to wrap around a moving ball or absorb the pace of an incoming ball. Children can then naturally progress to moving, sending and receiving a ball with a partner in a five-metre grid area, initially slowly and lightly so that they learn how to respond to a moving ball and player and retain possession. This introductory possession play in grids can be developed by moving in threes in order to introduce movement off the ball, so that there is a support player at the side and behind. The players off the ball are initiating options for the movement of the ball. The players quickly learn to pass and move either to the side or behind in order to retain possession and move the ball. This layered approach supports children in understanding the key elements of a movement situation, which can later be applied in new contexts.

MANAGING THE LEARNING SPACE

Physical education takes place in spaces that are different from normal classrooms. The large space of the school hall, the playground or the field can be challenging for both the teacher and the children, so it is important to think about how to manage the learning environment to promote positive progress for all.

In a large space, it can be helpful to agree approaches to communication with your class. You may choose to give silent messages through clear actions or to utilise a whistle or other audible device but, whatever you choose, it is important to be clear about this in advance of activities getting started: once the class has dispersed over the school field is not the time to wonder how you will get them all back together again.

Similarly, it is often valuable to define the space the children are working in. Existing playground markings, cones or beanbags can all be used to help children to understand the parameters of their working area; for example, when playing two-on-two hockey, cones can be used to divide the playground into a number of small 'pitches'. It can also be very helpful to the children if you define the amount of time that they will have to work on different elements of the lesson, particularly when working in pairs or small groups to plan sequences in dance or gymnastics, for example, or when applying skills in mini-matches.

In planning how to manage the learning space, it is important to consider how you might make adjustments for individual learners, in terms of the space, equipment, time, communication and other factors. For example, a child may have a particular sensitivity to noise, struggle with co-ordination or tire quickly. Every child brings a unique set of prior experiences and personal resources to a physical education lesson, including their health, fitness and well-being; they can all make good progress if the learning environment communicates values and respects individual and diverse needs. A teacher should be highly sensitive to the individuality of every child.

CRITICAL TASK 11.3

Defining the learning space

In this example, Dave, a School Direct PGCE student teacher, has thought carefully about how to organise and manage the learning space, in order to support children's knowledge and understanding of invasion play, to:

- learn where to move in the space with two other players in order to retain possession
- understand the significance of exchanging spaces
- understand the significance of supporting the ball player 'wide' and 'behind'
- learn to make decisions based on spatial knowledge and understanding.

He has set out cones to divide the space into three equal parts, each three metres wide. Three children run slowly down these wide lanes: the one in the

(Continued)

left-hand lane holds a beanbag and sets the pace; the one in the right-hand lane tries to stay level with the child holding the beanbag ('wide'); the third child aims to stay three metres behind the child holding the beanbag ('behind'). All three children try to develop an awareness of the pace and relative position of the other two. Once the children have shown sound understanding and are working well together, a dynamic element is introduced, as the beanbag is thrown from one player to another, and the three children aim to create a new triangular arrangement, with one leading, one running level and one behind.

Consider how the approach to divide or define the learning space might be beneficial to the learners in relation to their layered understanding. What might be the next step in the teaching and learning sequence?

PEDAGOGIC FOCUS FOR THIS CHAPTER: MEETING INDIVIDUAL AND DIVERSE NEEDS

In the following, we will explore how a teacher can promote inclusive practice in physical education, through establishing an inclusive environment, identifying and understanding individual needs and providing access to the curriculum.

CRITICAL TASK 11.4

Values

Consider the personal and professional values that underpin approaches to inclusive practice.

AN INCLUSIVE LEARNING ENVIRONMENT

An inclusive learning environment embraces every child on equal terms and is underpinned by values. It communicates human rights and brings children to the heart of the teaching and learning process. Children have more common needs than different needs (DfE, 1978) and all children can experience varying degrees of difficulty and competence in learning in physical education (Ainscow, 1991).

Central to an inclusive learning environment is a teacher's ability to access all children to learning and make good individual progress. Ofsted (2013) and Ofsted and Spielman (2017) are clear that high-quality teaching is pivotal in ensuring that every child in every classroom can enjoy the best learning opportunities in order to make the best progress. Every teacher is responsible for every pupil in their class, is accountable for every pupil's progress and should understand the individual needs of all their pupils (Carter, 2015).

The teacher is key to enabling all children to access learning and, for some children, it is necessary for a school and their teachers to work in collaboration with a range of professional personnel, such as physiotherapists or speech and language therapists, in order to appropriately help a child to access and progress in their learning and development.

UNDERSTANDING INDIVIDUAL NEEDS

Understanding the individual needs of each child enables a teacher to help them to access learning and promote individual progress. Progress is highly individual to each child and this informs the way that we provide personalised guidance in lessons and manipulate information so that each child can understand, know and apply knowledge to their own development. In order to understand the developmental needs of children, it is necessary to engage in formative, qualitative assessment and evaluation strategies that provide evidence-based information to inform personalised guidance and drive individual progress (Wiliam, 2018).

Segmental analysis (see Figure 11.1), as a form of focused observation, can be employed by a teacher in order to understand how the segments of the body are moving in response to a movement situation and then use this to inform their guidance. It is not necessary to make notes in every box, but the model can serve as a helpful reminder to observe every segment of a child's body in order to analyse their developing knowledge, understanding and skills in relation to their movement.

In the case of the example in Figure 11.2, the purpose of segmental observation and analysis is to help the child to achieve a mature movement pattern in skipping.

Following observation of James' skipping, the teacher can personalise guidance through appropriately sized steps and strategies: 'move your shoulders down and remember to keep your head still', 'open your hands a little' or 'remember to look at the end of the rope'.

Formative assessment information should be used immediately within teaching, as well as feed forward to the planning and teaching in the next lesson, so it is important for a teacher to know what they want to focus on and devise an assessment strategy that will meet the outcome. It can serve to help a teacher to:

- understand problems that a child might be experiencing in movement learning
- understand how a child's body is moving
- assess a child's knowing, understanding and applying in a movement situation
- assess the standard and quality of a child's movement response.

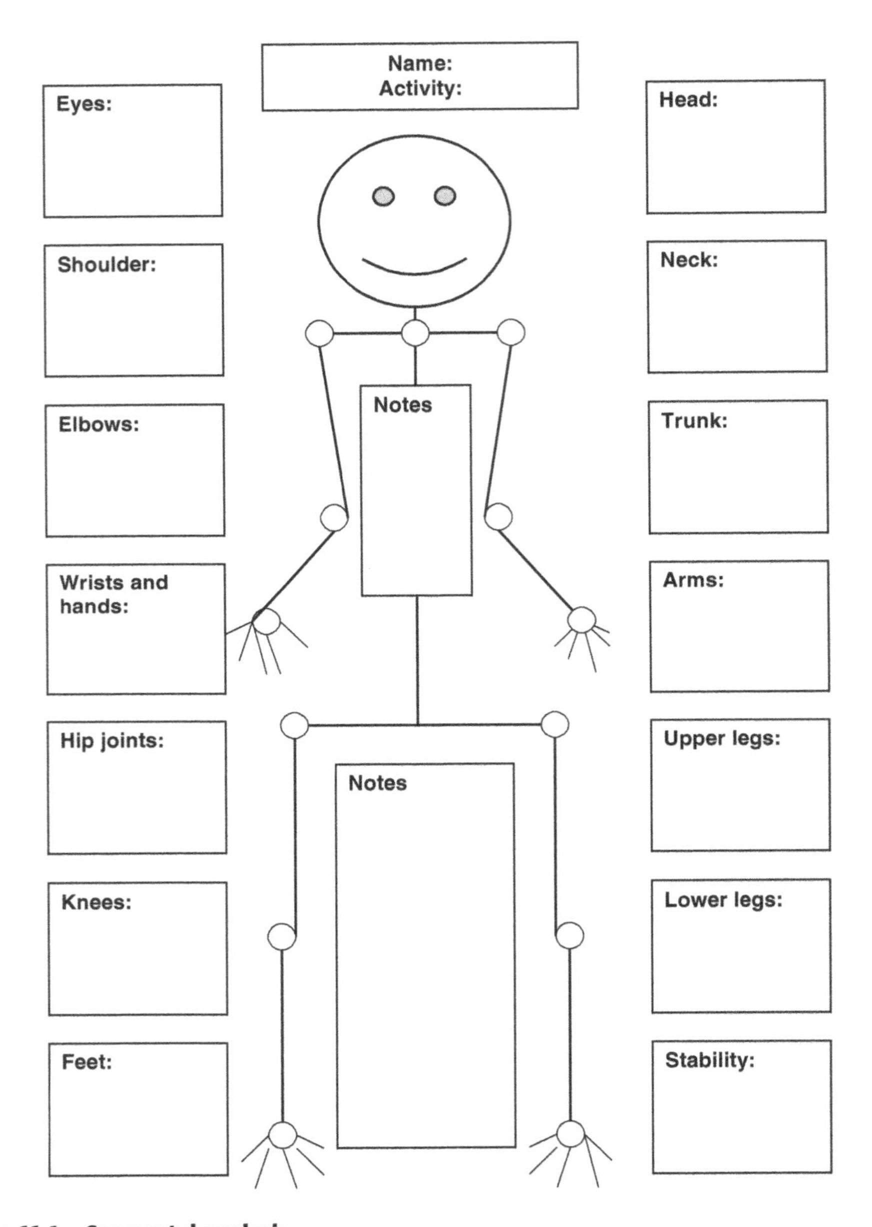

Figure 11.1 Segmental analysis

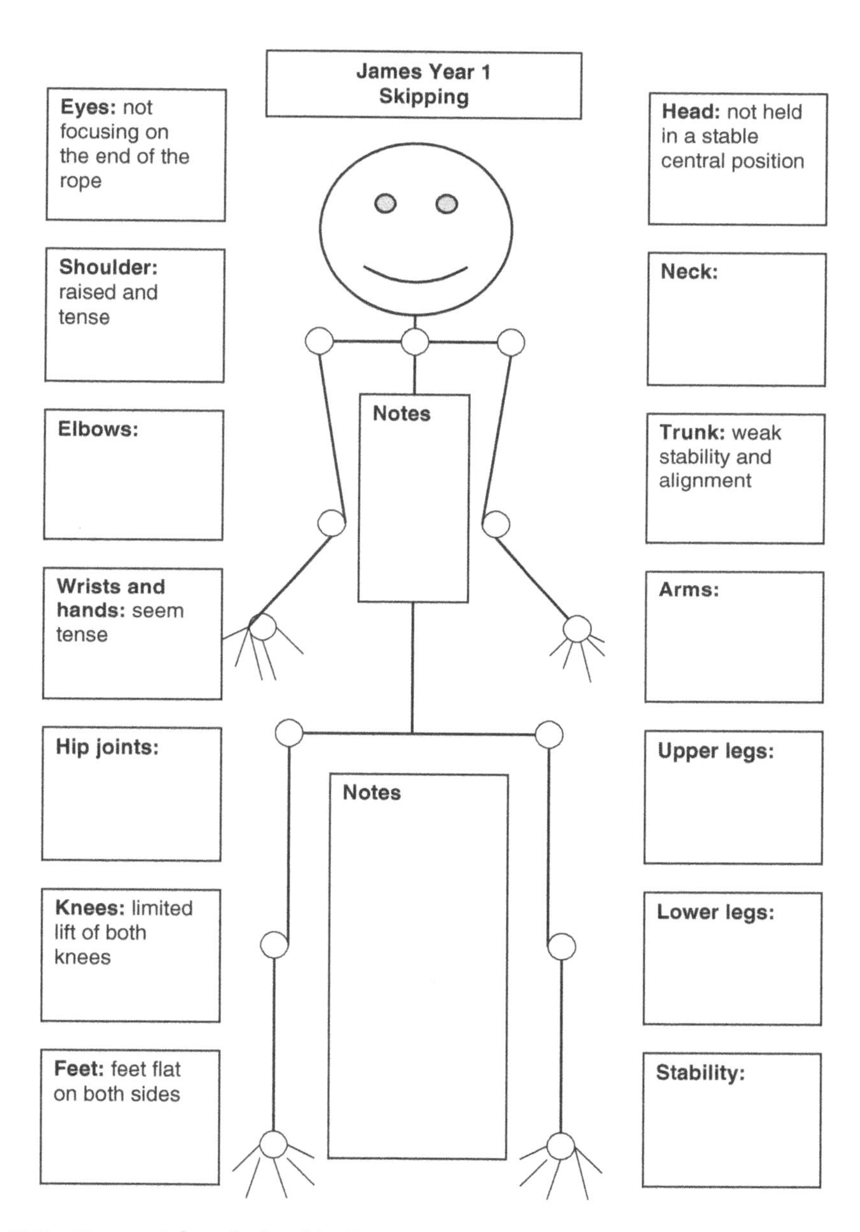

Figure 11.2 Segmental analysis: skipping

The greatest learner should be the teacher, with an ongoing quest to know and understand to the benefit of all children.

PROMOTING ACCESS TO LEARNING

Teachers have to be able to understand learners in order to interpret the curriculum appropriately for the developmental status of the children, and then how to manipulate information so that the children can understand how to learn, how to move and how to improve (Gallahue et al., 2011; Cleland Donnelly et al., 2016). This means 'unpacking' the curriculum, in order to both develop a progressive sequence of lessons for the diverse range of developmental needs in the class, and to personalise the demands of a movement situation for a child so that they can access learning that is developmentally appropriate for them. As a child knows and understands more, so changes can be made to the task and learning environment.

For example, in short tennis, a child is learning how to play a groundstroke on the open side with the body in a sideways position. First, the child is learning how to send the ball up the sideline to the opposite back corner: a straight forehand drive. The child is learning how to release the ball from the non-racquet hand, while bending the knees and swinging through the ball in line with the sideline, with the eyes on the target corner and with an appropriate degree of pace and weight on the ball, with the racquet hand wrapped softly around the handle in order to achieve accuracy. Next, in order to make a small, developmental change to the task and environment, the ball is sent down the sideline to the child, who is required to read the incoming ball and time the preparatory back swing and follow through in order to return the ball up the sideline to the opposite back corner.

To help a child to understand how to respond in a movement situation, knowledge can be presented and developed in a personalised, sequential way. Moving and guiding a child initially can be followed by key word(s) in sequence for the child to say as they prepare to do the appropriate action. For example, when catching an incoming ball, key words can be identified in sequence, as in Table 11.1.

Table 11.1 Actions and key words

Body parts	Action words	Amplification
Eyes	Look	Track the ball through the air.
Toes	Move	Behind the line of the ball.
Knees	Bend	When reaching for the ball.
Fingers and elbows	Give	In towards the body when receiving the ball. Soft fingers.

It is important not to overload the senses when a child does not understand how to move: the tendency is to talk at a child, whereas moving with them or modelling allows an understanding to be established through experiencing the sensation of the movement. When modelling to a class or an individual, the teacher might manipulate information so that the children can understand and access the learning. If a teacher or pupil models a movement situation that is scaffolded with key information, presented in a sequential way, it allows the children to access it, relative to their development. Sequenced, focused questions with focused modelling and observation enable a child to understand, step by step, how to move and how to improve.

For example, when moving along the baseline of a short tennis court:

Table 11.2 Focused questions and modelling

Question	Modelling
What part of the foot am I moving on?	Balls of the feet/toes
Am I moving heavily or lightly?	Lightly
Am I sidestepping or running?	Running
Where are my toes pointing?	Direction of travel Towards the baseline corner

It is also necessary to understand that the size of the personalised steps will vary in a shared movement situation and the teacher can identify key aspects appropriately for a child as they engage in personalised guidance. For example, when a child is learning to receive a ball that bounces, the information could relate to body parts, such as toes, knees, fingers, eyes. Action words can also be used, such as, 'What do my knees do when the ball bounces?'. Focused questioning with focused modelling and observation enables a child to know and understand that their knees should bend when the ball bounces. Responding to a moving ball requires a child to manage how their body is moving in order to play the ball, as well as read the ball so that they can control it skilfully and successfully. They have to learn how to manage their moving body in a controlled way, as well as read the flight or pathway of the ball, how fast it is travelling, how best to play it and where to send it, and then where to reposition themselves.

The teaching strategies should reflect the range of development across the class. It is all too easy to instruct the activity without due consideration to the range of movement skill development of the children. The requirements to meet the contextual demands of, for example, team games can take over without due consideration of the movement learning needs of the children. Casbon et al. (2005) propose that a 'games for understanding' approach, through the principles of game play, allows for the development of spatial strategies in well-defined, appropriately sized grids, to enable children to progressively know where and how to move effectively in the space. For example, in an invasion game, the space is defined with cones to enable a child to know and make decisions about where and when to send the ball and where and when to move. This graduated approach allows for the game to be appropriately scaffolded to promote knowledge and understanding of how to play the game: individually, with a partner or as a small unit of players. Similarly, understanding the complexities of moving with others in dance and gymnastics should inform the way a teacher develops children's knowledge and understanding so that they can learn how to enjoy sharing movement situations, as well as moving effectively with others.

CASE STUDY 11.1

In this example, Jenny, an undergraduate student teacher in the final year of training, is working with John in Year 3. He is exploring the making of different shapes with his body while balancing on his bottom: tuck, pike, straddle and twist (see Critical task 11.2). Through careful modelling of specific movements, Jenny enables John to understand how to move the segments of the body into and out of a different shape, to feel the point of balance, and understand the feedback from his body segments in order to develop an improved sense of balance. In developing a static balance, John is learning how to focus on the movement of his body segments in a sequential way so that he can learn how to hold the balance for a moment and then move into a different shape.

Student teacher evaluation: Jenny was pleased with the way in which she had identified some of the key aspects of John's learning about his body. In future lessons, she intends to develop John's understanding of how to develop and refine:

- the clarity of the shape and line (pike and straddle) of the body
- the degree of stretch through to the toes in each shape and fingers in the pike and straddle shapes
- the focus with the eyes on the fingers or toes.

Expert critique: This focused movement learning situation enabled Jenny to learn the significance of personalised guidance on John's ability to know, understand and apply. She was able to see how her guidance had driven good progress for John in learning how to move and improve. Her modelling strategies enabled him to know and understand how to improve and apply the strategies when undertaking other static balances. The strategies and guidance from Jenny enabled John to achieve a very good standard and quality of performance in this movement phrase. In future lessons, Jenny should seek to develop the qualitative aspects of this movement task with John, through focusing on the following:

- Time: is it appropriate to move quickly or slowly in this movement task?
- Weight: can the child focus their strength to hold the bottom balance while changing shape from tuck to straddle to pike to twist?
- Can the child hold the shape for a moment (pause) before changing shape?
- Can the child feel a sense of stretch in their toes in each shape?

A child recognises when a teacher understands them in a movement learning situation, at whatever point in their development. This way of teaching means that children will want to learn with a teacher and in lessons they will seek guidance because they want to learn how to move. The important message here is that the teacher is the key to access for all learners, wherever they are on their learning journey, and understanding all learners is the foundation of becoming an effective and significant teacher.

RESPONSE TO CRITICAL TASK 11.1

Developing physical literacy

We asked you to suggest ways in which you might respond to Dan and Emily, both in Year 5, who do not know how to receive and redirect a ball with control in a one-two possession play situation in hockey. Here are some suggestions of ways in which you might support them to develop their physical literacy in this context:

- Move alongside the child; encourage them to focus on the sensation and sequence of the movement of stopping then pushing the hockey ball.
- Include key words, layered in sequence, that relate to the action of the body at each incremental step: 'watch the ball all the way', 'bend the knees', 'move the right hand lower'.
- Try not to talk too much: be neat with words. Encourage children to observe others and to concentrate on the sensation and developing control of their movements.

RESPONSE TO CRITICAL TASK 11.4

Values

In this task, we asked you to reflect on the personal and professional values that underpin approaches to inclusive practice. It is important to identify your values and apply them in the day-to-day work of teaching. For example, if you believe that every child is worth investing in, this will impact significantly on your practice in every lesson, as you seek to make adjustments so that all children can access the learning and make appropriate progress. The challenge is that the children who need us to invest in them the most are sometimes the most challenging to work with, so hold on tight to your values and do not give up on any child.

APPLICATION OF THE PEDAGOGIC FOCUS TO OTHER SUBJECTS

The key principles of meeting individual needs are the same in all teaching situations and are based on the values of respect and inclusion for all. Whether teaching athletics or adjectives, high jump or haiku, cricket or creation, the teacher seeks, first, to ensure that the learning environment is positive, welcoming and supportive of all children, and then seeks to understand the emotional, physical and learning needs of each child. In religious education, this might mean establishing a positive and respectful environment, in which every child's religious or personal beliefs are valued and in which all children are able to answer questions, without criticism or fear of criticism, about their faith or lack of faith.

In English, the teacher might seek to understand why a child finds letter formation challenging or why they dislike reading, as gaining these insights will make a huge difference in helping to identify a supportive way forward. For example, if the teacher identifies that the child who finds letter formation challenging has poor pencil control, the task and/or resources can be adapted to support fine motor development. The teacher may also work alongside the child, modelling appropriate pencil grip and hand movements for formation. If the teacher of the child who dislikes reading discovers that the child is not interested in the texts on offer in the classroom, the teacher can then have a further discussion to find out what the child is interested in and can then source texts that might appeal. Identifying potential barriers to learning and taking resourceful approaches to overcome these is central to meeting individual needs, whatever the subject.

SUMMARY FOR THIS CHAPTER

In this chapter, we have considered the distinctive nature of physical education and the importance of developing children's knowledge and understanding about their own physical literacy and their next steps in learning. We have explored some of the challenges, such as utilising the physical learning space effectively, and considered ways in which the new teacher can manage the learning within physical education in a way that is consistent with inclusive values and practice. The important message is that the teacher is the key to access for all learners, wherever they are on their learning journey, and understanding all learners is the foundation of becoming an effective and significant teacher.

When teaching physical education, do:

- develop children's understanding of their physical literacy
- provide children with the knowledge and understanding required to develop their movement competence
- utilise a layered approach to the development of knowledge, understanding and skilfulness
- plan how to utilise the learning environments to promote learning.

When meeting individual and diverse needs, do:

- establish a values-based, inclusive learning environment
- seek to understand the learning of every child
- explore ways in which each child can access the learning.

FURTHER READING 

The following texts may be helpful in developing your understanding of effective teaching and learning in physical education and in exploring the principles of inclusive practice.

Lawrence, J. (2017) *Teaching primary physical education*. 2nd edn. London: SAGE Publications.

Physical education is an important part of the primary curriculum and one that provides unique challenges for those involved with its teaching. This book offers a balanced and comprehensive overview of the subject, covering issues such as safe practice in physical education, inclusion, subject leadership and cross-curricular approaches, supported by an accessible theory-informed approach.

Pickup, I. and Price, L. (2007) *Teaching physical education in the primary school: a developmental approach*. London: Bloomsbury.

This is a comprehensive yet accessible guide to the teaching and learning of physical education in the primary school. Readers are encouraged to plan lessons that are individually relevant, worthwhile and motivating for children, and to ensure that learning is at the heart of the physical education experience.

Vickerman, P. and Maher, A. (2018) *Teaching physical education to children with special educational needs and disabilities*. 2nd edn. Abingdon: Routledge.

This text provides a thorough overview of the challenges and opportunities for inclusion in physical education lessons. Combining a theoretical framework with practical strategies for teachers, the title covers a diverse range of issues that teachers need to address in order to provide high-quality learning experiences for children with SEND.

REFERENCES

Ainscow, M. (ed.) (1991) *Effective schools for all*. London: David Fulton.

Carter, A. (2015) 'Carter review of initial teacher training (ITT)'. Available at: https://assets.publishing.service.gov.uk/government/uploads/system/uploads/attachment_data/file/399957/Carter_Review.pdf (Accessed: 23 April 2019).

Casbon, C., Spackman, L. and British Association of Advisers and Lecturers in Physical Education (2005) *Assessment for learning in physical education*. Worcester: BAALPE.

Cleland Donnelly, F., Mueller, S. and Gallahue, D. (2016) *Developmental physical education for all children*. 5th edn. Champaign, IL: Human Kinetics.

Department for Education (DfE) (1978) 'Special educational needs: report of the committee of enquiry into the education of handicapped children and young people'. Chairman: Mrs H.M. Warnock. London: HMSO.

Gallahue, D., Ozmun, J. and Goodway, J. (2011) *Understanding motor development: infants, children, adolescents, adults*. 7th edn. New York: McGraw-Hill.

Harris, J. (2018) 'The case for physical education becoming a core subject in the National Curriculum'. Association for Physical Education. Available at: www.afpe.org.uk/physical-education/the-case-for-physical-education-becoming-a-core-subject-in-the-national-curriculum/ (Accessed: 23 April 2019).

Maude, P. (2001) *Physical children, active teaching: investigating physical literacy*. Buckingham: Open University Press.

Ofsted (2013) 'Beyond 2012: outstanding physical education for all'. Available at: www.gov.uk/government/publications/beyond-2012-outstanding-physical-education-for-all (Accessed: 23 April 2019).

Ofsted and Spielman, A. (2017) 'HMCI's commentary: recent primary and secondary curriculum research', 11 October. Available at: www.gov.uk/government/speeches/hmcis-commentary-october-2017 (Accessed: 23 April 2019)

Wiliam, D. (2018) *Embedded formative assessment*. 2nd edn. Bloomington, IN: Solution Tree Press.

12

PERSONAL, SOCIAL, HEALTH AND ECONOMIC EDUCATION

DEVELOPING EMPATHY

JUDE PENNY

OBJECTIVES

- To explore the distinctive nature of personal, social, health and economic education (PSHE).
- To consider how primary school teachers can support the development of children's empathy.
- To reflect on the opportunities to develop children's empathy in some other subjects within the primary curriculum.

In this chapter, we will consider the distinctive nature of personal, social, health and economic education (PSHE). As well as knowledge acquisition and skills development, PSHE concerns the instilling of values, moral principles, behaviours and attitudes that can enable children to live confident, healthy and productive lives as members of society. As such, it is not helpful to view this area of learning and development as a 'curriculum subject'; rather, it is better viewed as an embedded aspect of children's learning.

As a pedagogic focus, we will identify the ways in which teachers can utilise good quality PSHE to help children to develop *empathy*. According to Raundalen (1991), our primary task should be to help children develop the capacity to empathise and it is thought that, as children's language and capacity to take the perspective of others develops, their capacity for empathy also increases (Berk, 2018).

WHAT IS DISTINCTIVE ABOUT PSHE AND WHY IS IT IMPORTANT?

CRITICAL TASK 12.1

Reflecting on your personal experiences

Please consider the following questions:

- Did you receive PSHE lessons during your primary education? If so, what can you remember about them?
- What about secondary school? What was your attitude towards these lessons? Were they beneficial and impactful?
- To what extent do you think your personal experiences have influenced your perception of PSHE?

When student teachers reflect on their experiences of PSHE in their own education, it is interesting to hear the details that they remember:

> 'I remember the "Life Bus" coming to my primary school where they used a giraffe puppet to teach us about smoking and things.'
>
> 'At secondary school, it was sex education and drugs awareness – the "facts of life".'
>
> 'They were boring/easy lessons.'
>
> 'The teacher seemed embarrassed: they didn't seem to want to be there!'
>
> 'In Year 6, we had a one-off lesson where we were asked to "draw jealousy".'
>
> 'It felt really weird and I didn't understand what to do or why we were doing it.'

These reflections on their experiences consistently reveal a paucity in the regularity and frequency of PSHE lessons and that PSHE teaching and learning seem to occur on a 'need to know' basis (e.g. children are about to reach puberty; therefore, sex and relationships education is required) or when 'time-filler lessons' are required. A diverse range of experiences has resulted in student teachers holding diverse, subjective views of PSHE, ranging from enjoyment, to apathy or, even, dislike. However, when student teachers have the opportunity to explore the fundamental principles of PSHE education and learn about the depth, breadth and importance of this area of learning and development, many are surprised by the narrow provision that they received during their own school years. They are also surprised to learn that PSHE does not have a prescribed programme of study within the National Curriculum. However, it is important to note that section 2.5 of the National Curriculum states: 'All schools should make provision for personal, social, health and economic education (PSHE), drawing on good practice' (DfE, 2013a: 5).

The DfE recommends the good practice of the PSHE Association, whose website contains current developments, resources and a comprehensive programme of study to aid planning. In addition to the recommendations in section 2.5 of the National Curriculum framework, the Department for Education guidance states that PSHE is 'an important and necessary part of all pupils' education' and that:

> 'schools should seek to use PSHE education to build, where appropriate, on the statutory content already outlined in the National Curriculum, the basic school curriculum and in statutory guidance on drug education, financial education, sex and relationship education (SRE) and the importance of physical activity and diet for a healthy lifestyle.' (DfE, 2013b)

As the result of recent curricular developments, all primary schools will be required to teach health education, in addition to relationships education, from 2020:

> 'This makes the majority of personal, social, health and economic (PSHE) education mandatory for all pupils, in all schools. While falling short of mandatory status for the whole of PSHE, this measure will greatly encourage schools already prioritising PSHE and help level-up standards across all schools, for all pupils.' (PSHE Association, 2018)

The PSHE Association (2018) describes PSHE as 'learning to live life well'. While knowledge acquisition is important, equally important are opportunities for children to acquire and practise *interpersonal* and *intrapersonal* skills and the *attitudes* and *values* that support these. If children are to 'develop resilience, manage change and have a realistic sense of their own worth and capabilities' (Boddington et al., 2014: 5), these skills, attitudes and values are essential. The PSHE Association programme of study explicitly refers to these essential skills and they should be taken into consideration during the planning stage, alongside knowledge development (PSHE Association, 2017).

THE IMPORTANCE OF THE 'AFFECTIVE DOMAIN'

Bloom's 'cognitive taxonomy' of higher order thinking skills is a well-established guide for thinking about meaningful teaching and learning. What is less well-known is that Bloom also devised an 'affective taxonomy', related to the manner in which we deal with things *emotionally* (feelings, values, appreciation, enthusiasm, motivation and attitudes). In fact, it is believed that 'the affective domain can significantly enhance, inhibit or even prevent student learning' (Osler, 2013: 36). This provides further endorsement of the importance of personal, social and emotional development for academic achievement; it also indicates that teachers should not view PSHE as a curriculum 'subject'. This area of learning and development cannot be taught and assessed in the same way as most 'subjects': it is about human development and is, therefore, complex and non-linear. As teachers are human beings who have been (and are still) on their own personal and social learning journeys, PSHE can be incredibly interesting and intriguing to teach. Effective PSHE teachers allow the children to explore, ponder and articulate their life experiences, ideas and learning and there is no reason why teachers themselves cannot participate, through considering and sharing their own experiences and ideas. The important thing to understand is that PSHE is not a set of measurable standards to be 'delivered' or 'covered' and planning and teaching should be approached with sensitivity and respect for children's individuality as human beings.

Cambridge Primary Review (2007: 3) found that children as young as four years old think deeply about world issues that affect us all, including family turmoil, crime, the effects of climate change and the gulf between rich and poor. It is, therefore, important that children are presented with opportunities to engage in critical thinking in PSHE and, for the purpose of this chapter, *questioning*, *reasoning*, *reflective judgement* and *problem-solving* are some key thinking skills that will be considered.

SUPPORTING CHILDREN TO THINK DEEPLY AND TO EXPLORE AND ARTICULATE THEIR IDEAS, EXPERIENCES AND LEARNING

According to Goddard et al. (2013: 7), personal education is 'concerned with self-knowledge, self-acceptance and valuing of the self as well as acquisition of skills in keeping well and safe'. Good quality PSHE should always include opportunities for children to explore their ideas, perhaps through elicitation activities, such as drawing (and sharing) their 'self-concept' (a self-portrait annotated with personal likes, dislikes, special people and places, achievements and goals). This activity not only encourages children to reflect on their lives and what is important to them, it also provides a forum for teachers to encourage individuals to offer *reasons* for their ideas and take time to consider other children's ideas and experiences too.

'Circle time' is an approach that is widely used as a vehicle for class discussion and debate (Mosley, 2005). It can be timetabled or used spontaneously in response to an issue that may arise within the class. The children and adults form a circle on chairs, cushions or carpet and this helps to create a bond between the participants where eye contact and a feeling of intimacy and collaboration is possible. Often, a story or stimulus, such as a video clip, photograph or a puppet's story is used to prompt a discussion. Circle time rules, such as the importance of turn-taking, respecting everyone's opinions and showing others that they are being listened to, are established and important transferable skills of looking, listening, speaking, thinking and concentrating can be supported and developed (Mosley, 2005).

Circle time can be particularly valuable in developing children's *interpersonal* skills, such as communication, assertiveness and compromise, emotional literacy and empathy. Group games and activities provide excellent opportunities to develop important transferable social (and emotional) skills. For example, as a circle time warm-up, 'Eye Contact Shuffle' is a silent game in which, on the word 'go', children simply change places with others they make eye contact with and keep going until the teacher says 'stop'. This game can help children to practise and develop a range of skills: those who find eye contact uncomfortable can experience it in a safe and fun way; children learn that they do not always have to use their voices to communicate; skills of spatial awareness and compromise (if two children go to the same chair) are practised. Children can be encouraged to reflect on the skills that they were using and how they felt during the game, and offer some reasons for actions and feelings. This is an important aspect of all PSHE activities as it provides teachers with deeper insights and can support children to clarify (and sometimes adjust) their ideas.

It is also very important that children are encouraged to ask questions if they do not understand or want to know more, and to reflect upon their learning in terms of what it means to them *personally*. For example, they might ask a talk partner:

- Is anything puzzling you? (reflection)
- Do you have a question about/for … ? (questioning)
- Do you have an idea about how we can help [e.g. Susan]? (problem-solving)
- Why might they have acted in that way? (reasoning)

To close a circle time session, passing a speaking object (only those holding the object can speak) for 'last words' (the opportunity to share final thoughts) is good practice: often, children who have not spoken in the session decide to contribute at this point. 'Last words' also gives the children a chance to articulate and share their developing thoughts or ask questions to clarify or extend their understanding (e.g. 'can bullies also be victims?'). Diaries and journals can provide an opportunity for older children to engage in deeper, more private reflections following a discussion.

ENACTING PSHE VALUES OUTSIDE OF PSHE LESSONS

It is very important that the values and attitudes that the teacher seeks to develop within PSHE lessons should also be enacted throughout every part of the school week. There is little point in leading a circle time session on the theme of 'respect' if children are later belittled by the teacher or spoken to with impatience or frustration.

PEDAGOGIC FOCUS FOR THIS CHAPTER: DEVELOPING EMPATHY

WHAT IS EMPATHY?

Have you ever witnessed a family member or friend stub their toe or bang their head and did you exclaim 'Ouch! I bet that hurt!'? It is thought that this capacity to 'feel' another person's pain, without having to experience it ourselves, could have been a very effective mechanism for survival and at the centre of this capacity is *empathy* (Boddington et al., 2014). As social creatures, humans are naturally empathetic. Hodges and Myers (2007) suggest that many of the most noble of human behaviours, such as aiding strangers and stigmatised people, are thought to have their roots in empathy. Interviews with non-Jewish rescuers of Jews in Nazi Europe have revealed that their commitment to act did not suddenly appear under the threat of brutality; altruism was integrated into their lives long before the war began through caring relationships and the shared values of their parents. Empathy is important because it is our 'social radar' (Goleman, 1998: 133); it is the ability to read and 'tune in' to other people's feelings, a core skill in letting people feel acknowledged and valued (Sharp, 2001). Empathy can also help children to respect those who are different from themselves and adopt caring, supportive and sensitive attitudes towards them (Brown, 2001). So, when we empathise, we think about how other people might be feeling, which can lead to *changed behaviour* and *better relationships* (Equality and Human Rights Commission, 2016).

BEING AN EMPATHETIC TEACHER

Sharp (2001: 27) suggests that 'people in the caring professions usually show a high degree of empathy, but it is a core skill in all work involving people'. After their primary carer, teachers are possibly the most significant and influential adults in a child's life: it is important that, in their interactions with children, teachers enact the skills and attributes that they would hope to develop in the individuals in their care. Demonstrating empathy may require the suppression of one's own personal mood and affective state, as well as subjective feelings towards others, and so we may need to make a conscious effort to *develop* this important skill, as well as enact it.

CRITICAL TASK 12.2

Developing empathy

Consider the following questions:

- Am I compassionate enough to care about/understand another person's feelings?
- Can I put myself in the other person's shoes so completely that I do not criticise or judge them?
- Can I let myself enter into the other person's feelings and personal meanings to see these the way they do?

If you answered 'no' or 'not sure' to any of the questions in Critical task 12.2, perhaps a conscious effort to practise these daily can help you to develop your capacity for empathy. Avery (2011) believes that we can use both verbal (words) and non-verbal (actions, physical cues) ways of communicating to help us be perceptive of children's thoughts and feelings (see Table 12.1).

Table 12.1 Verbal/non-verbal encouragers (adapted from Avery, 2011)

Verbal encouragers	Non-verbal encouragers
I want to understand more about your experience	**I am listening**
Asking related and relevant questions to collect more information . . . such as 'Can you tell me more about that?' or 'I am curious about . . .'	Eye contact, nodding of the head, smiling.
So what I am hearing you say is that . . .	**I want to listen**
Reflective listening: simply reflect what you think you heard and ensure that you refer to the child's feelings; they will feel as though you have *really* listened and that you understand them.	I am not checking my watch every five minutes or rolling my eyes, sighing, etc.

ESTABLISHING AN ENVIRONMENT WHERE EMPATHY CAN FLOURISH

Ultimately, creating empathy comes down to leading children by example, so enacting the non-verbal and verbal cues (Table 12.1) can certainly contribute to a classroom ethos where empathy can flourish. However, it is important to consider other factors such as classroom ground rules and the extent to which they include being consider-ate and respectful to each other in a positive manner. Hold discussions with the children to emphasise the idea that behaviour that is respectful, fair, kind and empathetic, and treating others in the way you want to be treated, are good 'rules' for the class. Make celebrating successes a regular part of your classroom life, through sharing and celebrating achievements (not just outcomes, but processes and effort too). A positive, caring, empathetic environment can be established if we take time to notice, share and praise the day-to-day occurrences in our classrooms.

Gordon (2010, cited in Beach, 2010) advocates an 'ask don't tell' approach, which is based on the premise that we never know, for sure, what another person is feeling, so it is really important that we *ask* how a child feels and don't *tell* them how they feel. Avoiding phrases such as 'I know how you feel' and replacing them with 'I imagine that you feel this way, am I right?' can make a world of difference. Gordon (2010, cited in Beach, 2010) also advocates making 'thank you' part of the classroom culture, because she believes that gratitude is inextricably linked to empathy. From a simple thank you for holding the door, to a bigger thank you for sharing something, regular use of 'those two small words' creates a culture of gratitude and so empathy in a classroom.

STRATEGIES TO HELP CHILDREN DEVELOP EMPATHY

Persona Dolls are special dolls with individual personalities. They come with a 'persona', a culture, family background, likes and dislikes, which they share with the children that they 'visit'. It is important that the dolls share commonalities as well as differences so that the children can identify and interact with them. A doll can visit children to share their happy, and sometimes unhappy, experiences; the story can mirror a current issue or incident that requires 'airing'. Having listened to the doll's story, the children are given the opportunity to listen, reflect, talk and engage in some reasoning and problem-solving. Persona Dolls are 'perfect vehicles for promoting active empathy' (Brown, 2001: 1). By examining the feelings of the dolls, children have the opportunity to understand why the doll thought and behaved as they did. This, in turn, empowers the children to express their own feelings and attempt to solve both the doll's and, eventually, their own problems. Through sharing stories, children are able to identify, evaluate and, possibly, feel what the dolls are feeling. They may be comforted by the fact that they are not the only ones who have experienced these events and feelings.

CASE STUDY 12.1

In this example, Polly, a PGCE primary student teacher, is facilitating circle time with a group of Reception children. There has been a recent incident in the role-play area, in which a boy was 'not allowed' by other children to play at cooking because 'only mummies cook in the kitchen'. After a discussion with the class teacher, Polly has decided to use Charlotte, a Persona Doll, to address the issue by creating a 'similar but different' scenario. This is good practice because, when addressing an incident that has occurred in the setting, it is important to change the character and story so that it does not exactly mirror the situation and avoids placing a 'spotlight' on the children involved.

Polly: Children, we have a special visitor to our circle time today. This is Charlotte. Say hello to Charlotte.

Children: Hello Charlotte!

[Polly puts her ear to Charlotte's mouth.]

Polly: Charlotte has come to tell you a story and to ask if you would like to help her. Would that be ok?

[The children nod.]

Children: Yes!

Polly: Well, yesterday at nursery, Charlotte wanted to play with the garage and cars but the other children said, 'no Charlotte, you can't play because only boys play with cars!'. What do you think of that, children?

[Silence for several seconds.]

Ellie: The children were being naughty.

Polly: Thank you Ellie, does anyone else have an idea?

David: Anyone can play with the cars . . . Charlotte can play with the cars.

Polly: Thank you, David. She says that makes her feel a bit better. So you would let Charlotte play with the garage?

[David nods.]

Polly: How do you think this made Charlotte feel? Perhaps tell your partner…

Polly: Shall we share our ideas? How is Charlotte feeling?

Libby: Sad.

(Continued)

Polly: Thank you. She is feeling sad. Does everyone agree?

[Some children nod, some shake heads.]

David: She feeling cross *[makes a cross face]*.

Polly: Yes, you do look a bit cross with that face, David.

Ellie: Upset and mis rubble like this *[makes a face]*.

Polly: Thank you Ellie.

[Polly 'listens' to Charlotte.]

Polly: Charlotte says she did feel sad, a little bit cross, upset and miserable. She feels better already because you understand.

Student teacher evaluation: Polly said that she was rather nervous of using the Persona Doll, as she had never tried this approach before. Undertaking some research beforehand gave her an idea about the sorts of things to say and do. Polly said: 'Overall, I was pleased with how the children responded to Charlotte's story, as if she was another child. I did feel a bit stuck when I didn't get an immediate response to some questions and looking back, I think my initial question (What do you think of that?) was too open, hence the silence that followed. Also, I should have made more of some of the children's responses so that they felt that their contributions were valued. For example, when Ellie said the children were being naughty, I thanked her and moved on, whereas there may have been an opportunity to explore the notion of naughtiness and behaviour towards each other. I think I would like to work on how I respond to the children's ideas so we explore them together, in more depth. I was trying very hard not to lead them to the answers and outcome that I wanted and I do think that they were able to empathise and to come up with some solutions that were their own, which is great.'

Expert critique: Given that this was Polly's first attempt at using a Persona Doll and that she was addressing an incident that occurred in the setting, there is much to be positive about. She reversed the gender and situation and she did not refer to the real-life incident or the children involved. She also allowed the children to share their ideas in 'talk partners', which was a great opportunity for them to clarify their thinking. However, it is also a good opportunity to provide some thinking time and 'listen in' to gain a sense of what the children are thinking. In developing her responses to children's ideas, Polly could ask children to give their reasons for their ideas, as this can lead to deeper thinking, sharing of experiences and the airing of possible solutions. Polly encouraged emotional literacy through telling the children, 'Charlotte says she did feel sad, a little bit cross, upset and miserable. She feels better already because you understand.' It is good practice to share the doll's persona with the children, before introducing the story or problem, so Polly should aim to do this next time.

The children care about the Persona Dolls and what happens to them, so a helpful next step for Polly might be to revisit and share what happened when they followed the children's advice. For example, 'Charlotte has been enjoying playing with the garage and the other day, the children that left her out joined in! She asked her mummy if she could go and visit a garage one day'.

ROLE-PLAY AND 'HOT SEATING'

Role-play is an appropriate and engaging strategy when exploring empathy with older children. For example, the children could consider the feelings and experiences of a character from a well-known story, film or fairy tale; an anonymous letter from a school child or a video clip of refugees could be suitable stimuli for some questioning, reasoning, reflection and problem-solving that could support the development of empathy. Scenarios depicting issues such as bullying, gender stereotypes or difficulty with accessing learning can be practised and acted out.

'Hot seating' is a way of developing (or deepening) character and empathy. If you are in the hot seat, you answer questions from others while you are 'in role'. Possible questions for characters in a scenario might be:

- How long has it been going on?
- How does it make you feel?
- Why do you think they are treating you this way?
- How often does it happen?
- Have you spoken to anyone?
- What would you like to happen?

Reflection points for children when out of role:

- How did you feel playing the different roles?
- How was it imagining and acting out the feelings?
- What made some more difficult than others?
- Were you surprised by how you felt in any of the roles?

Questions such as these allow children to reflect upon, articulate and understand their own and others' experiences, which are key facets of empathy.

APPLICATION OF THE PEDAGOGICAL FOCUS TO OTHER SUBJECTS

There are opportunities to develop children's empathetic understanding and skills in many subjects of the primary curriculum and, in doing so, to further develop their understanding of key ideas within those subjects. According to Foster and Yeager (1998: 1), historical empathy is seen as 'a powerful tool for understanding history' and central to the construction of historical meaning. History is not a collection of cold, dry facts about the past, but an exploration of the ways in which real people lived and, in some cases, died. In seeking to understand the lived experiences of our ancestors, 'tapping into' their emotional journeys helps children to see the relevance of the study of history as the story of humankind and to understand why some historical events developed as they did.

In English, reading stories with great characterisation is a good way of developing empathy. According to Empathy Lab (online), 'As we read, our brains are tricked into thinking we're genuinely part of the story and the empathetic emotions we feel for characters wire our brains to the same sort of sensitivity towards real people'. Teachers can make skilful use of questioning about shared texts, both to develop children's reading comprehension and to develop their empathy, by exploring events and emotions from the story. This might be particularly powerful when considering the actions of a 'bad' character, where the motivations for their actions may be unexpected or surprising.

SUMMARY FOR THIS CHAPTER

In this chapter, we have learnt about the power of the 'affective domain' to support children's intellectual development and academic progress and some key principles and strategies involved in the effective facilitation of PSHE. We have learnt that PSHE can provide valuable and purposeful opportunities for children to develop interpersonal and intrapersonal skills, and that the teacher plays an important role through enacting these skills and attitudes and providing opportunities for children to explore and develop them. The importance of supporting children to develop empathy was explored, alongside establishing an environment conducive to this and in which there are plenty of opportunities for questioning, reasoning, reflective judgement and problem-solving.

When teaching PSHE, do:

- remember that it is not helpful to view this area of learning as a 'curriculum subject'
- provide children with the opportunity to explore, ponder and articulate their experiences, ideas and learning
- encourage the children to give reasons for what they say and to ask questions if they do not understand or want to know more

- enact the PSHE skills and attributes that you are aiming to develop, in your everyday interactions with children.

When supporting the development of empathy, do:

- be an empathetic human being
- establish an environment where empathy can flourish, and aim to understand the children's backgrounds, thoughts and fears
- use stories, characters, Persona Dolls, puppets and familiar situations to support the children's capacity for, and development of, empathy
- plan questions that help children explore situations, emotions and reasons for these.

FURTHER READING

To further develop your knowledge and understanding of effective pedagogy in PSHE, the following sources are recommended:

Boddington, N., King, A. and McWhirter, J. (2014) *Understanding personal, social, health and economic education in primary schools*. London: SAGE Publications.

This useful book is aimed at student and early career teachers. It is full of practical strategies and case studies and offers clear guidance on how to approach sensitive issues.

Stanley, S. and Bowkett, S. (2004) *But why? Developing philosophical thinking in the classroom*. Stafford: Network Educational Press.

Philosophy for children (P4C) is a powerful approach that has a very positive impact on children's work across the curriculum, giving them the confidence to speak and discuss ideas to a high level. P4C has far-reaching benefits that touch all parts of the curriculum and every aspect of school life by creating a climate for learning, increasing motivation, developing communication skills, boosting creativity and imagination, teaching moral citizenship, developing confidence, self-esteem and emotional identification. *But why?* provides everything you need to introduce philosophy into your classroom.

The PSHE Association website: www.pshe-association.org.uk

The PSHE Association is the national subject association supporting the field of personal, social, health and economic education. The website contains quality resources, up-to-date guidance, training and support for schools.

REFERENCES

Avery, T. (2011) 'Empathy training'. Available at: www.slideshare.net/taverypsyd/empathy-training (Accessed: 23 April 2019).

Beach, M. (2010) 'Creating empathy in the classroom'. Available at: http://teachmag.com/archives/1115 (Accessed: 23 April 2019).

Berk, L.E. (2018) *Development through the lifespan*. 7th edn. Boston, MA: Pearson.

Boddington, N., King, A. and McWhirter, J. (2014) *Understanding personal, social, health and economic education in primary schools*. London: SAGE Publications.

Brown, B. (2001) *Combating discrimination: Persona Dolls in action*. Stoke on Trent: Trentham Books Ltd.

Cambridge Primary Review (2007) *Community soundings: the primary review regional witness sessions*. Cambridge: University of Cambridge.

Department for Education (DfE) (2013a) *The national curriculum in England: key stages 1 and 2 framework document*. London: DfE.

Department for Education (DfE) (2013b) 'Guidance: personal, social, health and economic (PSHE) education'. Available at: www.gov.uk/government/publications/personal-social-health-and-economic-education-pshe/personal-social-health-and-economic-pshe-education (Accessed: 23 April 2019).

Equality and Human Rights Commission (2016) 'Lesson 2: developing empathy'. Available at: www.equalityhumanrights.com/en/secondary-education-resources/lesson-plan-ideas/lesson-2-developing-empathy (Accessed: 23 April 2019).

Foster, S.J. and Yeager, E.A. (1998) 'The role of empathy in the development of historical understanding', *International Journal of Social Education*, 13(1), pp. 1–7.

Goddard, G., Smith, V. and Boycott, C. (2013) *PSHE in the primary school: principles and practice*. Abingdon: Routledge.

Goleman, D. (1998) *Working with emotional intelligence*. London: Bloomsbury.

Hodges, S.D. and Myers, M.W. (2007) 'Empathy' in Baumeister, R.F. and Vohs, K.D. (eds.) *Encyclopedia of Social Psychology*. London: SAGE Publications, pp. 296–8.

Mosley, J. (2005) *The circle book (circle time)*. London: The Positive Press.

Osler, J.E. (2013) 'The psychology efficacy of education as a science through personal, professional and contextual inquiry of the affective domain', *i-Manager's Journal on Educational Psychology*, 6(4), pp. 36–41. Available at: https://files.eric.ed.gov/fulltext/EJ1101776.pdf (Accessed: 23 April 2019).

PSHE Association (2017) *PSHE education programme of study (key stages 1–5)*. Available at: www.pshe-association.org.uk/system/files/PSHE%20Education%20Programme%20of%20Study%20%28Key%20stage%201-5%29%20Jan%202017_2.pdf (Accessed: 23 April 2019).

PSHE Association (2018) 'Government takes "major step" towards better PSHE for all'. Available at: www.pshe-association.org.uk/news/government-takes-%E2%80%98major-step%E2%80%99-towards-better-pshe (Accessed: 16 July 2019).

Raundalen, M. (1991) *Care and courage*. Stockholm: Radda Barnen.

Sharp, P. (2001) *Nurturing emotional literacy: a practical guide for teachers, parents and those in the caring professions*. London: David Fulton Publishers.

13

RELIGIOUS EDUCATION

DEVELOPING CHILDREN'S UNDERSTANDING OF LIVED EXPERIENCES

SIMON HYDE-WHITE

OBJECTIVES

- To explore the distinctive nature of primary religious education.
- To consider how teachers can promote pupils' understanding of lived experiences within primary religious education.
- To reflect on opportunities to develop an understanding of lived experiences in some other subjects within the primary curriculum.

In this chapter, we will explore the distinctive purpose and nature of primary religious education in contributing to children's development of new knowledge and personal perspectives. To this end, we then move on to exploring the central theme of 'understanding lived experiences'. This refers to understanding how people's beliefs can directly impact upon their motives and how they live their lives. We will examine examples of primary practice to discover how primary teachers can best promote this understanding in young learners. The chapter will conclude by suggesting how understanding lived experiences may be utilised to support effective learning in some other curriculum subjects.

WHAT IS DISTINCTIVE ABOUT THE PURPOSE AND NATURE OF RELIGIOUS EDUCATION?

Since 1944, all schools have been required to teach religious education as part of a broad and balanced curriculum. However, religious education has traditionally resided outside of the National Curriculum. Instead, schools under the remit of a local authority have to follow a locally agreed syllabus, determined by the local Standing Advisory Council on Religious Education (SACRE), which sets out the statutory requirements. Free schools and academies have freedom to adopt an alternative agreed syllabus or to devise their own curriculum, so long as it reflects the requirements of the 1996 Education Act that recognises 'the religious traditions in Great Britain are in the main Christian, while taking account of the teaching and practices of the other principal religions represented in Great Britain' (Education Act, 1996: 213).

Despite its omission from the National Curriculum, the importance of primary religious education should not be underestimated. In seeking to explore significant religious and non-religious worldviews of how people experience and respond to the world, the subject is uniquely placed to promote a healthy regard for others in the community. Children should rigorously and critically engage with religions and worldviews, not to promote or nurture a specific faith (or non-faith), but to counteract common misrepresentations of religions which may lead to ignorance or, even, fear. Moreover, young people told the Commission on Religious Education (2018) that gaining a better understanding of other people's beliefs enabled them to form better friendships and helped them to deal more knowledgeably with controversial issues and acquire a deeper sense of their own place in our increasingly diverse society.

IDENTIFYING AND UNLOCKING CORE CONCEPTS

The aspirations for religious education outlined above may seem ambitious, but they can be realised if teachers are clear about the subject's purpose. However, many primary practitioners fail to realise its potential, often replacing a rigorous study of religions with hasty and tenuous links to PSHE (Ofsted, 2013). Indeed, the requirement to explore a breadth of religions in meaningful depth presents challenges for a crowded curriculum (Chater, 2018). The answer lies in teachers resisting the temptation to 'cover' vast swathes of material in a superficial manner. Instead, prioritising only the most significant concepts within each religion will leave space for the desired depth of learning, while still exposing children to an appropriate range of content.

An example within Judaism would be to focus on the key concept of the centrality of the *Torah* (teaching), since almost everything a Jew does is in an effort to obey it. Consequently, children can reinforce their understanding of this central idea by exploring a range of Jewish practices. Jewish families attach a metal case containing two sacred chapters of the Torah (called a *mezuzah*) to the doorway of their homes, which they touch on entry to remind them of God's teaching. In addition, male Jews often wear a shawl (*tallit*) of 613 tassels when praying, to symbolise the 613 laws contained within the Torah. An exploration of the weekly Jewish Sabbath (*Shabbat*) will also reveal how it satisfies the Torah's command to set aside a day of rest to honour God. An in-depth enquiry into one key concept can then form a natural link to another, namely the special covenant God made with the Jewish nation, promising to protect and prosper them if they followed the Torah's commands.

Table 13.1 shows other examples of concepts central to religions that should dictate appropriate content.

Table 13.1 Relating teaching content to religious concepts

Religion	Core concept	Supporting content
Christianity	*Incarnation*: God coming to Earth in the form of his son, Jesus.	• How and why Christians observe advent and celebrate the nativity story. • Examples of Jesus demonstrating his divinity through his teaching, acting with authority and compassion, and performing miracles.
Islam	*Submission*: willing obedience to God (Allah).	• Expression of worship (*ibadah*) through obeying the Five Pillars of Islam outlined in the Qur'an. • Praying five times daily with head bowed on a prayer mat in willing submission, and other expressions of self-discipline and modesty.
Hinduism	*Moksha*: liberation from this world.	• Belief in multiple reincarnations of one's soul (*samsara*) residing in plants, animals and humans, before achieving release and merging with God or ultimate reality (*Brahman*). • Living by a moral code since *moksha* is achieved by pursuing one's religious and moral duty (*dharma*).

CRITICAL TASK 13.1

Identifying appropriate content linked to core concepts

Can you think of relevant religious content (stories, practices and festivals) to help unlock children's understanding of 'salvation', a concept central to Christianity? You might find it helpful to look through a locally agreed syllabus for religious education.

CULTIVATING A RESPECTFUL ATTITUDE

Since religions explore delicate questions concerning purpose and existence, teachers must sensitively navigate the diverse opinions existing within a classroom. To do this, teachers of religious education should possess certain open-minded attitudes and values:

- an abiding interest in questions and issues raised by religious education
- awareness of their own prejudices and bias
- openness to amend their own beliefs and values through recognition that other people's views may have equal validity to their own
- avoiding all ridicule of others' beliefs while being willing to challenge harmful or discriminatory views
- valuing diversity, particularly in the children they teach.

(Adapted from McCreery, 2004: 27–8)

Since these attitudes are also required of effective learners, teachers should seek to cultivate them by providing frequent opportunities for children to form their own views on subjective issues. Providing a safe classroom space to raise questions and debate opinions, therefore, becomes a shared responsibility; pupils must feel their responses are just as valid as the teacher's and each other's, provided they are well considered and informed. Cumulative dialogue that attempts to evaluate issues and form reasoned conclusions underpins high-quality religious education.

To this end, incorporating Philosophy for Children (P4C) is extremely effective, since this dialogic approach seeks to increase pupils' collective understanding of the world around them. In order for children to develop and express personal insights, the teacher must ensure the stimulus selected for P4C is appropriately challenging and linked to the intended religious education outcomes. For example, when helping children to enquire into the nature of the Jewish God, you could use the thought-provoking stimulus of the story of God asking Abraham to sacrifice his only son, Isaac

(Genesis 22:1–19), before ultimately providing a ram caught in a thicket to take Isaac's place. Children raising a question such as 'Why would God say to kill someone when it is written in the Ten Commandments not to murder?' might well provoke discussion on a range of issues, from the distinction between 'sacrifice' and 'murder' to the question of humans having free will. One would hope this would lead to children concluding that the story is in essence about Jews trusting and believing in a faithful, all-knowing, all-loving God who has good plans for them. However, irrespective of the final outcome, just as important is developing the children's ability to be able to 'disagree agreeably' by avoiding personal criticism of others when voicing alternative opinions.

CHALLENGING ENQUIRY

In successive inspections of religious education teaching, Ofsted found that children were rarely encouraged to develop their skills of enquiry into religions (Ofsted, 2013). Yet as we have just seen, effective religious education teaching demands that children grapple with significant issues raised by religion. Typical examples might be 'Why do Christians remember the day Jesus died as *good* Friday?' or 'Should Sikh children be allowed to conceal a short symbolic sword (*kirpan*) under their school clothes?'. Such matters go beyond just finding out what believers do, to examining the significance of such practices. Providing opportunities for children to 'linger longer' over their enquiries to arrive at genuine understanding should prevent teachers from relying on closed worksheets. For example, when studying contemporary Muslim practice, merely matching religious objects to their correct place on an outline of a mosque, and then using prompts to describe these objects, makes little intellectual demand and leads to superficial understanding. Such simplistic approaches will not suffice. By contrast, a careful examination of an actual prayer mat can reveal genuine knowledge and understanding concerning the people who use it. By speculating on its texture, appearance and purpose, pupils can discover why Muslims orientate the mat to face Mecca, why they remove their shoes before standing on it and why they place their heads down on it in submission.

INTERROGATING PRIMARY SOURCES

Since enquiry learning lies at the heart of religious education, children should indeed be challenged to discover the knowledge located in religious sources for themselves. Examples of primary sources include sacred stories and texts, artefacts and works of art. However, Erricker's (2011) research highlighted that children cannot always be expected to fully interpret them alone, due to the often abstract and searching nature of these sources. To judiciously guide the enquiry, teachers should:

- pose a key question linked to the insights located within the source
- respond to pupils' speculations, observations and questions surrounding the source in ways that facilitate further thinking
- stimulate 'deeper thinking' and critical debate by providing 'sorting', 'identifying' and 'ranking' tasks
- provide timely subject knowledge that further challenges and extends the children's comprehension.

For example, when enquiring with a Key Stage 1 class into 'Why Christmas matters to Christians', a teacher could follow a retelling of the Nativity story by asking the children to select the 'odd one out' between God, angels and Father Christmas. If a child responds to this thinking task by suggesting 'Father Christmas' because he is the only one who brings people gifts, the teacher could challenge them by asking whether Christians might also consider the angel's announcement of Jesus' birth to be a special 'gift' for Mary and the shepherds. Further, the teacher could introduce some Old Testament knowledge to suggest that God himself can deliver 'material gifts' just like Father Christmas, for example, the food or 'mana from heaven' to the Jewish people when journeying through the desert. The point is, with such a task, there is no right or wrong answer; its purpose is to provoke a more critical examination of the selected primary source.

EXPERIENTIAL LEARNING

Visiting a real place of worship is often a highly effective stimulus for learning, since it generally arouses personal interest and brings the subject alive. To maximise the opportunities offered by such visits, teachers should consider:

- how to incorporate multi-sensory experiences, such as role-play or interaction with religious objects
- how children can best encounter and respond to the atmosphere of the place, free from the constraints of fact-filling worksheets.

Secular locations can also provide wonderful opportunities for exploring religious concepts. A local community walk can reveal signs of peace, kindness or faith, as well as issues of concern, addressed by religions. A valuable response for pupils would be to use their knowledge of Jesus, Muhammad or a Sikh guru to speculate on what these leaders might think and say if visiting the locality themselves. Similarly, exploring parks, hills, beaches and cities can be 'spiritual' experiences since they have the potential to provoke responses of awe and wonder. Children are often struck by the beauty and mysteries of the natural world that can take your breath away and leave you feeling incredibly small, really grateful or deeply moved.

Myatt (2018: 133) suggests humans are a 'challenge-seeking species' and as such, children should readily respond to such deep enquiries into primary sources that can expose their misunderstandings and precipitate new insights and informed opinions. The next section explores how engagement with real people is fundamental to deepening these enquiries.

PEDAGOGICAL FOCUS FOR THIS CHAPTER: UNDERSTANDING LIVED EXPERIENCES

We have emphasised that primary children should be encouraged to infer meaning from well-selected sources. However, since religious beliefs can sometimes appear rather complex and unfamiliar, we shall now explore how teachers can utilise real people to provide greater clarity about beliefs and their impact upon daily lives.

ENQUIRING FROM A POSITION OF KNOWLEDGE

There is no substitute for people of various faiths and worldviews visiting the primary classroom to make religious education both fascinating and tangible. However, as Selway (2018) asserts, visitors should be primed to respond openly to questions raised by pupils concerning the realities of living in today's society, and avoid merely delivering a pre-prepared 'talk'. To maximise this encounter, children should have some prior awareness of the visitor's faith in order to prepare for a meaningful exchange. One way to achieve this is to take the learners on a 'mystery journey', prior to the visit, in order to generate curious questions.

CASE STUDY 13.1

In this episode, Alice, an undergraduate student teacher, is reflecting on her use of a mystery journey approach with a Year 5 class to generate questions concerning the Jewish festival of Passover, or *Pesach*, and how families celebrate it today. After familiarising the children with the central story of Moses leading his people out of Egypt, she sets up a mystery table of food to recreate the first evening of *Pesach*, when Jewish families remember the story.

Alice: What do you think these different foods might represent?

Sophie: There are crackers and parsley, and an egg and some lamb.

(Continued)

Ben: Is all this stuff on the plate representing something from the ten plagues?

Charlotte: Does the lamb represent when the angel came to kill the Egyptian sons?

Alice: Fantastic. You are drawing on your knowledge of the Moses story.

Izzy: Why are the different types of food quite small portions?

Alice: Really good question. Has anybody got any ideas?

[Six second pause.]

Harry: Because when travelling through the desert after the escape, maybe Moses and the Israelites hardly ate anything at all.

Alice: Fantastic; really good thinking.

Ben: Why is this story so important, and do all families celebrate it with this meal?

Alice: Ooh, good questions, I wish I knew. Anyway, looking again at the table, is there a certain place around this table that's different to all the others?

Izzy: Yes, that one, it doesn't have a place name. It's got a cup and also a cushion.

Ben: Is it the guest we heard about?

Alice: So you think it's the guest that sits there? Any ideas who?

[Four second pause.]

Harry: God. Or maybe a poor person that couldn't afford to eat this food.

Alice: Lovely idea. In fact, that place is left for Elijah, an important Jewish prophet, to sit there.

Sophie: Who is Elijah?

Student teacher evaluation: Alice commented that the children were really interested in the mystery table, and drawing on their prior knowledge helped them to 'form good questions' and begin to make some suggestions. She identified that her subject knowledge needed to be a little more in depth to truly answer some of the questions. She was unsure whether all Jewish families celebrate in the same way and why Elijah is invited, noting that 'all I could say was he is there in spirit and not in person'.

Expert critique: In recreating the Passover meal, Alice clearly grabbed the pupils' interest and sparked their curiosity. She also consciously used 'pause' and 'prompt' strategies to involve more children in asking and responding to questions. Allowing the children to smell and taste the foods later in the lesson also shed further light on their symbolic connection to the story. However, since some questions were subjective concerning the enduring importance of the story and how it is celebrated by families, they could only be fully addressed by a practising Jew. Hence, this was a prime opportunity to invite along a local Jewish representative to field the questions and even recreate the Seder meal for the children.

CRITICAL TASK 13.2

Generating questions

After finding out about the modern day festival of *Pesach*, what further questions would you want to ask a Jewish visitor? How would acquiring some prior knowledge of the festival deepen your questioning?

For example, would knowing that Jewish families link Elijah's presence at the table to the imminent arrival of the Messiah prompt you to ask questions concerning the precise nature of this longed-for Messiah, when he might come to Earth, and for what purpose?

RAISING 'BIG' QUESTIONS

In Roald Dahl's memorable story, *The BFG*, eight-year-old Sophie finds she cannot stop firing a plethora of questions at the 'big friendly giant' to discover more about his character and experiences. Her curiosity to build on her existing knowledge of giants by seeking personal answers from someone intriguing and quite different from herself is insatiable. It should be the same for religious education: children should be inspired and encouraged to ask questions with a similar urgency. And just as Dahl's heroine discovered, the answers to initial questions often prompt even 'bigger' questions to arise. The very nature of religion generates questions of ultimate significance concerning life's meaning and purpose, suffering, the existence of God, the after-life and so on. Plater (2016), therefore, advocates that practitioners must be sensitive to the children's preoccupations, in order to balance pupils' knowledge acquisition with satisfying their personal curiosities.

CASE STUDY 13.2

In this example, Lucy, an undergraduate student teacher in her final year of training, invited a local Muslim chaplain, Asif, into the classroom as part of a Year 6 enquiry into the existence of God. Having explored 'evidence' from a range of religious texts, and having considered the views of humanists, the class was keen to engage with a real-life faith believer.

Lola: Why do you believe in God?

Asif: My family taught that everything has been created by God's work through countless processes we call nature and science. What we see is the precision of God's planning and commands.

Harisa: What do you think God is like?

Asif: I don't think he looks like a human or that any shape or form contains God. Allah is one of those things the human mind cannot comprehend. It's like we all know the sun is there because we feel its heat and see its light. But none of us can look directly at the sun and say I have 'seen' it.

Mikey: If someone lives a good life but doesn't believe in the Muslim God, will they still go to heaven?

Asif: The fundamental requirement of God is that you must believe that he exists. And if you live a good life, and are on a journey to improve yourselves, your families and the wider community, then you will ultimately go to heaven.

Mia: Is the God of Islam the same as the Jewish and Christian God?

Asif: Yes, God says so in the Qur'an in several places. Muslims call him Allah because this is the Arabic name for God, as do Arab Christians and Jews.

Tom: If God really loves us, why would he be silly enough to answer all our prayers?

Asif: It is purely because God loves all humans that he *doesn't* answer all our prayers. God's wisdom is far superior to our wisdom. If we got everything we asked for we would probably not be able to cope. I'd rather be patient and see what God has in store for me.

Student teacher evaluation: Lucy identified that the children loved asking the visitor lots of questions and that 'they felt like real detectives'. She commented that she had wanted to ask some follow-up questions, but didn't want to take over. Lucy felt she could have asked Asif to comment on some of the other views the children had explored so far about God's existence, since this may have helped the children to compare opinions and even begin to form their own conclusions.

Expert critique: The decision to include a faith expert was highly beneficial since his answers clearly provided considerable knowledge of Islamic beliefs, while remaining child friendly. However, Lucy could have encouraged children to raise follow-up questions to ascertain how the visitor personally related to the Muslim teaching, since many of his responses appeared more 'factual' than 'experiential'. It would be revealing, for example, to discover whether Asif has ever received confirmation of God's existence by hearing from him 'personally', rather than just 'knowing' of his existence, or whether he is ever frustrated or confused by Allah's responses. I wonder, too, how Asif reconciles his own certainty of going to heaven with the Qur'an's teaching that Allah will ultimately be the judge of all people.

INTERROGATING LIVED EXPERIENCES

To be fully dynamic, children's learning in religious education should allow them to explore how people's responses to big questions actually impact upon their everyday lives. What is it really like to 'live out one's faith' in a society that seems to champion materialism and personal gain over humility and self-sacrifice? Examining religious texts clearly highlights the potential challenges faced by believers. For example, Jesus' teaching in the 'Sermon on the Mount' (Matthew 5–7) urges people to turn the other cheek when facing adversity, and 'love your enemies and pray for those who persecute you'. Since much of what Jesus taught about one's conduct appears counter-cultural, it is highly appropriate to hear the experiences of followers today.

CASE STUDY 13.3

James, an undergraduate student teacher, invites Sarah, a local Christian chaplain, into his Year 4 class to field questions on how she tries to apply Jesus' words in her own life. Prior to the visit, the pupils consider what most intrigues, inspires or challenges them about Jesus' teaching, precipitating a host of eager questions for the chaplain.

(Continued)

Tamid: How does your faith make a difference to how you live?

Sarah: I became a chaplain because I felt God led me to do this. Also in the way I get on with the people I meet.

Laura: What is the best thing about being a Christian?

Sarah: Knowing that I am loved, just as I am.

Frank: What is most challenging about being a Christian?

Sarah: For me, it is keeping God at the centre of my life when there are many distractions.

Farah: We learnt God tells Christians not to worry; how does God provide for you?

Sarah: He's given me people who love me, a direction for my life and the joys of living in this world. I don't tend to think so much about material things, but I am thankful for a home and food and having enough money.

Emma: How do you feel when your prayers aren't answered?

Sarah: It's tough. I know people who have to live with illness and other problems even though many people have prayed for them. I have seen God help people even when things are very hard for them.

William: How easy is it to 'love' and make peace with someone who's hurt you?

Sarah: It's a challenge, but I ask God to help me with it. What I really like is to have a good discussion with someone who disagrees with me!

Student teacher evaluation: James commented that he was pleased that he had been in touch with the chaplain in advance about the session to share some of the questions with her, so that she had time to think about the more challenging ones. He noted that what also worked well was that Sarah was really open and honest, meaning the children gained a real insight into what life might be like for a Christian today.

Expert critique: James was right to identify the value of sharing the expectations with the chaplain prior to the visit. In relating the interview to the perceived anomalies in Jesus' teaching, the power of religious education became evident in not shying away from addressing real issues and relationships. However, some of Sarah's responses would require further illustration for all pupils to comprehend them fully. James could have asked children to generate subsequent questions to clarify meaning or address new curiosities. How, for example, did Sarah feel 'led' to become a chaplain, and what does she precisely mean by being 'loved' by God? Also, what has been her best discussion ever with someone who disagreed with her views?

It is also important to provide pupils with the opportunity to weigh up the personal relevance of the thoughts and actions described by a visitor. Would individuals ever see themselves reacting calmly to those who tease or upset them, and if so why? Would they be perceived by others as weird and weak, or courageous and self-controlled?

RELATING TO THE CHILDREN'S OWN EXPERIENCES

As suggested in Case study 13.3, children need to form a 'bridge' between the lives of people they learn about and their own personal experiences. Any information gleaned can then be allowed to challenge their own thinking. As Teece (2015: 30) explains, learning *from* religion should 'enrich the experience of the learner' when reflecting on perspectives gained from learning *about* a religion. It is important, however, for these new perspectives to be sufficiently broad to offset the danger of forming generalisations from just one particular viewpoint. Exposing children to the lives of so-called 'inspirational' people can be particularly interesting. Nevertheless, identifying with someone you know little about can be superficial and frustrating. Children should therefore thoroughly examine blogs, websites and published interviews of contemporary people to help properly evaluate their decisions and actions.

The experiences of Moe Sbihi, the first ever Muslim to row for Britain in the Olympic Games (London, 2012), provide a good example. Since the Games fell during the month of Ramadan, some Muslim athletes decided to fast during daylight hours, but others, like Sbihi, felt this would not be possible. Instead he decided to provide sixty meals a day for poor people in Morocco, equating to 1,800 meals in total. Learning of these events can challenge children to decide whether they think Sbihi made the right choice, before considering whether abstaining from something themselves for a while, be it television or social media, or showing some generosity towards others, would be beneficial for them also.

Similarly, the famous adventurer Bear Grylls, who is a Christian, offers potential relevance for children while also deviating from the norms of his faith. Long periods of time away from home prevent regular church attendance, but the extreme challenges he faces on the mountains lead him to pray with gratitude every day. He finds it a great source of strength and comfort to know that God is always right beside him. In response, children could consider whether the values of faith, enthusiasm and courage are in any way important for them. Might they be inspired to engage more with nature, or strive to achieve something they find challenging but highly rewarding? To further stretch children's thinking, they should also identify the possible limitations of 'inspirational' people. For all his courage, might Bear Grylls have to be slightly reckless on occasions?

CRITICAL TASK 13.3

Researching inspirational people

Consider other modern day inspirational people who can add depth to pupils' appreciation of lived experiences, while offering some potential relevance for their own lives. Aim to research people from a range of religions and worldviews, including some notable females. One suggestion is Chanda Vyas, the first female Hindu priest in the UK. Try to establish what might be considered inspirational about such people, how their beliefs influence their actions, and how they might relate to pupils' lives.

RESPONSE TO CRITICAL TASK 13.1

Identifying appropriate content linked to core concepts

This task asked you to consider possible beliefs and practices which could be explored to unlock the key Christian concept of 'salvation'. Table 13.2 provides some suggestions.

Table 13.2 Linking content to the core concept of 'salvation'

Religion	Core concept	Supporting content
Christianity	*Salvation*: Jesus' sacrificial death to rescue humans by opening the way back to God.	• The meaning and practice of Lent, during which Christians reflect and mourn for six weeks. • Recalling and interpreting the events culminating in Jesus' death and resurrection. • Belief that Jesus as 'saviour' offers the gift of forgiveness to all and relationship with God. • How Christians celebrate this at Easter.

APPLICATION OF THE PEDAGOGIC FOCUS TO OTHER SUBJECTS

We have considered the importance in religious education of children beginning to understand the experiences of others. It is also important for pupils to develop an appreciation of what motivates contemporary people in other curriculum subjects. One of the aims for art in the National Curriculum (DfE, 2013: 176) is to 'evaluate and analyse creative works'. This necessitates gaining some knowledge of the artists themselves in order to understand what personal experiences and challenges may have inspired them to produce their work, and what their art reveals about them. James Brunt, Julie Mehretu and James Martin are three examples of contemporary artists whose styles reflect their passions, experiences and beliefs, and whose work conveys certain messages.

Jonathan Sacks, the chief Jewish Rabbi, once said, 'God is the music of all that lives, but there are times when all we hear is noise'. Similar to when children engage with religious stimuli and places and with people of faith, engagement with music can also be a spiritual, personal experience. In both subjects, it is important for pupils to spend unhurried time responding with open minds. Learning to identify and evaluate the moods of musical pieces can reveal expressions of joy, celebration, sorrow and thankfulness, all akin to religions. Music is also a form of communication, often embraced by faith believers to help them communicate with God and show their appreciation of him.

SUMMARY FOR THIS CHAPTER

This chapter has emphasised the importance of pupils developing some understanding of why people believe and act in particular ways. To support pupils in this quest, enquiry-led approaches are highly appropriate, since they cultivate deeper, more personal learning. In handing the intellectual space over to the pupils, teachers must establish and maintain the direction of the enquiry by selecting thought-provoking stimuli and thinking tasks. To fully grapple with the meaning and significance of religious practice, children should raise important and intriguing questions to be addressed by each other and contemporary people of faith. Finally, children must be encouraged to consider the beliefs and practices they see in others that might help them reflect upon their own ideas and ways of living.

When teaching religious education, do:

- identify and pursue the essential foundations of each religion
- promote an inclusive and respectful climate in which pupils can 'disagree agreeably'
- adopt an active, enquiry approach to learning
- incorporate and interrogate primary sources such as sacred texts, religious stories, artefacts and sacred places.

When promoting understanding of lived experiences, do:

- develop children's knowledge of a religion before expecting them to become curious about the impact beliefs have on people's lives
- enable the children to raise 'big questions' about how having a faith impacts on the lives of different people
- utilise people of faith to share their lived experiences with children
- provide opportunities for children to make connections with their own lives.

FURTHER READING

The following sources may be helpful in further developing and exemplifying your knowledge and understanding of effective religious education pedagogy.

Baumfield, V. (2002) *Thinking through religious education*. Cambridge: Chris Kingston Publishing.

This wonderful resource provides examples of how to challenge children with collaborative deeper-thinking tasks in religious education, helping them to develop and express their personal understanding and opinions.

NATRE's Spirited Arts website (www.natre.org.uk/about-natre/projects/spirited-arts/spirited-arts-gallery/2018/) showcases children's religious and spiritually inspired artwork and poetry.

It is a very useful resource for showing examples of how pupils have responded with awe and wonder in a personal way to their religious education learning.

RE:Online website (www.reonline.org.uk/) provides a wealth of subject knowledge and pedagogical support for practitioners. It includes 'Research for RE', an online tool facilitating research-informed practice, and 'Email a believer', where experts from a range of religions and worldviews answer pupils' questions and post their own blogs.

REFERENCES

Chater, M. (2018) 'Why we need legislative change, and how we get it' in Catelli, M. and Chater, M (eds.) *We need to talk about religious education: manifestos for the future of RE*. London: Jessica Kingsley, pp. 71–84.

Commission on Religious Education (2018) 'Final Report. Religion and worldviews: the way forward. A national plan for RE'. London: Religious Education Council of England and Wales.

Department for Education (DfE) (2013) *The national curriculum in England: key stages 1 and 2 framework document*. London: DfE.

Education Act 1996, Section 375. London: The Stationery Office Ltd. Available at: www.legislation.gov.uk/ukpga/1996/56/pdfs/ukpga_19960056_en.pdf (Accessed: 23 April 2019).

Erricker, C. (2011) 'Why conceptual enquiry? An introduction to the methodology' in Erricker, C., Lowndes, J. and Bellchambers, E. (eds.) *Primary religious education: a new approach*. Abingdon: Routledge, pp. 52–90.

Genesis 22:1–19, *Holy Bible*. New International Edition.

Matthew 5–7, *Holy Bible*. New International Edition.

McCreery, E. (2004) 'Developing the "religiate" primary RE teacher: where are we starting from and how do we get there?' *Journal of Beliefs and Values*, 25(1), pp. 15–29.

Myatt, M. (2018) 'Making the case for more demanding religious education' in Catelli, M. and Chater, M. (eds.) *We need to talk about religious education: manifestos for the future of RE*. London: Jessica Kingsley, pp. 133–42.

Ofsted (2013) 'Religious education: realising the potential'. Available at: www.gov.uk/government/publications/religious-education-realising-the-potential (Accessed: 23 April 2019).

Plater, M. (2016) 'The aims and outcomes of RE: embracing diversity', *RE Today*, 34(1) pp. 57–9.

Selway, C. (2018) 'Encounters, engagement and experience: making RE real'. Available at: www.reonline.org.uk/blog/encounters-engagement-and-experience-making-re-real/ (Accessed: 22 July 2019).

Teece, G. (2015) 'Creative learning about and from religion: principles underpinning effective RE planning and religious understanding' in Elton-Chalcraft, S. (ed.) *Teaching religious education creatively*. Abingdon: Routledge, pp. 18–30.

14

SCIENCE

QUESTIONING SKILFULLY TO PROMOTE INTELLIGENT ANSWERS

COLIN FORSTER AND JUDE PENNY

OBJECTIVES

- To explore the distinctive nature of primary science.
- To consider how teachers can make effective use of questioning within primary science.
- To reflect on the application of effective teacher questioning to some other subjects within the primary curriculum.

In this chapter, we will explore the nature of primary science, identify the ways in which it is distinctive from other curriculum subjects and consider what it has to offer children as a part of their primary education. We will also examine the role of questioning as a key teaching skill and engage with research to identify ways in which primary teachers can employ questioning effectively and, just as importantly, identify some pitfalls to avoid. We will conclude the chapter with some consideration of ways in which effective questioning can be applied to some other curriculum subjects.

WHAT IS DISTINCTIVE ABOUT TEACHING AND LEARNING IN SCIENCE?

Let's start with a simple question: *what is the name of the female part of the flowering plant?* Struggling? You probably 'learnt' this fact at some stage in your education, so why might it be difficult to recall? We'll explore this later in the chapter.

Science has been a core subject in every version of the National Curriculum since its inception in 1988 and, in the latest version, science is still seen as an important aspect of a child's rounded education. It enables children to draw on their innate curiosity (Dewey, 1963) about the world, to raise questions, to solve problems, to explore and experiment, to discuss big issues and apply their knowledge in various contexts. However, in any curriculum, there is a danger that the 'content' of what children 'should be taught' can overwhelm the opportunities afforded to develop children's ability to think. It is not written in the National Curriculum that recall is the most valued of intellectual skills but the bullet-point nature of the programmes of study can easily lead to a content-focused approach to teaching and learning. This can give rise to the teaching of 'random' science facts (such as the name of the female part of the flowering plant) that are remembered just long enough to pass a test but do not enter the long-term memory and do nothing to develop children's science-related intelligence. By 'intelligence', we do not mean the ability to remember lots of specialist knowledge but the ability to use mental faculties in a range of ways.

HIGHER ORDER THINKING

Primary science offers good opportunities to develop children's ability to think critically and creatively and to develop what are often referred to as a range of 'higher order thinking skills'. Benjamin Bloom proposed a possible hierarchy of thinking skills, with 'remembering' as the lowest order skill on which others can be developed: understanding, applying, analysing, evaluating and creating (Krathwohl, 2002). This provides a way of thinking about the kinds of opportunities for thinking that children should be provided with through their science lessons. It is important to recognise that Bloom's framework is not itself the 'correct answer' about how children's thinking skills should be developed, as other intellectual skills can also be considered as higher order: being logical, being reasonable, anticipating (thinking ahead), being sceptical, being open to new ideas, being willing to change one's mind, being able to justify one's opinions and thinking about thinking (metacognition).

It is hard to develop a range of higher order thinking skills working on your own in silence. Engaging children in purposeful and intelligent talk is a key strategy for developing a range of intellectual skills. Remember, though, that these should be opportunities for children to talk, not the teacher.

CRITICAL TASK 14.1

Opportunities for developing higher order thinking

Here are some examples of questions that might promote some higher order thinking, adapted from Forster et al. (2010). Discuss the possible answers with a friend and evaluate the quality of the questions themselves.

Can you think of anything that isn't a solid, liquid or gas?

Why doesn't the Earth's atmosphere drift off into space?

If you jumped out of an aeroplane and, suddenly, all of the air in the world disappeared, what changes would you experience?

Come up with a question of your own that might promote higher order thinking in primary science.

WORKING SCIENTIFICALLY

'Working scientifically' is the part of the science programmes of study most closely aligned to our belief that science has to be about more than helping children to learn a few random facts. It should be thought of as the bedrock of the science curriculum, with all other content approached through working scientifically. This section of the curriculum sets out the key intellectual skills required for children to start thinking and working like scientists, such as raising their own questions, undertaking investigations, recording and presenting results, interpreting evidence and drawing conclusions.

Working scientifically should include explicit opportunities for children to examine evidence that they have generated themselves to answer their own questions. This enables them to grapple with the complex and, sometimes, conflicting ideas that may be developing in their minds and engage in deep and meaningful learning.

It is important to remember that children's learning is highly individual, as each child constructs their own knowledge and understanding, based on their own prior experience and how they have interpreted various sources of information (Selley, 1999). This can give rise to 'alternative conceptions': ideas that make sense to the individual but that are not, yet, fully aligned with scientifically accepted models. Gathering their own empirical evidence, through working scientifically, can enable children to experience cognitive conflict that begins to challenge their alternative conceptions, through interacting with the subject matter rather than receiving knowledge passively.

EMOTIONAL INTELLECTUAL ENGAGEMENT AND PERSONAL RELEVANCE

As we explored in Chapter 1, the role of emotions is often overlooked in teaching and learning, which is strange because humans are highly emotional beings: we process most things that happen to us on an emotional level first and foremost, with other intellectual processes following behind. Therefore, effective teaching in science must include approaches that acknowledge children have emotions and utilise these positively in the learning. This needs to go beyond just making sure that lessons are not boring: providing genuinely intriguing and stimulating lessons that promote curiosity are an essential starting point in primary science. Children's intellectual engagement can be stimulated through sensitively exploring emotive issues, such as the impacts of deforestation or plastic waste, and engaging with these through contexts that are closer to home, such as local recycling, food waste and composting. It is important to explore science topics in ways that have personal relevance for learners.

THE MEDIUM IS THE MESSAGE

Postman and Weingartner (1969) draw on the work of McLuhan to make the point that *how* children are engaged in their learning in school is significantly more important than the 'content' of the lessons. In every classroom and in every lesson, teachers make choices about *how* the learning will take place. For example, children can be encouraged to talk to one another and raise their own questions or required to sit quietly to listen to the teacher. They might be actively engaged with solving problems or copying a picture or some writing in their books. They might challenge the ideas they read on a website or be asked to memorise the content it provides; in short, they might be intellectually active or passive.

We see this as being a particularly important issue to consider in primary science, given that we see the aim of primary science as developing children's intelligence. In any science lesson, we can provide opportunities for children to engage in analysis, critical thinking and evaluation, or to be intellectually passive, requiring them to memorise relatively meaningless 'facts'. For example, a lesson's 'content' might be about the life cycle of a flowering plant, but how we organise the teaching and learning will have a significant impact on what the children learn. We could ensure that they are passive by asking them to copy a diagram into a book: this would keep them quiet and give us a nice neat page of work to mark. Alternatively, we could aim to promote higher order thinking by providing flowers for them to observe closely, to take apart, to discuss with others and to raise their own questions about.

Postman and Weingartner (1969) suggest that children will learn what we have them do: we can have them sitting quietly, accepting our answers as the 'correct knowledge' they should memorise, or we can have them do activities that help them develop a range of thinking skills. In this context, in the following, we will explore the challenging issue of how teachers ask questions.

PEDAGOGIC FOCUS FOR THIS CHAPTER: TEACHERS' QUESTIONS

It may seem obvious that teachers should ask questions to engage children in the learning, probe their understanding and stimulate their thinking. However, teachers' questions can be double-edged and, like all teaching strategies, must be carefully evaluated. In many cases, teachers ask too many questions, ask poorly thought-out questions, give children limited time to consider their answers and fail to think carefully about how they respond to children's answers. We will consider these issues in more depth.

THE NUMBER OF QUESTIONS TEACHERS ASK

Perhaps the biggest challenge for teachers related to their questions is regulating the number that they ask. In a seminal study on this issue, Rowe (1986) found that, on average, teachers asked dozens of questions every hour and hundreds every day. While this may seem to be a dated source, in our own research (Forster et al., 2019), we found that student teachers can ask as many as eighty questions in half an hour. Wood (1998) found that there is an inverse proportionality between the number of questions that teachers ask and the depth of thinking engaged with by learners. To put that another way, the more questions that teachers ask, the less children think. This is a significant (and possibly surprising) finding but one that makes sense: the more the teacher fills the available 'intellectual air time', the less opportunity there is for children to engage in intelligent talk. If you aim to be a teacher who promotes children's higher order thinking, you need to ensure that you do not ask too many questions.

CRITICAL TASK 14.2

How many questions?

To think about: how many questions would it be reasonable for a teacher to ask in a science lesson that is forty-five minutes long? What would be the optimum number you would like to ask and what would be the maximum number?

Challenge: audio-record yourself teaching and count the number of questions. Review the quality of your questions and, most importantly, the quality of the children's responses.

KINDS OF QUESTIONS AND THEIR IMPACT

It is often said that there are two kinds of teacher questions: closed and open. Closed questions, where there is normally just one 'right answer', require children to use the lower order thinking skill of recall. Open questions are questions that have more than one answer and give more scope for children to utilise a range of thinking skills in answering them.

However, it may be better to think of questions as being of these two kinds: those that require children to do some thinking, which should be utilised frequently, and those that do not require children to do some thinking, which should be avoided or used sparingly. This is because *some* closed questions, in which there is only one correct answer, can be intellectually provocative and require the application of prior knowledge or some higher order thinking in order to be sure of the answer. Take the following two examples:

> 'How many legs does an insect have?' This is a closed question that merely requires recall. Boring.
>
> 'What is the gas in the bubbles of boiling water?' This is also a closed question, as there is only one right answer, but, because it is not an answer that most well-educated intelligent adults can immediately recall, it gives rise to some thinking about the gases that might be plausible answers and whether the application of any prior knowledge might help to answer it.

In any science lesson, aim to use questions that promote genuine thinking rather than recall.

ENGAGING CHILDREN WITH QUESTIONS

We have established that, in order to hand the intellectual activity over to the learners, it is important for teachers of primary science to think carefully about the kind of questions they ask and to regulate the number of questions they ask. We will now consider what to do after asking a great question that might help promote genuine intellectual engagement in the children.

In her early research on this, Rowe (1986) found that some teachers waited less than a second for a child to answer a question before rephrasing it or asking another child to answer and, again, this is supported by our own research in 2017. Wragg and Brown (2001) found, somewhat unsurprisingly, that children will give better, more considered answers if they are given time to think before an answer is expected from them.

There are several ways to give children this 'thinking time', including pausing after asking a question and counting silently up to five. A more effective 'thinking strategy' is to give children the opportunity to discuss their ideas with someone else. This has a few benefits, in addition to giving time to thoughtfully reflect on the question. It also gives children the chance to hear the thoughts and ideas of other people, which in itself may stimulate further thinking and exploration of the issue. It also has the added advantage of encouraging all children to participate in whole-class discussions, as they may feel more confident about sharing an idea with the whole class once they have discussed it with a peer.

Remember that, in any class of children, there will be some who will readily answer questions and some who are quite happy not to say very much at all, so it is a good idea to develop some ways of working to ensure that you hear every voice in your science lessons (but do not be tempted to seek multiple short answers to closed questions to achieve this).

RESPONDING TO CHILDREN'S ANSWERS

When researching types of talk within British classrooms, Alexander (2008) reported a scarcity of interaction that challenged students to think for themselves. He also observed that the majority of teacher questions were closed and that the Initiation, Response, Feedback (IRF) model was dominant: teacher asks, pupil responds, teacher quickly evaluates the response for its closeness to the 'right answer' before moving on.

Just as it is important to give children thinking time after asking them a question, it is also important to give yourself thinking time when responding to children's answers. Before responding, it is essential to make sure that you have really listened to what a child has said, so pausing before speaking will give time to focus on the children's words and consider their answer before offering the next stimulating part of the interaction.

CRITICAL TASK 14.3

Responding to children's questions

In this short extract, Jane, an undergraduate student teacher in her final year of training, is showing a group of Year 2 children a runner bean that has begun to germinate.

Jane: So we're going to learn about how that bean grows into a runner bean.

Arjen: Within ten days, would it grow into a runner bean?

Jane: Yes. Well done.

It is relatively rare for a child to raise an unsolicited question so it is worth making the most of it when it happens. In this example, Jane praises the child for asking the question but gives the erroneous impression that the bean could grow into a runner bean in ten days. It may be that Jane was unprepared for a child to ask a question of their own.

To consider: How else might Jane have responded at this point?

CRITICAL TASK 14.4

Improving closed questions

In Table 14.1 are some closed questions: in the column on the right, suggest some better questions or better approaches that might promote more intellectual engagement from the learners.

Table 14.1 Improving closed questions

Closed question	Your suggested improvement
What is the name of the female part of the flowering plant?	
What is the correct term for the process when liquid turns into a gas?	
What is the main factor that affects the rate of evaporation?	
How many legs does an insect have?	
Which is the best material for making a table?	

CASE STUDY 14.1

In this example, Julie and Lynda, undergraduate primary student teachers in their final year of training, have been reflecting on the impact of their questions. In preparation for teaching, they have explored the existing research about good practice in questioning and have decided to limit the number of questions that they ask: they have agreed an upper limit of fifteen questions in half an hour of teaching. They are teaching a group of Year 2 children about germination and are looking at some pictures and discussing what would help plants to grow. In this extract, which in the audio recording lasts almost exactly one minute, the group is looking at a picture of some rotten food.

Julie: Do you think that plants will need this to grow?

Ben: Yes. They need food.

Julie: They need food. What type of food is it?

Ben: Actually they don't.

Lynda: They don't. Ben, can you read it? What is it?

Ben: Rotting food.

Lynda: Rotting food. So why don't plants need rotting food to grow?

Francesca: Because probably plants don't like rotten food.

Lynda: You don't think plants like rotten food. Have you got anything to add to that?

Julie: Do you think plants need that to grow? Why don't you think they need that to grow?

Lynda: Is it going to be good for them?

Ben: No.

Lynda: No. When you put your seeds into your pots did you put rotting food into it?

Ben: No. We didn't even give them food.

Julie: What did you give them?

Ben: Water.

(Continued)

Student teacher evaluation: Julie and Lynda felt that the quality of their questions was mostly good in being aimed at particular children to involve them in discussion. However, they recognised that they asked a lot more questions than they had originally planned and suggested that this could have been improved by allowing more opportunities for discussion among the children without teacher involvement, as it seemed that the children became quite reliant on their questioning.

Expert critique: There are several important aspects worth reviewing here, including the number of questions that the student teachers asked, the quality of those questions and the extent to which they listened and responded to the children's answers.

In one minute, Lynda and Julie, between them, asked eleven questions, well above their ambition of asking, on average, one question every two minutes. They seemed to have a limited ability to draw on other strategies to reduce the number of questions that they asked. In their evaluation, they quite rightly noted that the children became reliant on their questions and that it was difficult for them to break this pattern of interaction.

Many of the questions were closed questions ('Is it going to be good for them?'), in which the children knew that they were required to guess the 'correct answer'. Some of these were dressed up to look less like closed questions ('Do you think that plants will need this to grow?'), but it is most likely that the children still saw these as questions requiring a 'yes or no' answer, only one of which would be deemed to be 'correct'.

It is also interesting to note the extent to which the student teachers did (or did not) carefully consider each child's contribution. Ben started by asserting that plants need food to grow and then appeared to change his mind, probably because Julie's response made him think his initial answer was not correct. It may have been best for Lynda and Julie to stay quiet at this point, to see whether Ben would say more about what he understood about plants needing food.

Finally, it is worth noting that it is easier to be confident in your teaching approaches if your subject knowledge is secure: this enables you to welcome children's questions and take a more dialogic approach in thinking and talking. In this case, it would have been good for the student teachers to be clear about the difference between germination and plant growth and to know that rotten food is on its way to becoming compost and can be used as a fertiliser to boost plant growth.

CLIMATE

In addition to the technical aspects of effective questioning that we have so far considered, it is also important for a great science teacher to think about the intellectual climate that they want to create in their classroom. This is hard to define, but will be reflected in the confidence that children have to express their own thoughts about scientific ideas, the number of questions that they ask, the extent to which they listen to each other and the way in which they respectfully challenge ideas or justify their own opinions. Above all, it might be seen in the way that children question and respectfully challenge the teacher about scientific issues, rather than accepting the teacher's answer as the only correct version. Encourage children to see you not as the font of all knowledge, the final arbiter of all answers, but as someone who is always willing to be intrigued by their questions.

CASE STUDY 14.2

In this example, Tim, a primary PGCE student, is reviewing his approach to questioning in his work on Earth and space with Year 5 children.

Tim: So why can't you see the Moon during the day?

John: It goes to the other side of the Earth.

Morna: But I have seen it in the day…

John: Maybe it was a bit early coming round.

Zac: Ooooo … is it because the light doesn't reflect off the Moon during the day?

Gemma: Or because there are clouds.

Student teacher evaluation: Having reflected deeply on his use of questions and his role in stimulating and guiding productive talk, Tim was pleased to have provoked so much response with just one question. In particular, he was pleased that Morna felt confident enough to raise an objection to his question and that John then responded to Morna's comment rather than to the original question. He felt that the children were thinking about the question and coming up with sensible answers, without him making further interventions.

Expert critique: On first reading, it seems that Tim has asked the wrong question to begin with, as the question includes a scientific misconception:

(Continued)

as Morna points out, it is often possible to see the Moon during the day. On reflection, however, this seems to be a very clever question, as the alternative might have been a closed question (Can you ever see the Moon in the daytime?), which might have closed down discussion. Tim has clearly created a climate in which children feel able to express any conflicts between the key message of the question and their own understanding, so asking a question that includes some factual ambiguity has stimulated some good thinking. One possible improvement might be to say, 'I wonder why we can't see the Moon in the daytime'. This could contribute to the children's positive affective response through Tim placing himself alongside them as an 'enquirer' and not the instructor or holder of knowledge.

RESPONSE TO CRITICAL TASK 14.4

Improving closed questions

In this task, we asked you to consider the closed questions presented in the first column and suggest some better questions or better approaches that might promote more intellectual engagement from the learners. Table 14.2 shows some of our suggestions.

Table 14.2 Improving closed questions: revisited

Closed question	Your suggested improvement
What is the name of the female part of the flowering plant?	Tell the person next to you four things that you know about the parts of the flowering plant.
What is the correct term for the process when liquid turns into a gas?	Tell the person next to you if you think there is a difference between 'evaporation' and 'boiling'.
What is the main factor that affects the rate of evaporation?	Make a list of the factors that might affect the rate of evaporation and tell the person next to you when one might be more significant than others.
How many legs does an insect have?	Discuss with the person next to you and make a list of all the questions that you have about insects.
Which is the best material for making a table?	Which materials wouldn't you use to make a table?

APPLICATION OF THE PEDAGOGIC FOCUS TO OTHER SUBJECTS

We have considered the importance of effective questioning in science and this is also an important teaching skill across all other subjects in the primary curriculum. For example, history is a subject that has many parallels with science, in terms of the critical thinking skills that children should both utilise and develop through engagement with the curriculum content. They should be offered opportunities to explore historical artefacts or secondary evidence and seek to derive meaning through analysis, inference, deduction and raising their own questions. As such, it is important that the teacher guides the process without dominating the children's intellectual activity, so a small number of carefully judged and well-focused questions will be more beneficial than a large number of closed questions.

In a very different subject, PSHE, the teacher's role is significant in providing carefully judged guidance in discussions about issues that are sometimes sensitive and personal. It is particularly important that the teacher listens very carefully to the children's responses and allows sufficient time and space for children to discuss their thoughts, feelings, problems and solutions before making well-judged and supportive interventions through non-judgemental yet provocative questions. Children may raise questions of their own about the issues being discussed; this should be encouraged and teachers should ensure that they handle children's questions sensitively, with respect for all members of the class. This may mean, on occasion, answering a question individually, rather than as part of a whole-class discussion.

SUMMARY FOR THIS CHAPTER

In this chapter, we have explored the power of primary science to support children's development as intelligent and creative individuals who can solve problems, analyse evidence and ask relevant and pertinent questions. We have learnt that teachers of science should aim to regulate their own speech, limit the number of questions that they ask, listen carefully to children's answers and aim not to dominate the learning experience.

When teaching science, do:

- engage children in higher order thinking
- plan to address content through working scientifically
- make learning relevant to the children
- engage children's emotions in their learning.

When asking questions, do:

- regulate the number of questions
- plan to ask some intellectually provocative questions
- give children time to think
- listen carefully to the children's answers
- encourage children to raise their own questions.

FURTHER READING

The following texts may be helpful in further developing your understanding of effective teaching and learning in science and exploring the complex issue of questioning.

Allen, M. (2016) *The best ways to teach primary science: research into practice*. New York: Open University Press.

This helpful book is useful for exploring a range of research-informed approaches to teaching topics across the primary science curriculum.

Fusco, E. (2012) *Effective questioning strategies in the classroom: a step-by-step approach to engaged thinking and learning, K-8*. New York: Teachers College Press.

This book considers a range of issues that teachers might need to grapple with in order to become confident question-askers.

Rothstein, D. and Santana, L. (2011) *Make just one change: teach students to ask their own questions*. Cambridge, MA: Harvard Education Press.

This excellent book challenges teachers to refocus their efforts, to make the switch from asking many questions to promoting question-asking as an important intellectual skill to be developed by all learners.

REFERENCES

Alexander, R. J. (2008) *Essays on pedagogy*. Abingdon: Routledge.

Dewey, J. (1963) *Experience and education*. New York: Collier Books.

Forster, C., Parfitt, V. and McGowan, A. (2010) *Science homework for key stage 2: activity-based learning*. Abingdon: Routledge.

Forster, C., Penny, J. and Shalofsky, R. (2019) 'Questioning the role of questions: new primary teachers' realisations of over-reliance on questions in scientific dialogue', Practice: Contemporary Issues in Practitioner Education, 1(2), pp. 173–85.

Krathwohl, D.R. (2002) 'A revision of Bloom's Taxonomy: an overview', *Theory into Practice*, 41(4), pp. 212–18.

Postman, N. and Weingartner, C. (1969) *Teaching as a subversive activity*. Harmondsworth: Penguin Books.

Rowe, M.B. (1986) 'Wait time: slowing down may be a way of speeding up!', *Journal of Teacher Education*, 37(1), pp. 43–50.

Selley, N. (1999) *The art of constructivist teaching in the primary school: a guide for students and teachers*. Hoboken, NJ: Taylor & Francis.

Wood, D. (1998) *How children think and learn*. 2nd edn. Oxford: Blackwell.

Wragg, E.C. and Brown, G. (2001) *Questioning in the secondary school*. Revised edn. Abingdon: RoutledgeFalmer.

15

CONCLUSION

RACHEL EPERJESI AND COLIN FORSTER

OBJECTIVES

- To review the purpose of primary education.
- To consider how to promote authentic learning.

In this chapter, we will remind ourselves of the purpose of a rounded primary education and return to our central themes, to conclude with some suggestions of how teachers can make life-changing contributions in their teaching by promoting authentic learning.

THE PURPOSE OF PRIMARY EDUCATION

By the time they start school, most children have learnt how to talk, walk, run, eat and dress, to name a few of their major achievements. In most cases, no one *taught* them how to do these things but, through observation and perseverance, and with encouragement, they worked out for themselves how to develop and progress. The main purpose of primary education, then, is not to start children's learning, but to support them to continue their independent development.

CHARACTERISTICS OF EFFECTIVE LEARNING (IN THE EARLY YEARS AND BEYOND)

Children, particularly younger children, are automatically 'wired' for learning. As outlined above, before they even come to school, they have learnt some fundamental skills that will stay with them for the rest of their lives, such is their capacity for learning. They have an in-built sense of curiosity, to explore and investigate, which, if responded to appropriately, can be almost insatiable; if you have ever spent any length of time with a three or four year old, you are likely to have faced a seemingly endless list of questions, many of which begin with 'why... ' and some of which you have no idea how to answer. So, if children have this natural capacity and thirst for learning, you might ask why it is sometimes so difficult to teach a particular concept or skill. There are probably a number of factors involved, including the quality of the teaching and the child's 'readiness' for learning that particular concept or skill. What is often overlooked, however, is careful consideration of *how* children learn, in addition to *what* they learn. When we tune into how children learn most effectively, it can have a significant impact on both our teaching and their learning. Bottrill (2018) suggests that teachers need to enter the children's 'universe', rather than expecting them to fit into ours, and goes on to suggest that teachers need to remember the 'magic' of childhood, harnessing this in their teaching in order to keep children's innate curiosity and desire to learn alive.

In addition to the themes of 'unique child', 'positive relationships', 'enabling environments' and 'learning and development' (DfE, 2017: 6), the Early Years Foundation Stage (EYFS) Statutory Framework (DfE, 2017) also outlines what it terms 'characteristics of effective learning', suggesting that there are three of these: 'playing and exploring', 'active learning' and 'creating and thinking critically' (DfE, 2017: 10). How children learn and developing their capacity to learn further seem to be as important as what they learn in EYFS, and that is a principle we can certainly agree with. However, the characteristics of effective learning are not explicitly referred to in the curriculum guidance for Key Stages 1 and 2, as if they stop being important once children have completed their time in EYFS. This is, of course, untrue, and many effective primary teachers place great importance on supporting children to understand themselves as learners and to develop their 'learning skills'. Many of the pedagogical foci explored within the previous chapters of this book align with at least one of the identified characteristics of effective learning.

ROUNDED INDIVIDUALS

Of course, we want our children to be knowledgeable about a range of topics across the curriculum, in current affairs and in areas of personal interest. We also want them to have good understanding of challenging concepts and a range of skills, based on the National Curriculum requirements. Most importantly, we want them to leave our primary schools as rounded individuals, with a range of personal and interpersonal skills and developing confidence.

As we identified in Chapters 12 and 13, a rounded primary education enables children to develop an awareness of the feelings of others, respect for the views of others and a willingness to learn from other cultures, faiths and people. As they learn about other people, children are also able to develop an awareness of themselves, their own feelings and their responses to experiences.

We also want children to be able to think critically about a range of issues, both within and beyond the curriculum, through identifying strengths and weaknesses in evidence or arguments and exploring complexities in a positive and creative way. In many chapters within this book, we have emphasised the valuable social and communication skills that can be developed through engaging in critical thinking tasks, as children learn to express potentially challenging opinions and questions in positive ways.

ASSESS WHAT WE VALUE

One of the major challenges in many education systems around the world is that measurement of the 'outcomes' of education focuses on a very narrow range of easily measured factors, typically in relation to children's subject knowledge, and mostly in relation to English and mathematics. The use of Programme for International Student Assessment (PISA) comparisons between countries has, in some cases, increased the pressure on schools to 'improve' results in these areas. The impact of this, in primary schools, has been to focus more curriculum time on

English and mathematics and to reduce the emphasis on foundation subjects and on the breadth of children's development.

Hopefully, at some stage in the future, the system of assessment in primary schools will receive a major overhaul, to focus on children's attainment not just across the entire curriculum, but also taking account of the range of intellectual and social skills and qualities that are so important in their development as rounded individuals: problem-solving, listening, questioning, having empathy, critical thinking, leadership and working as a member of a team, to name but a few. In the meantime, when teaching, aim to make children aware that you really value these aspects of their learning and make a serious attempt to assess them, so that you can celebrate the children's successes and report these to parents.

PROMOTING AUTHENTIC LEARNING

Throughout this book, we have explored the central importance of engaging children in meaningful, worthwhile, deep, relevant and valuable learning, and in the following we reflect on some of the approaches to teaching that will promote this kind of authentic learning.

POROUS SCHOOLS

We identified in Chapter 1 that the current model of schooling has one inherent, fundamental challenge: in order to prepare children for life in the real world we put them in a box, called 'school', for twelve years. One way of responding to this challenge is for teachers to aim to create 'porous schools', in which children get out of the classroom and into the real world as often as possible and in which members of the real world are regularly invited into the school building, as explored in Chapters 4, 6 and 10. School 'trips' do not need to be expensive or involve coach travel: get in touch with local businesses or voluntary enterprises that are within walking distance of your school and see whether they could host a visit for your class, with a clear focus on an aspect of curriculum learning. For businesses that are too far to walk to, invite them to come to school to talk about their work, the skills required and what the best aspects of their jobs are. Aim to ensure that your teaching of the curriculum is informed and enhanced by visitors for every subject (remembering, as much as possible, to avoid reinforcing gender stereotypes): poets, engineers, shopkeepers, nurses, accountants, refuse collectors, librarians and artists can all add value to your teaching and make the children's learning relevant to the real world.

Where it is not possible to organise a visit out of school or to invite an expert to visit your class in school, remember that it is still possible, and valuable, to contextualise learning, as explored in Chapter 4, through using real world models and applications to support understanding. Aim, too, to utilise the school grounds and other local outdoor spaces as contexts for meaningful learning, as discussed in Chapter 6.

HOLD ON TO YOUR VALUES

As we explored in Chapter 11, values underpin our approach to teaching and it is important to keep a careful eye on whether your values and your conduct are well aligned. If you find yourself acting in a way that is not in accordance with your values, it is time to take a deep breath, step back, reflect on what is happening and adjust your practice. For example, you will aim to treat all children with dignity and respect at all times. This can be challenging at times of high stress, when children are not behaving as you would like or when you know that a lesson is not going well. Resist the urge to speak harshly to children: it is not in the children's best interests and will not make you feel any better.

Similarly, aim to know your children well, by speaking to every individual regularly about their learning, about their life and about their interests. As noted by Kohn (1999), use of both punishments and rewards is shown to have significant limitations in managing children's behaviour, and an effective learning environment is based on positive and mutually respectful relationships that promote children's intrinsic motivation to learn about themselves and the world.

A key aspect of your values-based approach to teaching will be to keep in mind that children are intelligent and capable. As such, do not demean them by providing tasks of limited intellectual rigour or interest. As we identified in Chapter 14, children are emotional beings (just like adults) and we should aim to engage their emotions positively in their learning, rather than provoke feelings of boredom and frustration.

PLAN FOR LEARNING RATHER THAN TEACHING

As we outlined in Chapter 1, the National Curriculum document is just that: a document. As teachers, we can make decisions about how we interpret it, so that learning is the driving force, rather than delivery of curriculum requirements. Effective early years pedagogy starts with teachers observing and making assessments of the current attainment of each child, as a 'unique learner', before then planning how to move learning forward. This puts the child at the heart of the learning journey, with the curriculum adapting to meet the needs of the child, rather than the other way round. While formative assessment practices go some way to mirror this in Key Stages 1 and 2 (and beyond), all too often the curriculum requirements are still the starting point for the journey, rather than the child. If we wish to teach for authentic learning and make a significant and holistic impact on our learners, we need to start with them, by finding out their attainment, their strengths, their interests and any barriers to their learning, so that we can plan for progression.

Throughout this book, we have explored a range of pedagogic foci, intended to promote deep and meaningful learning. Each one has been explored in the context of a particular subject and the transferable nature of each has also been considered. Another transferable pedagogical approach that can have significant impact on learning is play. One of the underpinning principles for early years pedagogy is that learning and development should be founded on 'planned, purposeful play' (DfE, 2017: 9), whether adult-led or child-initiated. The Department for Education (2017: 9) identifies that 'play is essential for children's development, building their confidence as they learn to explore, to think about problems, and relate to others'. If it is 'essential' for children in foundation stage, one might question why play-based, or 'playful', learning is not more explicitly promoted as an effective pedagogical approach for children in Key Stage 1 and beyond; despite this, though, many effective primary teachers already recognise the potential value of play-based approaches and are embedding these in their practice across the curriculum.

Planning for learning, by starting with the children, does require more work and skill than simply 'delivering' the curriculum, but is worth the investment, both for the children's learning and for your own motivation. You may find that you do not always get it quite right, but stick at it. This will undoubtedly take you on a learning journey of your own and, as you develop your skills in planning and teaching in this way, you may find it helpful to make use of an approach such as action research, to support you in examining and adapting your own practice, in an informed and evidence-based manner (Forster and Eperjesi, 2017).

CRITICAL TASK 15.1

How will children remember you?

You may remember some of the teachers from your own primary education and your own experiences of being a learner in their classes. Some of these memories may be very positive and others may be less so. Now consider how you would like children to remember you. What words might they use to describe you and your teaching? What would you like them to tell others about what it was like to be a learner in your class? What might they say about the impact you had on them, both as a learner and as a person?

Remember these considerations: if children are to remember you in the ways that you would like them to in the future, your actions and reactions in the present are crucial.

SUMMARY FOR THIS CHAPTER AND THE BOOK

In summary, we return to the cohering theme of this book, introduced in Chapter 1: in order to be a great teacher, do not dominate the learning.

REFERENCES

Bottrill, G. (2018) *Can I go and play now? Rethinking the early years*. London: SAGE Publications.

Department for Education (DfE) (2017) *Statutory framework for the early years foundation stage: setting the standards for learning, development and care for children from birth to five*. London: DfE.

Forster, C. and Eperjesi, R. (2017) *Action research for new teachers: evidence-based evaluation of teaching*. London: SAGE Publications.

Kohn, A. (1999) *Punished by rewards: the trouble with gold stars, incentive plans, a's, praise, and other bribes*. Boston, MA: Houghton Mifflin.

INDEX